WITH PASSION: AN ACTIVIST LAWYER'S JOURNEY

WITH PASSION: AN ACTIVIST LAWYER'S JOURNEY

by
Michael Meltsner

TWELVE TABLES PRESS
XII

T

www.twelvetablespress.com

P.O. Box 568
Northport, New York 11768

© 2017 by Michael Meltsner
All Rights Reserved

Library of Congress Cataloging-in-Publication Data

Name: Michael Meltsner
Title: With Passion: An Activist Lawyer's Journey
Description: Northport, New York: Twelve Tables Press, 2017
ISBN: 978-1-946074-10-2
Subjects: Law—United States/Biography
LC record available at https:lccn.loc.gov/

Twelve Tables Press, LLC
P.O. Box 568
Northport, New York 11768
Telephone (631) 241-1148
Fax: (631) 754-1913
www.twelvetablespress.com

Printed in the United States of America

For Lucy, Anna, Will, and Tessa

Contents

Author's Note

This is *not* a work of fiction. Names, characters, places, and incidents, including references to legal matters, are not products of the author's imagination and are not to be construed as fictitious or as composites of various realities. The depiction of events, locales, organizations, or persons living or dead is intended to be an accurate representation of what actually occurred. Occasionally, the text contains material that I have published elsewhere but which seems appropriate to include here. Wherever possible, documentary and other historical sources as well as interviews have been consulted as a check on memory but should readers have a contrary view be assured that the systematic clash of interests that characterizes our politics (and our legal system) supports the presence of different stories, voices, and points of view.

To understand the creating forces is to understand what is important.

(Adam Nicolson)

The pull that justice and its absurd procedures has for certain minds. . . . Find the explanation.

(Albert Camus, *Notebooks*, January
1942 to September 1945)

Preface

One dazzling spring morning in the early 1960s, a woman I knew from the neighborhood stopped me as I was walking briskly down Broadway toward the Eighty-Sixth street subway that would take me to my Columbus Circle office. She asked if she could interview me for a local newspaper that was just getting started in the hope of finding favor with Westside advertisers. Barely a year into working as a lawyer for the NAACP Legal Defense Fund, I was flattered by her attention. It was a time, before the passage of the 1964 Civil Rights Act, when the disgust of Northerners for the antics of Southern segregationists ran high but the Kennedy Administration, worried that passage of its legislative program was vulnerable, was totally confused about where to pledge its loyalty. A week later, I sat down to answer her questions about the cases I was working on. Then I forgot about our conversation until I saw the article that followed—introduced by a large-type, bold headline announcing "He Helps Them Overcome."

I felt like a fool. No one should think my choice of work was some sort of bending down to help the downtrodden. I was there for myself as much as for others. Wasn't it George Orwell, a man whose essays I read slavishly as a young person, who said saints should be presumed guilty until proven innocent? I wanted immediately to go to the few Broadway newsstands that carried the paper to seize every copy before anyone saw it. Of course, my ardor soon cooled; I was forced to examine the embarrassment and shame I'd felt. Where did it come from? Why was I doing what I was doing, unlike almost every other member of my law school class safely settled in the womb of prominent private law firms? I had trained to be a lawyer and wanted to practice my craft. That must be it.

But it wasn't nearly the whole story: almost every day I realized that ending up as a civil rights lawyer, especially a white civil rights lawyer, was no accident, though the way I found the job was pure serendipity. Signals from my parents had a lot to do with my choice of work but so did growing up in New York City. Sometimes it was observed that many white civil rights lawyers and activists were Jewish. I was often asked about whether I was doing the work for that reason. Feeling a bit defensive, I'd reply that plenty of Jews had different views about civil rights and race than I did. Privately I believed that if any trait in my ethnicity brought me closer to the work I was doing it was that historically some Jews thought that not having a nation state of their own survival depended on taking personal responsibility for the condition of the society in which they found themselves. In the early 1960s before she was a celebrity, Susan Sontag told a New York audience that Jewish liberalism was a gesture of self-legitimization—Jews legitimized themselves through a political stance; homosexuals, she added, through the aesthetic. It doesn't take much unpacking of her terse formulation to understand why both groups keep a keen interest in the paths taken by the body politic.

What follows is a zigzag search for the reasons that compete with the accidental to serve as an explanation but also a chance to excavate the meanings buried in the stories that served my passions for an improbable sixty-year life in the law. And I am driven toward discovery by mortality.

Reports from cancer patients are a growth industry; though heartrending, most are formulaic, and ultimately boring. I'd leave mine aside but I'm convinced ennui stands as a dam behind which emotions mass; to that bit of supposed wisdom, I add my belief that the deeper the sense of boredom, the more intense the rush of feelings crashing against the walls trying to break out. Six years ago, I was diagnosed with esophageal cancer. No surprise, having grown up in a household of smokers, starting myself at fourteen, and putting myself through college as a paid ($50 bucks a month) representative of the Philip Morris company by distributing free Marlboro's to overeager fellow students. Of course, I'd stopped smoking years before like everyone I know and my doctors were adamant: "There's no hard evidence the smoking had caused the cancer." But I thought this annoying doctorspeak and not at all persuasive. The cells have a history.

I'd been on the lookout for death for years, though my certainty that it would come when I was young disappeared over the horizon when I passed the early age (forty-seven) when my father died. It turned out that in my youth I believed deeply if unconsciously that he and I were linked in everything that mattered. As a child the only distinction I was aware of was that he was bald and I was not. But it was clear when he faltered so would I. That I had no inkling of his real condition was not important; it was enough that there was a message of doom packed in the hidden crevices of his life that a son took in, no less powerfully for him being a most happy fella, a great lover of his wife, a doggerel poet, an optimistic gambler, die-hard liberal, and a covert outsider even though (after a struggle) a great success in his commercial doings. Because he believed most things were tentative and unsettled, a persistent looker under masks—a deconstructionist before there was deconstruction—I guess I learned to imagine what was behind his.

My expectation of an end in my forties passed because of my shrink. He put aside his Viennese-trained recessives and had me bring him my father's autopsy. When I arrived weeks later with the dim photocopy and passed it to him, he immediately handed it back.

"Read it out loud," he ordered in his Viennese-inflected English. As usual I complied with this former student of Freud's commands, though this time reluctantly:

"Patient admitted in shock . . . blood pressure 40/0." "Febrile . . . presence of amyloid . . . jaundice . . . Massive G.I. bleeding . . ." and so forth. After an agony of pathologist's jargon and more grim particulars—brain weight (1375 g), spleen (750 g) "markedly enlarged," "a number of Alzheimer's glia"—he passed judgment:

"Nothing in the least inheritable. Nothing genetic. Whatever is wrong with you his body is totally blameless."

I took this verdict as settling the matter. Indeed, if I had once been long obsessed with death the way the famous subjects whose last days are closely and evocatively rendered by Katie Roiphie in *The Violet Hour*, my preoccupation soon disappeared. To my amazement, I also lost a fear of flying that had haunted my air travel to Southern courtrooms during the civil rights era. No more did I have to counter and control the turbulence with alcohol or chain smoking, when, of course, I wasn't flying the plane in my head.

When the first endoscopy revealed the tumor, a team of amigos—a radiologist, a surgeon, and an oncologist— entered my life. They sent the cancer away for enough years so that I thought I had escaped. Just as I was ready to dismiss them, it returned. They reconvened again, came up with a new protocol, and cured me a second time. I suspect they were greatly surprised (certainly I was)—though given their professional faith in cures, they would probably deny it. The chemo and radiation, the tests and tubes, were awful but ordinarily awful so the details are unremarkable. You know them. I only retail all this because, as seems to regularly occur in cases like mine, the stories that follow are fused with an energy that comes from deciding that death is on the way and that dying is both hateful and unfair but also totally normal. Not much into denial or extreme edge of the abyss methods, I found myself in the middle of the road, much like, I suspect, most of my fellow patients on the ninth floor of the Beth Israel Hospital in Boston.

My words to family and friends were something like, "I've made my peace." I want no obituary to report death "after a long and courageous battle with cancer." Maybe better, "He relied on the best science, doctors and nurses; then he let go." If you spend enough time suing bastards, contrarian impulses never go totally away. The taint of end-game heroism is, I believe, just another convention to leave behind. No Dylan Thomas "Rage, rage against the dying of the light." I didn't want to "burn and rave at the close of day"; certainly had no taste for "And Death Shall Have No Dominion." Nor was this the arrival of the last Kubler–Ross stage—acceptance—but rather simply death on my own terms. This dying business was, I thought, like a job and I usually loved my work.

Roiphe found a profound beauty in what she saw in the last days—"deranged seeming courage," "mad love"—of her main subjects—Susan Sontag, Freud, John Updike, Thomas, and Maurice Sendak. It's likely, I think, that immersion in the details of most of us at the end, not just the famous, will reveal and even fascinate. A steady reader of full-scale obituaries, a memorial service auditor, will not be surprised at what is told there or of one's ignorance of the lives lived by both celebrities and even close friends.

The courage and love, the missteps and misalliances, transcend the clichés of death notices.

But for me any drama was muted. In the months of treatment the observer was as strong as the participant. I gave my body over to the work but I also watched it happen. Perhaps this distracted me from thinking about the likely ending, which when it didn't come released a brief flood of tears. And disbelief. Of course, it took a while to get there. Was I kidding myself? Was I just pretending to be a good patient by showing a good front? I certainly doubted my resolve the whole way. Just like a death row prisoner, I fought off reality by visiting faraway places. Laying there on various slabs, beds, and scanner platforms while waiting for treatment, I counted the best orgasms I could remember, tried to recall the countries I'd visited, hikes taken, lectures given, cases both won and lost, clients I thought I'd helped, memorable books read, students who'd taken something of me away, encounters with friends and enemies, the regrets that remained from stupid mistakes, and the triumphs that had smothered some but not all of them before finally coming to rest on the joyous tangles, the ups and strange downs, of my incredible marriage in a way it was "arranged" (by the two of us) but only in the sense that we'd been together less than a month before it was settled, and then the images of my sleeping daughters when they were young, an even deeper connection with them as they came into their own.

This was, of course, life trying to push the inevitable away but then when it stepped forward in the unmistakable dress of endoscopy camera images and hospital paraphernalia, as opposed to previous murky fantasy and nebulous anxiety, to my utter surprise I actually believed I was ready to go.

A man I admired, the great doctor and drug researcher, Norman Zinberg, died in 1989 a short time after collapsing on an exercise machine at a Mexican health spa. At his home a few days later, fumbling over how to express my profound regrets, out of nowhere came the question I asked his widow, the Harvard lecturer Dorothy Zinberg:

"Did Norman feel he'd lived a good life?" (When asked a similar question after he was disgraced, Richard Nixon responded that "He didn't get in to that crap.")

Dorothy paused a few seconds before fleeing from my intrusion to the assembled mourners but she left me, indelibly, with a message I didn't want to hear—she wasn't at all sure he did.

That's the question I consoled myself with decades later passing time on the cancer floor while the bag of chemo emptied drip by slow drip into my left arm, and the sweet oncology nurses—I always fall in love with them—smiling their always-smiling smile, the most important question—how to live?—and if we can answer it well, then it's the best revenge—but really the only one we've got.

War

Wars are not accidents in history, but integral and even normal parts of the process of history.

(James Burnham)

I go to New York City now as a visitor. Brutality that once thrilled me is now too often a chaos of noise, dirt, and ugliness, although some of this is time's wicked distortion—the redoubtable Jim Dwyer wrote recently in *The Times* that in the 1960s "you could touch the air in New York. It was that filthy. No sensible person would put a toe in most of the waterways." Still a world where the poor had some purchase, weak as it was, now favors only the moneyed. It was my grandmother who gave these feelings permission, as James Salter would put it, "born to the city and thus free not to love it," but when I was a citizen pride, even arrogance, overrode the critic.

No matter where I am, the City is with me always, folded into the daily fabric of my life. Dodgers and Giants could escape; I never could. In the seacoast town where I have spent part of over fifty summers, there is a large shore-side granite quarry, once in private hands but now part of a popular state park. A bizarre conglomerate structure looks down at the dazzling blue rainwater that fills its depths, long ago the source of building foundations and curbstones in Manhattan and San Francisco and later, after reinforced concrete doomed the granite trade, the best swimming hole in a hundred miles. My eye travels from the suggestion of a Dutch gambrel-style house to an ugly five-story concrete tower said to have been the site for an antiaircraft weapon guidance system during World War II. Above the tower sits a frame cupola that looks like it could have been lifted from a salvage yard specializing in demolished churches. Glancing up at it while I jog on the gravelly path that circles the quarry, I wonder what its designers could have been thinking: I conclude only a committee of bureaucrats could have produced such improbability.

The house is now a visitor's center and an exhibit gives up the answer. In an effort to camouflage the tower's function from the air, military planners placed the fantasy of a gabled cupola as might top a New England Congregational Church above the flat roof of the tower. Whatever the illusion fostered in the mind of a Nazi reconnaissance pilot banking his aircraft to get a look, assuming any German aviator ever made it to this coast, the view from the ground today probably reminds visitors more of a Disneyland concoction than a national defense asset. On my way down to the nearby seaside path, I never take in this remnant of years increasingly few remember without being reminded of the whitewashed gun emplacements set out to protect us from enemy invasion as they lined the fringe of the beach in the Rockaway neighborhood of Queens, New York, where I lived until age twelve.

For what to him were totally mysterious reasons, and a constant embarrassment, my father was rejected for military service in World War II by the local draft board. Because he felt he had to do something to support the war effort, he volunteered as an air raid warden. Proudly donning what looked like a white construction worker's hard hat and carrying a chrome-cased flashlight, many nights he walked our street from one end to the other, from Jamaica Bay to the boardwalk facing the Atlantic Ocean, calling out when he saw shafts of light from only partially darkened houses: "Pull those shades all the way down. Please dim those lights."

Or more stridently: "Air Raid Warden. We are by the ocean. Kill Those Lights!"

His voice carried over the insane buzzing of the cicadas to my bedroom in the tiny house near a sandy lot my parents had bought for $5,000 shortly after I was born. It was strangely comforting to hear him call out in the night even when he varied the injunction with a scary warning like, "Remember those U-boats." I knew what a U-boat was because I had seen a picture of a submarine in the *World-Telegram*, one of the many newspapers he brought home from his work an hour train ride away in Manhattan.

My mother's contribution to the war effort may have had its origins in her sense of guilt because she was solely responsible for his rejection by the draft board but she soon embraced her role as a home-front warrior for its own sake. Suddenly, Alice became a proud woman in uniform, regularly delivering sandwiches to soldiers stationed for up to twelve-hour shifts in the gun emplacements she called Pillboxes. The concrete huts were studded along what in summer was a hugely populated public beach developed close to Brooklyn in the 1930s by Robert Moses, the man who controlled the highway and parkland development in New York State for decades. Moses wants to give blacks, immigrants, and working-class folks a respite from life in the slums but only so long as they keep a good distance from the more affluent whites who occupy the high-class venues of Eastern Long Island. Because of its location facing the open ocean at the edge of the City, Rockaway Beach is considered an important home-front defense perimeter as much as a summer playground. Residents are told they live near a dangerous entry point. There is a critical need to protect against clandestine landings from saboteurs and infiltrators.

The Pillbox soldiers are supposed to protect us from the enemy. They are lodged back from the water's edge near where dunes turn into scrub, protected from the tidal flow. The men come from a nearby army post called Fort Tilden, later converted into a Nike guided missiles site, where each morning the sandwiches are prepared. Across the bay from the narrow Rockaway peninsula, which here lies flat and exposed like a knife in the water, is New York City's first municipal airport, converted because of the war into a busy naval air station, Floyd Bennett Field.

My mother is dressed in a smart blue uniform, a neat cap set carefully in the center of her dark brown hair, displaying the eagle insignia of her sponsor organization, a group called The American Women's Voluntary Service, known everywhere by its initials, AWVS. Swelling the fabric, her breasts emerge from above a trim waist to convey as much officially sanctioned power as a woman was permitted in those days. Compared to her, my father's air raid warden garb looks phony. Ira is dressed more like an amateur actor trying out for a role in a local theatrical production.

How I know the importance of my mother's looks at this age is a mystery, but I do. I suppose some of it comes from the way men treat her; like the mother in Jess Walter's story "Mr. Voice," men would stop "on the street to watch her walk by." But she betrays little awareness of this or interest in shaping her appearance. At this time of her life there is no fuss, no long stares at her mirror, although I notice she does carefully apply her bright red lipstick. Only years later after she works as a cosmetics publicist for a French perfume house and worries about her sun-driven creases and wrinkles, only after I require excision of some precancerous cells from my forehead, do I understand that we were both young together, both totally heedless of tanning, of the perils that come from living hard by the glare of an ocean beach.

She picks me up from my ancient reddish stone grade school building, directing me to the back seat of our wood-paneled Chrysler station wagon where I find sacks stuffed with ham, cheese and chicken sandwiches on mayonnaise, or mustard-slathered bulky rolls, each tightly wrapped in wax paper. I am to hug these sacks as she drives out Rockaway Boulevard, making sure none spill. Eventually, she turns left toward the beach, pulling up near a line of white-washed emplacements half hidden in the dunes. My job is to grab as many of sacks as I can carry and then pad across the sand shouting, "AWVS sandwiches, AWVS sandwiches," passing them out to the men who crawl from little door holes on the landside of the bunkers like ants freed from under a rock. Their faces are vanilla ice cream pale, without any of the suntan; almost everyone shows in this community wedged between open-ocean and the huge, brackish, sewage dump of Jamaica Bay. They blink in the sudden light. The men pause, taking in the car, its motor still running, as they inspect the wrapped sandwiches. Prolonging, I suppose, a brief release from what must be airless, cell-like conditions. A soldier often idly pats my head or gives my arm a friendly punch. "Heh, kid," one says, "What room can't you go in?" And not waiting for an answer, "What's black and white and red all over?"

When in old age Alice begins to show signs of the anarchical randomness that will fundamentally alter our relationship, it becomes clear—the thought arrives while pouring over faded childhood photographs—that I have an important role to play on these jaunts, greater than merely handing out lunch. Why does she never leave the car? My adult fantasy decides the sight of this well-endowed, neatly uniformed young woman slipping across the sand, whose image I now recapture with her arm wrapped closely around my seven-year-old shoulders, would have driven any conscripted, heterosexual, enlisted man forced to spend days in enduring tedium, imprisoned in a white box staring at the waves, watching for invaders who never come, mad with desire. So by my presence I am her unknowing protector. But not fully trusting such suppositions, I also wonder if she just didn't think she could make it across the sand in high heels.

The first recognition that there was something called "The War" comes from the grinding, groaning sounds of single-engine fighter planes. Although they mostly land from the Brooklyn side of the airfield, planes taking off from Floyd Bennett seem to aim at a point high over my street in borough of Queens directly across the Bay from the runway. As they soar and climb, pick up a course, they seem to hover. At first, I believe they notice me. I run to the sidewalk and wave my arms wildly. Their wings, I am certain, wiggle back in recognition. But older, I learn war is too serious a business to permit casual contact with waving children. Discovering the trading cards that come in packages of chewing gum feature not only pictures of the planes but also aeronautic specifications, I become a student. My first truly intellectual act is to distinguish between Grumman Wildcats and Hellcats, Curtiss Avengers, North American Mustangs, and P41s. The different silhouettes make it look easy. Scanning the sky from our backyard or even leaning far out of my bedroom window, I have a clear view of the underside of aircraft seeking altitude. They each have a distinctive bulk or so I imagine. I challenge my friends to match my skill. But it's the sound that does me in.

Someone tells me that kids really in the know are able to identify in a few seconds the make and model of the aircraft from the groan of the engine noise alone. Jimmy, the flabby bully who lives down the block, claims he can do it but I certainly cannot. I don't believe him and tell him so. He turns away and then comes back with a hard punch. This is the first time I've been in a real fistfight and while defending myself I start to cry. We end up brawling on the patch of grass that is my front yard and he with a father who scowls and older brothers who probably work him over regularly, Jimmy seems to know what he is doing. He is a war veteran at nine. A slow-moving, fatted cow, but bigger and older than I am and calm at his work, which is aimed at methodically taking me apart.

My tears flow, not so much from his parried blows because I find I'm a lot faster brawler than he is, but from the tension of it all, the bodies, the smell of fear, of sweat, and the surprising hate in my heart. Violence when it comes, I will learn later, is all consuming but actually uninteresting because it is always the same, always the same agitation of the brain whether the source is a bear or a bullet. In the future a professional prizefight worth millions will stand as one of the more celebrated public events in which I have a hand but what I remember most vividly about that boxing match is not the raining blows, not even the last-round fall to the canvas of my client, but my own barely suppressed yawns. I was amazed at the famous writers—A. J. Liebling, Norman Mailer, and Joyce Carol Oates—who found some important take away from prizefights. At the Mohammad Ali versus Joe Frazier "fight of the century," March 8, 1971, after watching the battle intently for a few rounds, I found more interest in the pimps who had sequestered many of the ringside seats and their amazing floor-length furs.

Alice comes to the porch and stands watching. She is dressed in perfectly ironed white slacks and a colorful flowered print shirt. Compared to the women in this neighborhood most of whom dress like they never leave home, she stands out. I have learned by comparing her to other mothers that she must care a great deal about how she looks even if she doesn't show it or spend much time or money on her appearance. But her hair is pinned back and covered with a checkered kerchief, a sure sign that despite her clothing she has been disturbed while doing housework.

She looks down at the turmoil for what seems like an eternity but probably is just a few seconds as we flail away and I mumble insults to Jimmy through my tears.

I cannot believe her silence. I want and expect her to intervene; it is what adults are supposed to do, isn't it? But she takes her time. When she finally speaks, her voice cracks like ice. A voice that has nothing to do with "Eat your vegetables," or "Clear your place," or "Time for bed." Not the gentle voice that says, "Be careful with those sandwiches." A voice not meant for children or even distracted men. A command coming from somewhere beyond her beauty, a somewhere the men who flirt with her will never visit.

"History," William James tells us, "is a bath of blood." In one of the greatest essays in the English language, he writes, "Our ancestors have bred pugnacity into our bone and marrow and a thousand years of peace won't breed it out of us." And he must be right. Why did Jimmy and I fight? There was no "gold, women, slaves, excitement" to be gathered. But there must have been pride, another motive on his list, and, of course, now educated by the wider world, I know that weakness is the flip side of pride and by defending pride—respect is what it is called on the mean streets—the voice of weakness is muffled, if never fully silenced.

"Stop crying."

It's a simple order but it comes with explosive passion. It does not ask but demands. "Stop crying. NOW." Then a pause after obedience, after a tear-free punch, after a screaming Jimmy grabs at his jaw and runs home.

"Good. Fight if you want," she says, "but no crying. Never." What living has hardened a calcified core from a woman who so often has held me against the softness of her body? Of course, the child doesn't know enough to conceive the question, much less divine the answer. It will be a long time before I find out but the fierceness in her voice has passed into my body.

When Alice is dying, actually when I leave her to die in a Florida hospital room, I remember the injunction against crying. Dead in every way but officially, after days of not eating, drinking, and speaking, eyes closed, inert, aged, and creased, the one hint of her beauty left as she lays there immobile—hair a snowy white, brilliantly combed by an attendant, as light as fluff.

"Goodbye mom. Thank you. Thank you for bringing me up despite hard times. Thank you most of all for recognizing me, for finding a way to let me know I mattered. For showing my how to fight." I kiss her but there is no sign she knows. It feels strange to leave after so many days, strange not to stay at her bedside for as long as it takes, disloyal to go before some ritual act confirms the end of life, strange that I never say, "I love you." In the centuries since man left the caves, has death ever been attended such? Am I just a miserable son or simply another nameless artifact of social change?

"There is nothing you can do." The woman who has recently become her doctor says repeatedly. With this official blessing, I am now permitted to let her die alone.

Relieved, free to go, but also self-doubting, I take the first plane I can get North; the next day I teach a class and go to a faculty meeting. I try not to think of her but there is no avoiding the call to the hospital. Taking note of tangled feelings is, in fact, all I can do. Inevitably I start to beat myself up for not staying as long as necessary but then remember that she flew from Florida to New York for some pretend medical appointment as her last husband lay dying. Alice just couldn't attend another death; she arranged to return only when he was done for. So once again she has shown the way, crooked as it may be. There is no terror and no tears; certainly, no tears. "Never."

But in their place I am left with a memory of flight—blunt, cutting, failure.

After my father died, there were for us a few good years. Ira lived for nineteen after Alice was told he had a cancer that should have killed him within five at the very most. "He is the world's record holder," one doc awkwardly told her. Ira struggled for most of these years with a general fatigue that he cannot name because he is kept from the knowledge of its source. Alice and his doctor have decided that they simply cannot pass on the message that there is no cure. They become co-conspirators, concocting a series of phony diagnoses that ostensibly require treatments that are really meant to palliate the primary lesions. They get lucky when he develops jaundice from a blood transfusion. Now they are able to treat a real threat, one that conveniently masks the greater one.

His doctor finally recommends the crude chemotherapy of the time. Nitrogen mustard, first developed by the Germans, converted to poison gas that seeps through the skin to kill and maim tens of thousands in World War I trenches. By the 1940s its capacity to kill white blood cells has led scientists to turn experience with a devastating and illegal chemical agent into an injectable drug named mechlorethamine that for a time proves modestly effective in treating certain malignancies. Unfortunately, the right dosage for the drug is uncertain. In my father's case, it's as if he actually did serve in the trenches of Ypres—the poison does as much harm as good to his body.

Ira's response to the bouts of fatigue and the medical interventions that follow is classic macho. There are no complaints. Much clenching of teeth and looking away. That he is never told the truth somehow makes this easier to understand. In fact, he seems to double his exertions against the tide of weariness, never missing work, rarely saying he is tired, whenever he can going to the theater at night. He fires up the sources of his strength with a chain of Benson & Hedges Parliament cigarettes, extraordinarily hard to find during the war years. Even when his willingness to play catch or shoot baskets with me is diminished, he implies it's because he is working so hard. It has nothing to do with any illness.

Internalizing what must be seen now as the family norm, I go along with the total denial that anything is wrong. If there are cracks, I quickly fill them. The one exception is his coughing fits, hacking sounds that seemed to go on forever, often after midnight. They wake me from sound sleep. I lie in bed and just listen silently. Pretend I am asleep. Although my mother also smokes and doesn't cough, they both claim the coughing is "only" a smoker's cough. But she does urge him to cut down. He agrees readily but evidence of him actually moderating his habit is hard to find. The strain on his lungs continues. So does the noise in the night. Many decades later, after losing much of my esophagus to my own misalliance with tobacco, I develop my own cough. The sound of it brings me back to Ira, who I have almost forgotten.

When at last he succumbs, I am a college sophomore studying for exams in Oberlin, Ohio. Alice calls one early December evening. Her voice is flat. She tells me he is hospitalized and that I should come. I get a ride to Hopkins Airport in time to catch a late-night transcontinental flight on a Dutch airliner briefly stopping at Cleveland before going on to New York. I am the only embarking passenger. The blond stewardess takes one look and brings me a milky cup of coffee from the first class galley. I have never tasted such good coffee before and I am hooked for life. In my drugged state, I want to marry her.

In the hospital, Ira looks in bad shape. Wrapped in blankets, his head is slightly raised but he doesn't move or talk. He seems to nod at my entrance and I believe even winks. Then he closes his eyes. I sit in the room for hours while

Alice gets some sleep and try unsuccessfully to study for my exams. The next morning, a handsome young surgeon comes by. He briefly hovers over Ira's comatose body, insisting everything is as it should be. He says Ira is on the mend but cautions that recovery will take time. Alice tells me to return to Ohio. All will be well. I want to believe her so I go.

Two days later he is dead. At first, the hospital tells us they aren't sure of the cause but then it's ultimately attributed to internal bleeding resulting from a poorly executed surgical intervention. I hide my grief behind a furious feeling that I was tricked to leave. Years later, my own doctor, a perceptive Boston internist, speculates that the original cancer diagnosis was erroneous; Ira may have been mistreated for much of his adult life! Arriving at the funeral, the casket is open. For a moment, I have the bizarre feeling that my father is really alive. He should get out of the box! Alice is shocked; she shouts something and the casket is quickly closed. There is only one speaker, a family friend, but he's not really especially close to Ira, just the husband of a woman who went to school with Alice. I realize that, in fact, there are many Ira calls friends but none who are truly intimate. Alice is this only child's one close friend. The speaker describes my father pretty much as I expect—an amiable man who went out of his way to help people, who had an infectious sense of humor—but he ignores the toughness, the man who loves to unmask, behind the easy manner. He goes on about his great love for wife and son but with the mention of my name, I am no longer there. I stop observing. My thoughts are like the clapping of bricks and I go missing until the ceremony is over.

Back at school, a numbness comes over me. I am surprised at the many who offer sympathy until I realize that I am seen as a first—few of them have yet to lose a parent. Most of the time I mumble thanks and look away. I try to forget what has happened. But a few months after his death, home on a school vacation, I pick up the phone and hand it to Alice. It is the young surgeon who had done Ira's operation. She listens and hardly speaks. Emotions play across her face like a fast-moving set of storm clouds—shock, dismay, and finally I see embarrassment, maybe even shame.

"No, but thank you," she says nervously. "It is very kind of you to call, but no. Very kind and I do thank you."

She replaces the receiver and looks away. She lights a cigarette and turns back to her startled, staring son. "He asked me out . . . on a date." She disappears into her bedroom and shuts the door. I call up his face. Good looking, I recall. My stomach tightens; fists clench. This is the guy, I think, who killed him. Fuck. Fuck. . . . But the rage has nowhere to go.

Soon we go to see Ira's longtime doctor, who also happens to be Alice and my doctor. He is a miniature of a man with a tall reputation for wisdom among New York internists, although I always had my doubts. I never understood why I couldn't have my own doctor. Alice gave me a slippery reason—it would save time because we could all go together. When I was fourteen, he took me aside after spending time in his office with my mother and after the usual cursory questions about school that grown-ups resort to, met with my monosyllabic answers, issued his prescription: "Don't lie around in bed in the morning. Get up as soon as you awake; get on with the day."

Even at that age I understood he was crossing a line— telling me not to masturbate without telling me what was wrong with masturbation. I had actually read a page of the *Boy Scout Handbook* that recommended that on arising youths should take a cold bath so despite my confused youthful feelings I knew society condemned the act of pleasuring yourself. A decade later when I was a first-year law student, the Supreme Court excluded obscenity from protection of the first amendment. Justice Brennan defined the obscene as appealing to the "prurient" interest. Looking up a word I had never heard before, I realized immediately that while the opinion didn't say so explicitly, the Court was largely concerned with masturbation.

After this meeting, I turned wary of Dr. Weiss but he and my mother look very tight. Watching while pretending to read a sports magazine, I can tell they share something but have no idea what it is. I sat close by her, both of us across from him at the tiny desk in his office, as if to protect her. But they were talking only about medical records, test results, and cause of death. I flipped the pages of the magazine and tried not to listen. At first, I thought there was nothing here for me. But then I must have been brought to the meeting for a reason.

Dr. Weiss laid out a series of medical terms. At the end of his monologue, he said to my mother, "I'm comfortable with remission. I will report remission." He said it twice.

She was listening carefully and offered, "Then there shouldn't be a problem; the insurance company gave him a general exam before issuing the policy."

"What's the problem that isn't a problem?" I blurted out.

They looked at me, as if they had forgotten my presence.

Alice stared. Her face was near mine and she gripped the armrests of the chair. The story spilled out. Weiss said little but did a lot of nodding. The cancer. He would lose hope if he knew. Waiting for a cure. Nobody lived as long as he did. Death was expected within a few years. Lasted nineteen. Got to see you become a man.

I never knew, was not told; if I suspected, then I must have been good at selective amnesia. And I was kept from it. Until today, treated like a child . . . and he, must he have known? And couldn't say because they wouldn't give him a name? Or maybe he didn't know because he feared knowing. For a moment I wanted to strike her. And him too. Both of them. Light them up. Suddenly I saw them from a great distance. They are things, not people. Just disturbing objects. I wanted out of the room but I stayed seated, studying the carpet.

In the months that follow, her grief was balanced by freedom from the burdens of an exclusive, first-time love, from the gradual numbing of her life with a man condemned to die before his time. They had met when she was fifteen and

Ira a year plus older. Had never been parted. The two virgins secretly eloped in 1931, married by a skeptical justice of the peace in Greenwich, Connecticut, who thought they might be runaway kids but went ahead with the ceremony anyway. They did it to confound parental opposition. She was too young and he was broke but there was also class-based hostility between the two families common at the time—the Russian background of one side and the German on the other. It was characteristic of Alice and Ira's total assimilation that she wasn't ever clear about which side came from which place. "It wasn't important," she tried to explain years later. "Only immigrants cared about that stuff." But it was confusing. Even as an early teen I considered this nonsensical. Their parents had been born in New York and Philly, not Berlin or the pale of settlement. They weren't recent arrivals. But aside from Ira's mother, they were all dead and presented as shadowy two-dimensional figures. The way they saw the world was shunned. Lost or denied.

Two years after their Greenwich escapade they were married for show in a Manhattan hotel ballroom. At the last moment, the parents agreed to attend. Then the Great Depression controlled their fate. They were forced to move around the country while he looked for work, sharing what little money and space they could afford with those parents, whose businesses in the interim had gone bust. For the first time in their lives they had been poor and there were days when they were hungry. Long before I knew what

the Depression was, I understood that my parents had been
through something that had made them older and more
fragile than they had been before, tangles that they could
straighten out only if they could harden them into oft-told
anecdotes about going without a meal or walking fifty
blocks through Manhattan to avoid bus fare.

They must have been, I suppose, totally monogamous
from the day they met; there is implicit confirmation in that
now she and I are both seriously playing the dating game
for the first time. The $50,000 in life insurance money she
and Dr. Weiss worried over has come through; she gives
me $5,000 to pay for college tuition and whatever I want
thereafter. It's a generous gift. There isn't more coming to
her. Ira had tried for years to get life insurance and was
always rejected. Apparently they gave him cockeyed reasons for denying coverage but a few years before he died he
had finally been successful.

In response to her sharing what she has to live on while
she figures out how to support herself, I decide to take her
on a trip South with my savings from summer work. We
find a cheap flight and go to Havana for a long weekend.
Cuba is then in the control of the brutal dictator, Fulgen-
cio Batista, who treats the country as his own profit center
and has a cozy deal with the mafia. Fidel Castro will over-
throw the tyrant two years later in a move that, at first,
many Americans find appealing because of highly favorable coverage by Herbert Matthews, a *New York Times*
reporter who denies Castro is a communist. Matthews has

been taken to see Castro in his mountain camp at a time when many thought he was dead, heard Fidel describe himself as a committed democrat and believed he was supported by significant force.

But we don't discuss Cuban politics. This is a trip to get across to her that grief doesn't last forever. Because it isn't high season, we are able to stay at the most fashionable hotel in Havana, the Nacional, designed by McKim, Mead and White and probably controlled by the mafia. We gamble and win modestly. She suns herself at the pool for hours and surprises me by announcing that an old friend will hire her to do publicity for a French perfume house. She is lucky, she says, to have such a good son. This is repeated often. If she realizes how angry I am about her lying to my father, she hides it well. It's hard for me to separate whether I'm in turmoil for Ira not being told about the cancer, or for myself.

Just outside the hotel gates are clusters of pimps and hangers on ready to cater to every tourist desire. They shout out drugs for sale, their sisters are available, or if not interested how about a carriage tour of the City. When we go for a walk, a cabbie asks if we want him to take us to see the Superman show. We wave him off not having any idea what he is talking about. Later, an American standing next to me at the crap table tells me Superman is a folk hero and tourist draw. He has a penis the size of a baby elephant's. For a fee, he displays his talents with various female companions before a howling audience of tourists. In a club near the casino, Alice and I dance a modest foxtrot. I can tell guests who notice us wonder if we are lovers or mother and son. On this trip watching men follow her with their eyes to the roulette table or sizing her up while she stands next to me as I roll the dice, I realize my mother has no idea what to do with her looks.

When we return to New York, suitors start to appear sent by Alice's friends. Even I can see that most of them are total misfits, burnt-out divorce cases, professional bachelors, guys trying to hide their balding heads under fedoras, but then she is so awkward in their presence, so unclear about what she wants and what is expected of her, that I decide it's better I stay clear. And I am her son—plainly full of ambivalence of a Freudian nature. But she wants a companion and for some reason it's me who ends up playing the girlfriend. She talks about the men openly, with what I find a shocking innocence, and asks my opinion of each. My fear here is that she'll think that after she tells me her secrets I'm obliged to tell her mine. Still I try to meet her half way. I can't just nod my head.

"Mom," I ask finally, taking a deep breath, "what about the physical?"

"Oh, that's ok," she answers not revealing anything at all.

"That's what they've come for," I think but am afraid to say.

And a deeper thought confounds me, admitted and then instantly batted away: With a long-dying husband she probably hasn't had sex for years. To stay as separate as I can from her experience but also, of course, fascinated, I keep trying to be a good listener. When she asks polite questions about my own doings, they evoke only mumbled clichés but she isn't really interested in more. She wants permission and affirmation, not communication. It is at these moments of snatched conversation, actually her monologues and my deflections, that she begins to tell me stories. I had been sent to summer camp in upstate New York for July and August at seven years, old because they could then rent our Rockaway Beach house to vacationers from "the City" while reserving one bedroom for themselves. As a result, they'd clear enough from the renters to send me to camp and pay for a year's upkeep of the house.

"You know," she says, "Belle Harbor, that's what the real estate people have started to call Rockaway Beach. Well it used to be a prized summer destination for middle class New Yorkers." She tells this to a disbelieving me—Rockaway, in Queens County, within City limits, a desired summer destination!—over coffee in a cozy, well-furnished, Westside Manhattan apartment, a building with a doorman and a handy, on-call super. Proof, I suppose, that they had ultimately beat the bad years.

So now I understand my exile to swim endlessly in the chilly waters of Lake Oneida until late every summer afternoon giant-like counselors with hairy arms tenderly pull me out of the water, why I was eating unusual food including vegetables from tin cans, spending bad moments on the generous lap of a woman called The Matron, sleeping next to a kid nicknamed The Yellow Submarine whose sheets hang on the line every morning washed of his piss. They sent me to camp for daycare. To get me out of the house!

One night upstate I am given a part in a play. The recreation hall is filled with older campers and their parents. I am almost naked, having been dressed in a pillowcase, pinned across my middle like a diaper. I'm instructed to run on the stage several times and shout, "Where is my grandpa?"

Of course, I have no idea what this is all about, and I'm greeted by greater laughter, studded with applause, after each appearance. After the last, something I cannot see happens on stage and the audience erupts. Maybe one of my Grandpas has arrived but then I remember I don't have any. They are both dead. A counselor pushes me on the stage for a bow. There is even more applause. I am not certain why they like me but I do enjoy the attention. I will tell my parents the counselors put me in a show when they make their midsummer visit but after they actually arrive turn silent and totally focus on what food they bring.

"Green grapes, your favorite," Alice offers hopefully. Probably both of us know, though in a different way, that I am too young for this. The grapes are a seedless, slithery, and sweet refuge.

A Most of the Time Only Child

I was aware that unlike most of my schoolmates I had no sibling but it took a while before I inquired about the absence of a brother or sister. I don't remember what I said to my mother the first time I brought up the subject but her answer was unforgettable—"You're all one needs."

With a little perspective of the sort I was much too young to grasp, I could have concluded she was counteracting the usual reactions in those days to a singleton, which was to wonder why—was it perhaps the product of a troubled or failed marriage? Was it caused by a female health issue? Had it resulted in a spoiled, self-centered, and lonely child? But I was oblivious; certainly had no sense of being a victim, though it would have been nice to have a protective older brother or sister. After her secret had been exposed, Alice explained that she had been told early on that Ira was unlikely to survive; given their then perilous financial situation that meant no more children. But her "You're all one needs" was an early message; it plainly contributed to me wanting to succeed in the world, to satisfy my parent's hopes, and to confirm their judgment. If I was pampered, however, I wasn't in touch with it. I never consciously expected special treatment but wouldn't have recognized it if it was present because there was no one around for comparison. My cousins were older; they lived in a different city. Nor did my parents often convey the kind of anxiety about my safety or choices that could be expected in the sort of culture where a single male is viewed as a precious commodity. Of course, I wasn't totally dull to my status. There were the jokes. I heard my first Jewish Prince joke when we still lived near the beach. That's probably why I still remember how the Jewish mother is said to run across the sand toward the lifeguard screaming, "Help, help, my son, the dentist, is drowning." It never occurred to me that the boy supposedly flailing in the waves could have siblings.

While they never got specific in the way that friends often reported their parent's talk about grades, colleges, and choices of professions, knowing that I was "All one needs" produced a seriousness of purpose. Alice and Ira talked about the larger world; they paid attention to politics and policy and from an early age I followed suit. And by nurturing my independence my mother made me strong and self-directed beyond my years; she also inadvertently led me toward adolescent megalomania. I decided that not only I could create myself just as I wanted to be but also I should do so—a view of who I was that would flower when I began to practice law.

My mind went places I thought so strange that I could tell them to no one. A recurrent thought was that I could stand anything but death. I was aware that I thought about dying *and* avoiding it much too much. In time, such thoughts moderated, transitioning to dreams of glory: I would be a hero, one who would slay death. "[H]eroism promises immortality," as Charles Hampden-Turner once put it. Because in my world, there was no afterlife, no life after life, the childhood project would become defeating death symbolically and practically. Millions of others may approach their maturity with such fantasies, perhaps more so today spurred on by the computer gaming culture, but few are placed serendipitously, or otherwise, as I was to act it out when at age twenty-six, with special permission of the Justices, I argued a death penalty appeal before the Supreme Court. This would be my "immortality project" as Ernest Becker termed it in *The Denial of Death*, something that injects dignity and significance to life, and is thought to outlast it.

It wasn't until I approached my eightieth year that I had a concrete daydream of a life after life—it was that my ashes would be spread across a beloved bay faced by a family house where in the gooey world of such mental excursions my grandchildren and their progeny would be instructed that HE is out there.

I couldn't definitely answer the "Why an only child?" question until at age nineteen when I learned about my father's health but by then it was much too late to affect how I thought about myself. Hearing the story seemed to explain how I was treated, sometimes bizarrely, as if I was older than I really was, which in turn brought on a feeling that I was more like an adult than I had any right to feel. That led me to an undeserved belief in my own maturity as a man and a desire to do as my father did. How does a son take after his father when he is a concrete presence, tough at his core, full of virtues to imitate, but in an undefined but powerful way fading? I ended up tracking him by becoming an attentive son, as he was a husband, one who most importantly could anticipate his mother's wishes. This adaptation boils down to understanding your manly job is to take care of and protect the women in your life. I wondered about this in every serious relationship I've had, noting how often I worked—sometimes successfully, sometimes disastrously—to remain in friendly and supportive contact long after the passion had gone.

We tell stories like this about ourselves to support, I suppose, a sense of identity, a comforting belief that we know and can report at least to ourselves who we are. The blow that shattered this mirror image came in early December 1997. Alice was eighty-six years old; after the death of her third husband, she was in the process of leaving her New York apartment to live full time in a condo she owned in Sarasota, Florida. She had what appeared on the surface, at least, a successful widowed and retired life with volunteer assignments at the Florida East Coast Symphony and a branch library. She had friends in her condo complex but her most significant relationship was with an attractive local woman I'll call Janice. She had hired Janice to clean her condo unit but soon she became a confidant who invited Alice to her permanently placed mobile home for meals with her husband and children. She would run errands and with her husband take care of minor repairs to the condo. On a visit to Sarasota, I met her for the first time. She was full of praise for Alice—"what a wonderful woman." My mother, in the room at the time, glowed.

Until she turned eighty-five, Alice's health problems seemed more age appropriate than life threatening but two conditions that in the past had been troublesome but not critical began to cause her acute distress. She had surgery for glaucoma that was botched, leading to loss of vision in one eye, and back surgery for spinal stenosis that slightly improved her mobility and reduced the pain, though it offered no permanent cure. The surgeries themselves weren't particularly hard on her but during the recovery process she was often heavily drugged to deal with discomfort. For a time she was seriously depressed. Her memory suffered and she was easily confused. As a result of the back surgery, she took to using a cane. While the aftermath of the surgeries slowed her down and narrowed the range of her activities, they didn't compromise her strongly defended independence. She still lived alone in her condominium. When my wife and I told her that she could move close to us, settling in a Boston area assisted living facility, she rejected the idea immediately. Losing her independent way of life was out of the question. I was told by one of her acquaintances that she thought the suggestion was hostile. I should have been warned.

Then came the letter to me and my wife. It was from Roberta, whose friendship with Alice went back over forty-five years to a time when Ira was alive and Roberta was an isolated suburban mother with a demanding husband whose job as a New York publicist for Hollywood movies kept him constantly on the go and on edge. Alice was older, had been through her own stresses, and brought calm and comfort to the younger woman. "We have been through a lot and have always been there for each other," Roberta would say describing a relationship that was even more important to her once both women were widowed.

On a visit to Sarasota, she had been shocked. "I am writing to you about the goings-on that have taken place at your mother's home . . . I think you should be made aware . . . your mother has become more and more dependent upon this woman. . . . She and her husband did wonderful things for her, taking her back and forth to doctors . . . maintaining the house, the garden, painting and tiling . . . [but] I have always felt that this couple had motives that were not pure! Alice paid their mortgage, paid for medical care of their children, bought [Janice] a car, taking them both on trips. . . . The lengths she has gone to for these people . . . allowing them to redecorate their house at Alice's expense . . . she is getting older and has to be cared for."

My reaction as I read to this point was ambivalent. Roberta was calling attention to some things I was aware of, though much of the relationship she described was new to me. My mother is hardly rich, I thought, but she plainly has more money than this couple and maybe it's a fair trade to have folks around she likes who will help keep up the house and be available when she needs assistance. But then Roberta by questioning their motives was suggesting that she was in potential jeopardy of serious manipulation and abuse.

I had first heard of Janice a decade earlier when my mother told me she had lent money to the woman who cleaned her condo, whose family had medical problems. Janice was so grateful, Alice reported, that her family would do a variety of errands as well as all manner of repairs on the unit and look after it when she was in New York. I was pleased that there was someone my mother could call on for help if she needed it. On visits to Sarasota, I took Janice and her husband to dinner. The talk would bounce around from my mother's needs to Janice's children to local politics; it was superficial and unthreatening. But we had little in common other than an interest in Alice. I was there to thank them.

On occasion, Janice would try to become more intimate. Once she told me that her son from a previous marriage had read a book of mine and was thinking of law school. Would I counsel him about applying? I wrote him a letter about the process. During my mother's recuperation from her surgeries, Janice visited and ran errands. I asked her to call me collect immediately should there be any change in Alice's circumstances or needs. She readily agreed and shortly thereafter phoned to discuss installing a medical alert system so my mother could summon help promptly. I felt secure that my mother had someone nearby who was committed to support her if needed, though as it happened I never received another call from Janice.

So at first I was untroubled about what I was reading. Could Roberta, I wondered, just be jealous of Janice's place in my mother's heart? But as I read further, my attitude changed.

Alice "went to her lawyer and legally adopted Janice. In order to do this Janice had to obtain a letter from her biological mother, releasing her as to her relationship with the mother so she could legally be adopted . . . she had Janice's name added to her checking account . . . there was a discrepancy on this account . . . for $5,000 that Alice didn't remember who she gave it to. . . . The bank representative asked me to look into this, didn't like Janice and appeared not to want to deal with her under any circumstances. . . . The next thing I hear . . . [Alice] wrote into her will leaving the Florida house to Janice and her husband."

Reading this was torture. I tried to make a joke of it—no more an only child!—but I was furious. My first thought was "Here we go again!" This was a version of the secrecy that had kept my father's illness from him for nineteen years. Alice knew I had initially blamed her when I found out. But those feelings had been put to rest and I had assured her that I understood how difficult the decision must have been. But had she heard me? Was this latest dishonesty a payback for my disdain at the first one or simply the way she dealt with trouble?

With my wife's help, I tried to review our relationship to figure out whether I had done something wrong. I spoke to my mother regularly. It bothered me that I was the one who always called, but the conversations were mostly trouble free, though a bit formulaic. In trying to make sense of what I'd just read, I replayed the usual dialogue in my head. What clues had I missed?

We talked grandchildren. She was eager to hear of their development.

We often talked finances. Alice had been an independent investor for years and was proud of her acumen but she often asked me market-based questions. She liked to multiply her modest holdings in far too many different stock and bond accounts, as if the proliferation would protect her from fraud or dissolution of any one company. This made it difficult to keep track of how she was doing but she claimed that her assets were growing. She would often offer me some of her profits but I assured her I was doing well. She should keep her investments for her own needs.

Once she asked me to talk to her broker and get a reading on him and the quality of his advice. I was happily surprised when the young man knowledgeably answered all my questions, displaying awareness of the prudence needed to assist an aging widow.

I would ask her about her work for the symphony. She often replied how much she liked the performers who appeared at Sarasota's Van Wezel Performing Arts Hall. "Just as good as New York," was a frequent comment.

She did not often express any interest in talking to my wife, unless she wanted to lay the groundwork for a visit. We journeyed to Sarasota at least once year and would often see her in Manhattan when she came North in the summer. But the number of her trips to New York and New England, however, had slowly declined. Invitations to come to our house in Cambridge, Massachusetts, in other seasons were rejected on the ground that she "was done with the cold."

Had I failed my mother? Had I been willfully blind to what was plainly a mental deterioration? Or to whatever game Janice was playing? I tried to slay my guilt with knowledge that Alice's history had left her with a vulnerability I had not seen clearly enough—she had never been well mothered. Thirteen years younger than her sister, her mother an older woman when she was born, Alice had always claimed sister Frances had brought her up. Had her mother treated her as if she was a mistake? Did Janice offer the on-the-spot, on-demand caretaking that solved her practical needs as well as the attention she had craved from a caretaker? All this speculation paled before the basic fact of a secret adoption that gave credence to Roberta's fear that Alice was being manipulated and even robbed as well as compelling me to have a sister I did not want.

With dark humor, I mused that a real sister when I was fifteen might have introduced me to the girls I lusted after but was too afraid to confront but it was plain that when a woman in her eighties legally adopts a fortyish ex-cleaning lady, something is likely amiss. My fears climbed higher on a wall of worry when my mother flatly denied everything when asked directly—the adoption, the will, the car, the money, the co-checking account, even that Janice was more than a casual friend.

But I pressed her, sadly feeling like I was lawyering my mother. The evidence piled up and finally after a few weeks she surprised me by confessing, though never referring to her earlier disavowals. Alice wrote that she had done the adoption because Janice "saved my life"—apparently helping her while she recovered from surgery—and because "I need her," though adding that "by the way she expects no remuneration." The adoption means nothing—"I was the most important person in her life." She hadn't realized that "You would now have a sister, someone with equal rights to make medical and end of life decisions." Alice also admitted her new car—she'd totaled her previous vehicle—turned out to be actually owned jointly with Janice, who had gone shopping with her when she bought the car. And then she blurted out the thing that defined the matter: adopting Janice only meant it would be "binding her to me."

Later it came out that before Roberta's last visit, Janice had called Alice's stockbroker to tell him that a "poor relative" who might be after her money would be visiting. The broker professed shock and surprise that he would get such a call from someone he'd never heard of before on supposed behalf of a client but he never brought the matter to my attention. Alice confirmed that Janice was co-owner of her checking account and also admitted she had made mortgage payments on Janice's home. A few months earlier she had dismissed her longtime physician and a local gerontologist, replacing them with a doctor recommended by Janice. And then another bombshell, before the adoption Janice had secretly taken my mother to a psychiatrist to get proof while she adopted she was of sound mind.

At the time, I'd had been a member of the bar for almost forty years. I'd represented hundreds of clients in intensely litigated cases. Some in state courts, most in federal; sometimes in complicated administrative hearings. I'd hired my own lawyer when purchasing property and drawing a will but I'd never been a client myself in an actively litigated matter. Moreover, I knew nothing about Florida law or the Sarasota bar but luck was with me when I asked the advice of an old civil rights colleague who practiced across the state on the East coast but knew something of Sarasota legal community. Within months my new lawyers had the adoption voided and Jackie's mother's parental rights restored. At first, Alice resisted changing her will back to leave her estate to her grandchildren but ultimately she relented more I think because I asked her to than her own wishes. She tore up a new checkbook I'd arranged that replaced the one with Janice as co-owner but then opened a new account at the same bank without her, evidencing I thought mistrust of me as well as a desire to simply control as much of her life as possible.

These changes required that I become her court-ordered legal guardian. After taking a lengthy video training course and a passing a test ordered by a local judge, I hired two caretakers, one to deal with collecting Alice's income and paying the bills, and the other to look after her well-being as a companion. Both were remarkably caring and able people who stood by her as she declined. Medical examinations in the three years left in her life documented increasing dementia and a heart condition that ultimately took her away.

In a conference with the lawyer who arranged annulment of the adoption I was asked if I was asserting bad faith or any criminally abusive conduct on Janice's part. I made it clear that I would not make any such claims if Janice agreed to the annulment without further proceedings. He told me that would probably settle the matter with the court. Then feeling relaxed and comfortable I assumed my law professor stance. I asked him whether someone like Janice could be pursued by the law for taking advantage of an elder.

The well-groomed, white-haired lawyer leaned back in his desk chair, glanced out of the window toward the Gulf of Mexico, and slowly answered, telling me that Florida had few protections in place for senior citizens subject to manipulation. He told a story about a former houseboy from the Caribbean who had ended up inheriting millions from an elderly widow who doted on him. Her family had lost a legal challenge to the will.

"But," I cut him off, "it's a state with a huge population of older Americans. How can that be?"

"Ah," he said, pausing as if revealing a great truth to an innocent, "you know the people who move here to retire aren't thinking about their families all the time. Lots of them want to get away from you all, especially from the meddling of their adult children. Oh, they like visits on the holidays and regular phone calls but most of the time they feel they are now free to live as they want without interference or criticism from folks up North. That's why the state's elder protective laws are weak. They don't ask for them to be stronger because they don't want interference."

I must have looked shocked because he gave me a gentle smile and remarked, "Say look at your mother's case. In her last years she was in and out mentally but she very much wanted to be left alone. You may be a great guy but you were far away and she heard your concern as an effort to control her. Welcome to the Sunshine State."

Another Kind of War

Eight years old I am again sent to summer camp, this time to the Pocono Mountains of Pennsylvania. I feel experienced, more in control. I learn about color war and Capture the Flag but actually to my amazement, New York kid among suburbanites, Pennsylvanians, and Jersey boys, I already know. It's important not to let on that I've actually played Ringalevio. Well only three times but it's enough to feel New York superior. The game has taught the kind of tactical thinking I will employ as a litigator well before my time.

There are two teams. The kids in one scatter and hide. The other team searches the area and tries to catch any boy—there are no girls in sight—that can be found by grabbing hold, and then chanting "Ringalevio 1-2-3, 1-2-3, 1-2-3!"

If you're caught, you are taken to a place designated as base or jail—in my neighborhood the front porch of a local Victorian, a dark gray, usually unlit, house the neighborhood kids think is haunted. The place is decrepit, choked by wisteria, scary enough for me to wish the jail was an empty sandlot of which in the 1940s there are many, or a nearby playground, even a chalked area between parked cars. If a kid on your team is able to reach the jail area and run through it without being seized, he'll shout "Jail Break" and then the prisoners rush out screaming "Free. Free."

There is a frantic energy, a mix of fury and panic roaming the neighborhood until one team detains all the members of the other, or, more commonly, exhaustion sets in. These are the facts but as facts often do they totally fail to capture the feeling—crazy, chaotic, pure anxiety—of the chase. Ringalevio is brilliant and intense; once you've played, you never forget. It's cruel because running children are grabbed in flight, arrested with an unsupervised violence, and wrestled to the pavement or hard ground. Yet there are rules of engagement that are in everyone's mind even if they are not always followed because the game will fall apart otherwise. They are enforced with a random vengeance.

I am protectively tall for my age but younger and certainly greener than most of the players so the first time playing I only seize another boy when I am with others; often I hide out behind cars or on dark porches for safety. At times an angry energy overtakes me. I go out of my way to grab whomever I can; often it has to be done roughly. I am doing what the older boys do, which makes it ok. Somehow the game is, well, not so game like. It's the antithesis of sport but then just what kind of activity is it? Certainly, not something for parents to know about. It is never mentioned at the dinner table. Or at school. Some of the kids playing Ringalevio live on my street, others are from a poorer neighborhood, but all come together on those warm nights as if by magic. It may be something that kids do but also it's a simulation of war like chess. Only here the pawns are boys in motion.

In fact, the movements in Ringalevio are more like those of the combat soldiers I've seen in Pathé newsreels at the Park Theatre near the boardwalk on 116th Street than that of players in a sport. The films show how the American army captures French towns from the Germans. In Ringalevio we move across urban space like the hand-to-hand, house-by-house, combat of the advancing army. There are no time-outs, no referees, no spectators—indeed nosey adults in the vicinity will instantly lead to a pause in the game, even a cancellation. If there is pathology in the group, it will eventually be displayed; parents will only learn later from bloody noses, scraped knees, and visits to the emergency room what has happened when mobs of children congregate near the beach on June nights.

How summer camps came to adopt a form of Ringalevio as the often decisive contest to determine which group of campers wins the annual color war competition must be the subject of some graduate student's PhD thesis but it's still unclear to me. I wonder if it doesn't have something to do with the tendency of summer camps to mimic the identity and activities of American Indians. Camp fires, teepees, tribal designations, and Native American names are the stuff of my summers. Cabins are called after tribes. I've slept in Iroquois, Apache, and Winnebago. Imitation totem poles are raised in the meadows. Of course, the obvious urban roots of Ringalevio at first don't seem to suggest the connection but the camp authorities call their competition "Capture the Flag," which leads me to imagine a John Ford Movie with painted braves poised on their pinto ponies, high on a Western butte, watching the stiff-looking column of horse cavalry passing below. Regimental pennants are flying as the horse soldiers canter toward the inevitable bloody ambush.

The game, regardless of what it is called, liberates us from the strictures of the organized life. While in play we can be wild. Ringalevio has made me feel more powerful.

When I am hustled off to the Poconos for two months at this new camp, I have no idea what to expect. This place has strict uniform policies requiring camp-approved dark blue sweaters and shorts, each with name tapes my mother has sewed to identify my items when laundry is returned. At the new place there is remarkably little supervision. A girl's camp at the other end of the lake is the source of confusing comments; the counselors often act as if they have other things on their mind. But I can swim as long as I want, wander unimpeded past a woodland boundary and then down dirt tracks that connect the sprawling camp property to nearby dairy farms and cornfields. These are solitary walks of discovery. I chase salamanders, try to stab green snakes when they foolishly cross my path, and open the hatch of a wood-covered pit to a familiar acrid smell. Later I am told I have located the camp's septic tank.

Near the end of the summer when color war comes around, the mood shifts. A serious business lies ahead. The counselors look at us steadily, measuring our capacities to shoot baskets, run track, and lead others. The entire population of the camp is divided into teams, either Buff (a color I have never heard of) or Blue. Captains are chosen and you can tell there is bitterness among the older boys who aren't selected. Captains and counselor coaches then pick teams that will compete for points in basketball, baseball, tennis, and swimming over the next four days. There is also a group singing competition but the emphasis is on the physical, winning games while humiliating the other color. Campers bad mouth their opponents, even their best friends. When they can get away with it, during basketball games they push and shove. They resent, belittle, and insult. James writes that the military denies "neither the bestiality, not the horror, or the expense" of war, only saying these are the worthwhile and necessary costs, ultimately the protection against the "weaker and cowardly self." So are children taught.

But unlike real hostilities, in color war the teams are chosen to stalemate. The way things invariably come out, campers on each side are close enough in ability so that the victor must often triumph in the last event on the last day.

At some camps this is an all-in tug of war, and in others a race between two Native American–style war canoes. When I learn the clash that will decide our color war is called Capture the Flag, I think "Don't they know the right name?" I am a shocked eight-year-old.

A white line is chalked across the middle of the camp's immense acreage by the hand-pushed roller used to define the lines on the clay tennis courts, excepting only the dining hall and administration buildings. Each team is given a pennant with its color and a home base for a jail placed well back from the dividing line. The goal is to seize the other team's flag and bring it back to this base while keeping the enemy from seizing your team's flag. Players are free to roam anywhere but if you are tagged by a member of the other team in their home territory or even pulled across the dividing line you have to accept confinement in jail as a prisoner. You are out of the game unless a jailer can be forcibly taken into the prisoner's compound. That constitutes a jailbreak and every prisoner is released, free to roam at will unless tagged again.

Here's the thing. Ringalevio in the City is madness. No one is in charge. Rules must be taken seriously but their meaning really depends on individual conscience. Or more accurately what you can get away with or feel you must do, true to its New York tenement area origins. There are no umpires. Isolating bad actors happens later. Kids are grabbed and hustled into jail wherever they can be found. The goal is to get them all, or enough of them, in custody so that the few remaining will give up and go home for supper or dessert. Guerrilla warfare is the best metaphor for the city game. It's rough and dirty; stealth is the rule.

But at summer camp in the mountains where people able to afford the fees send their oh so promising children, the war takes place in sunlight; it is more organized, more civilized. The head counselor backed by his staff of college boys has promulgated laws of war, his Geneva Conventions. He watches the playing field like a war crimes prosecutor looking out for rule violators. Campers can be certain who is on their side and who isn't because everyone is wearing a uniform displaying team colors. There are captains, with insignia, symbols of military order, who are capable of strategic planning and enforcing discipline. The way to win Capture the Flag, they know, is to have a swarm of runners explode across the dividing line at the same time, sprint to the other team's base, overwhelm the defenders with sheer numbers, grab the flag, and evade the enemy long enough to return to home base.

At the same time one team has to keep enough of its own defenders back to prevent the other from pulling off the same stunt. Surprise then is the key but as both Buff and Blue captains understand despite the best strategies Capture the Flag is often a war without end. The teams of well-brought-up campers are cautious. They want to win but are already ahead in life's game, and don't want to risk losing what they have. In contrast to the disarray, the random violence of urban Ringalevio, the country game leads to sudden, unpredictable, yet regular asymmetries. Both the players and counselors can see what is happening because it always takes place in daylight; the city game, happening at dusk and sometimes going deep in the evening, is made for the daring, for special forces, who swoop down like invaders in a strange territory under cover of dying light.

Years later as I sue segregationists or defend civil rights workers under arrest, I know there are two different ways to litigate. One is the Ringalevio way and it is my way. The other is the civilized Capture the Flag way. Eventually I will find the former brings out a me I do not like and will leave the field but until then while I believe litigation is the moral equivalent of war it is also a practice engaged in without doubt.

But as a New York City–bred summer camper, it's plain that this is my game. I must star. So for most of the morning I dash along the line, slyly inviting the Blue team to pull me over, darting away as their front liners grab and grasp mostly at the air. I must star but I am out of control—a showboating kid who doesn't know better. Half the time my tongue is wagging. I dance away from hostile hands and feel the freedom of he who is not tagged.

A lean but muscular senior camper reaches out his long arms and almost has me by the wrist but I slip away. It's a glorious thing to escape but barely; to defeat in an instant an effort by a stronger force to control you. It is a brush with immortality. But then as any father playing tag with his kids knows, there is also joy at being caught and contained. I see pudgy Moon Monshein, the chunky one from the next bed in my bunk, hauled off and even Joe Finkel, the closest thing our cohort has to an athletic star, is wrestled down from his blindside and pulled away after he becomes absorbed in taunting one of the older blues. These Philly kids like Moon and Finkel, I think, remembering Ringalevio—they just don't play tough like New Yorkers.

But soon enough my turn comes. I am doing a fancy dance, taunting with my feet over the line then pulling them back, arms spread wide as if they are the wings of a glider, showing contempt for my pursuers, when I slip on damp grass and find myself slung over the shoulder of an older boy from the Blues who must weigh 200 pounds. He carries me like a sack of potatoes up the hill to their jail—a hard clay-surfaced basketball court—and after warning off the other inmates to stay clear dumps me on the ground near one of the foul lines. I get up to see that the compound already is occupied by about twenty others.

We are guarded by three junior campers who know they must stand out of reach, at least ten feet away. They are probably losers in the mind of their captain, doomed to low status guard duty. Instead of frontline fighters, they are assigned to make sure dummies like me stupid enough to get caught stay in jail where the rules say we belong until one team captures the flag of the other and claims victory. The guards must think jail duty demeaning as they present their backs to us as they face down the hill to watch the action at the territorial demarcation line that they are being kept from, as if that is where they think they should be.

"Heh, candy asses," we shout. "Come over here."

"Heh, chicken bluebirds!" My fellow prisoners call out but are mostly ignored.

As the noise of the game filters up the hill and the reality of jail hits me, even after just ten minutes of this confinement, I know I have to get out. I think to sneak away but the guards look back often enough to make that impractical; even if they couldn't catch me running away, I would be reported to the head counselor as a rule breaker. I can't risk it. I can only explain what I do next as coming from the lawyer hibernating in me, slouching toward a courtroom, waiting to be born. Or maybe it's the kid who's been taken away from his parents too early. After all, I am only eight years old so when I start to scream, "My knee," notice is taken, if not taken too seriously. I hobble toward the boundary. "Help me," I call, "I've gotta go to the Infirmary. It's bad. Please. It really hurts."

"Owwweeeoww!"

And it must be convincing. An Oscar-winning performance because the boy who has no name I know hesitates but finally his good instincts overcome the evil hydraulics of the game. This would never happen at home. It's like the movie where you know if the good guy goes for the sob story the enemy tells him, he is a goner. A bullet is waiting for him! The nice kid must be about twelve and he comes forward to save me and, of course, he is pulled in by my teammates, roughly pushed to the ground by the escaping throng, one of whom peels off to grab the Blue flag from its stanchion near a backboard, and run down the hill surrounded by an entourage of former jailbirds. Victory is ours.

One day thinking about Capture the Flag I came across a theorist named Ken Sanes writing on his blog "Transparency" about "acting out" through the combat-like game of Paintball. He described examples of intense simulations like video and computer games, pinball, and interactive computer porn. He called them symbolic arenas, "protected domains that make it possible to act out fantasies, embodying fears and desires, in ways that aren't possible in everyday life." Sanes also references maverick psychoanalyst, Robert Stoller, who is known to argue that symbolic arenas through art and imaginative eroticism allow mastery to replace trauma and, as Sanes put it, "create aesthetic excitement by presenting fictional dangers that seem real while allowing us to control the production to be certain it isn't real."

I don't know whether by playing Ringalevio and Capture the Flag my childhood wounds were being healed but the game was certainly part of a communal effort to create excitement through winning and losing, in a place where, wrongly or rightly, I felt danger was nearby. War in all its forms holds us tight and to free ourselves from its grip, as James insisted over a century ago, we must channel energy into "heroic" forms "that will speak to men as universally as war does." By doing so, Stoller would say we have contained a trauma: ". . . the story ends happily. This time we win." The war against war, as James biographer Richard D. Richardson noted, demands not the love of peace but the fight against war. We will have to kill war! Put Stoller and James together and the lesson is that through playing games as well as the play we call art we are searching and struggling for a way to defeat the most problematic part of our nature.

My work eventually draws upon such ideas but my own fight against war is more direct, and more self-serving. I admire the courage of people who fight for their country, especially those who volunteer, but I have never been in the service and haven't ever desired to be part of any armed conflict. I've spent years working on projects that were linked to avoiding violence but have never thought of myself as a pacifist. Pacifism, James explains, will never win over the military. To make peace, you must provide imaginative substitutes for the warring impulses. I try to explain to myself how someone so committed to the rule of law can justify avoiding service in the military that must be his greatest obligation but all such efforts seem false. They soon turn to dust in my mouth. It's a lack, one that is made no better (or worse!) by being based on fear. When called up for a selective service physical exam in the late 1950s, I approach the first doctor I see straight on, telling him plainly, "I don't want to join the army." I am proud of my audacity but don't expect much will come of it.

He is gray and small, almost shriveled. With his wire rim eyeglasses, he looks me over briefly. Presumably he sees a picture of physical health, a young man more than a head taller than he is with well-developed arm and leg muscles. I have worn glasses since age seven but don't look like a pushover, have even played a season of college football. But to my surprise he doesn't frown. Lectures me not on the obligations of law and citizenship. Doesn't ask me what I would do if we were still fighting the Nazis. It's as if he was waiting for someone like me. He grabs my papers, in seconds scribbles something in a box, waves me off, and calls for the next kid in line.

I flinch. For a wild second I wonder if I could be charged with some crime. What have I done? Will some Joe McCarthy type find out, call me a communist, and ruin my life?

I move quickly on to the next examination station before actually reading what the doctor has written. Amazingly, he has excused me; right there on the paper it says, "Unfit for military service." One of those moments where while you say "I just don't believe it" still there it is—you do believe! Your long shot bet has just won the Derby; the ticket says so. Maybe the doc was a reader of Thomas Mann's novel *Felix Krull*, about an antihero who evades German Army conscription by repeatedly insisting to his interlocutors that he is "perfectly fit" for military service. He says it so often that they decide he's crazy and send him packing. Just what he wanted. Maybe in the long line of potential draftees no one had told him what many of them were thinking.

As I hurriedly made for the exit, I looked again at the doctor's scrawl: I feel I have just turned over a Monopoly chance card and it says, "Do not go to War. Proceed to Go." It finally sinks in but not long after the inconsistency between my beliefs and actions makes me bow my head. I regret being called "unfit" but, curiously, I make no compensatory attempt to privilege (or denigrate) the military. I just feel like a fraud. While those who stand and wait also serve, they serve in safety. Well that's me, I decide. About all I can say in my subsequent imaginary conversation with a hostile interviewer is that if you have nothing in the history of your soul that has made you bow your head, you are very well defended indeed. But the lawyer in me knows immediately how weak an argument this is.

Of course, I do have to give myself a reason. (Sometimes I think education is most often about the ability to come up with reasons.) The excitement of a future I simply won't yield. I've learned something of war as a child and read enough about war to have an opinion and I have a life I want to lead, dim at this time are its outlines. Was the stupidity of men making war there to mask the fear or the fear present to distract from the stupidity? My template is the Spanish Civil War, a college thesis I have to research. I start with Orwell's *Homage to Catalonia* as almost everybody does but then drill down into the military details. I visit the Museum of Modern Art to see Picasso's "Guernica." I hear about the volunteers who join the Abraham Lincoln Brigade and the politics of Roosevelt's deluded neutrality policy. The violence disgusts me. So does my own fear. But most of all it's the powerlessness against the Fascists that breeds in my imagination.

The more I learn, the more I am grateful for majoring in history in college. The study of history is the great supplier of serviceable rationalizations, but then I note also that physical threats, real or imagined, to my children or my family immediately engage the angry forces of the amygdala. I hate war and the violence that is its fellow traveler but clearly I am no pacifist. I note the contradiction but have no idea what to do about it.

Manhattan

One late August day in 1949 my parents arrive at Centre Lake in Becket, Massachusetts, to pick me up at Camp Greylock where I have done little more than play basketball and baseball for two months. Without much of an introduction, they announce that we are driving to our new home, an apartment on Seventy-Ninth Street on Manhattan's Westside. An apartment in the City means a tall building, right? We won't be returning to the house near the beach? What can that mean? A different school, of course, but what else?

I am in shock and after a surge of questions say almost nothing as the car rolls South to the City on the Taconic Parkway. My mother, sensing I am frozen, nervously talks up the change. You'll have a larger room. Your father won't have to take two long train trips to get to his new office in Newark. You'll make new friends.

I mumble, "Ok, Ok" to shut off the sound of her voice. I spend the long ride from the Berkshires staring out the window of my father's green Chrysler, a step up for him, a model ironically called the New Yorker, pretending to myself I haven't heard a word.

Nothing will really change.

Years later I tell this story to my four female family therapist colleagues assembled at our weekly peer supervision meeting. After stepping down as a law school dean, I have a year off and use it to realize a long-held dream to acquire a second profession. With a serendipitous change in state law, I am soon licensed to practice as a family and couples therapist, able to spend evening hours each week seeing poor and low-income clients at a clinic run by a charismatic social worker named Anne Peretz.

When they hear the story of the move to Manhattan, my colleagues are aghast. No preparation. No goodbye to your old world. No transition plan.

"What lousy parenting," Claudia exclaims. "Did you feel a loss of self?" asks Eleanor Paradise. "You must have been furious," Mopsy Kennedy offers.

"Of course, of course," I agree, quickly conceding there must have been a traumatic reaction; otherwise the group won't take me seriously. They might think I am holding back or, worse, lacking insight. But actually I can't remember much about my emotional state in those first weeks in Manhattan. I must have stayed frozen, though I certainly had my worries. Growing up in Rockaway Beach, I am free of much parental control and fear it might be reimposed if not by my parents directly but by the constraints of real city living. Decades later an edgy novel will name the peninsula as a place where its characters can be free of constraints and the Ramones will sing how easy it is to get there from the mean streets.

My father works long hours; when he is around, he usually seems a very beneficent ruler compared to what I've seen in other families. He finds time to come into my room late at night, sometimes even waking me, ignoring that at best I'm half asleep. A favorite of his talk is describing the day's Barnaby cartoon in *PM*, the left-leaning daily paper he prefers. Still a school child I can understand only a part of what he is saying but he still delivers his views about the ways of the world. I wonder if this will change when we live in an apartment building on a busy street of apartment buildings instead of a house on a quiet street near the sea. It is only when I become a father that I fully understand the message my father is sending to himself. Crouching in the dark near the beds of my sleeping daughters, I hold back tears of unexpressed love and wonder, thoughts that will not be voiced. In the daytime fears of a dangerous world recede but I tell myself I will sacrifice myself for them should it be required; it's as if having the thought itself guards the girls, makes them secure.

I worry about a loss of freedom but, in fact, very soon I have too much of it. My mother treats my choice of where to spend time with respect bordering on indifference. At this time all I know is that for some reason I don't understand she likes to think I'm older than I am but until the secret is exposed I don't realize she just doesn't want my childhood to be fatherless. At this age I wonder why they rarely tell me what to do like other parents. They must have ideas and they aren't really shy. It occurs to me they are afraid of something like conflict or criticism from me but that's as far as I can go with the mystery.

I tell myself to feel lucky to be in the big city but I've grown used to roaming unhindered between the ocean and the bay. My bicycle is like a horse. The boardwalk out of season and the ocean beach with its color and texture changing daily is the Western prairie. Waves crashing against the jetties add drama. At Beach Ninety-Eighth Street there is an amusement park called Playland. If you avoid the summer, there are only a few visitors. The rides are cheap. There is a huge wooden roller coaster, a set of carriages that whip you around until you're dizzy, and a scary house of horrors. At the Rifle Range and Ring Toss couples keep playing to win cheap-looking stuffed animals.

There is something about walking or riding to school on the boardwalk thirty yards from the rolling surf or trolling the garish places in the amusement park that makes me feel strong and confident. And I believe in these feelings, believe they tell me something about myself. I learn to avoid the troublesome Irish kids from Saint Frances de Sales who can harass a boy alone, at least one they define as Jewish. Is this the sort of thing that happens in Germany? Certainly, Alice and Ira think so; they talk about the hotels, clubs, and companies that keep Jews out; my father says it's even worse for Negroes. One Halloween I am out for trick or treating.

A gang from another neighborhood tries to rob me and a few friends—none of whom happen to be Jewish—of the candy and pennies we've collected. I wonder why we were picked. I just walk away and no one tries to stop me. I must look tougher than I feel. This persuades me I can take care of myself and prevail. Fortunately, I never have another such an encounter because it may very well have proved otherwise.

In Rockaway Beach, I have gotten away with hiding things from my parents—sneaking on the train or using my allowance when I'm caught to go to Brooklyn's Forest Park where I secretly ride horses from the stable concession for three dollars an hour; going when I want to the Park Theatre double features on the local shopping street where you can watch the movies plus a newsreel and a *Perils of Pauline* serial for only a quarter. Next door to the theater is a penny arcade where I spend what money I've gathered sifting sand through a homemade device—a bottomed-out fruit carton lined with screening—where crowds of beach-goers have dumped their belongings on warm weather weekends. I lose it all playing pinball and roller ball games for prizes. I am suddenly a gambler—just like dad—but am unprepared for the feeling of shame when I lose.

I may not have been readied for the move to Manhattan and didn't know what to expect but tell myself it's not as if I am going to an unknown place. Still even though I've been there many times and know that politically speaking Rockaway is part of New York City, plainly life in Manhattan is going to be different. Living at the edge in the boonies was maybe closer in feel to the quiet, the emptiness of the West, than the neon and noise of the clogged city streets. I'm too young to realize that I fear the loss of my physical being, the pure pleasure, the freedom of a body in motion. All three of us had been born in Manhattan, my father having bought the Rockaway house when I was less than a year old because it made cheaper living possible, but that was over ten years earlier. My parents thought their decision to buy at the beach made them risk-takers, true pioneers having left a familiar place and a sophisticated life of music and theater for the primitive way of the far-off unknown land of Queens. Instead of a prairie schooner rolling West, they crossed under the East River on the Long Island Railroad.

But they never totally disconnected from Manhattan. Ira often drove us to his then midtown office near the majestic building of the main branch of the New York Public Library on Saturday mornings. My mother might go shopping at nearby Lord & Taylor's or B. Altman department stores while he completed the paperwork covering the sales he'd made during the week. The company he worked for and which was the source of family prosperity manufactured all sorts of paraphernalia—calendars, playing cards, desk sets—that he sold embossed with company names as advertising and business gifts. I was given free range to take what I wanted from the storeroom where the salesmen kept the samples they shopped to would-be customers.

For my parents the return to Manhattan was the end of exile. They soon spent their extra money on the theater and proudly displayed the *Playbill* programs of Broadway shows they'd seen on a living room coffee table. They fell in with a set of my mother's friends from Hunter College (now married) and exchanged regular dinner party visits. One complication was my ancient grandmother, Florence or Gornie as I called her, who had lived for a few years in the Rockaway house but was now settled in a Broadway residence hotel. My father was her sole support but he wanted as little to do with her as possible so the bimonthly contacts had to be arranged by Alice, who also disliked her.

Their feelings confused me. Gornie was old, wrinkled, cranky, and growing dim, though she would live into her nineties. She could be annoying because she thought she had been victimized by life in general and complained more about how unfair everything was as she aged. But I also found her fascinating, mostly because she spent much of her time talking about other worlds. While teaching me to play gin rummy and hearts, she would describe how she and her late husband, Charles, traveled the country in style while unbeknownst to them his brothers ran the family dry goods business into the ground. I imagined she lost count of the cards while telling about traveling in a Pullman car on the way West or visits to National Park lodges but she never lost sight of the game and would usually beat me. There was no letting me win. She made no allowance for a young grandson.

They had seen the whole country, Gornie said, dancing till dawn at the finest resort hotels and sharing late-night meals with "distinguished" guests. She had the long dresses and accessories she loved like jeweled mantillas and dark peekaboo fans moldering in two huge steamer trunks stored in the basement of the Rockaway house to prove that she'd lived that life. Still it took a good deal of faith to imagine her in high society; she was ugly in a porcine way, often crotchety, and her stories always ended with her in the right.

She had one habit that never failed to produce a smirk from Alice: Gornie's maiden name was "Dreifuss" and she would drop into a conversation about just anything that after all she knew well this or that fashion because she was a distant relative of *the* Captain Dreyfus of the famous faux French treason case. "In my family we are French-Swiss you know?" But she was never sure why some of her relatives were one-s Dreyfuses and others two-s Dreyfusses or how the i snuck into her name but of her pedigree she was absolutely certain.

Gornie was undeniably different than anyone else I knew. Even as she aged and cursed her wrinkled face, her decaying body, her poverty, and dependent widow's fate, she showed a kind of "the emperor's not wearing any clothes" shrewdness that made me believe there was a reason why she was my only surviving grandparent. Her stories hinted at a sleek world of drama and wealth more like something out of a movie than the polyglot Westside where I suddenly found myself a citizen. She was also an antidote to the New

York City boosterism and exceptionalism that her acid tongue and dreary single-room occupancy contradicted. It wasn't that we shouldn't love the City, honor its capacity to entertain and embellish lives, and respect how it did so much better than the rest of the country in finding ways to nurture the poor, the immigrant, and the illiterate, but she was steadfast in deploring the rhetorical excesses that never came close to acknowledging how losing was the fate of so many of these battles.

Yeah we were New Yorkers, tough, resilient, and smart, living in the "greatest City in the world." Ya, ya. We had Broadway, the Yankees, skyscrapers, and *The Times*, yet as Stephen Sondheim would later put it in his song "Another Hundred People Got Off the Train"—"It's a city of strangers. . . . Some come to stare, some to stay. And every day . . . Some go away."

Her eyes trained mine to see that the essentials that set us apart from the rest of the country were neither honorifics nor pejoratives but true differences that made us both despised and sought after. Despised because New York integrated others—internal migrants and foreigners, homosexuals, artists, radicals—imperfectly but regularly. Desired because it was free of Victoriana and the place where real money and fame could be gathered in. And where else, she asked implicitly, was there an architecture of destroy and build and destroy again curated so carefully? She didn't use these words but I got her point anyway. The habits of Manhattan stood against the complacence beyond the river, ironically a place sought after because the same conditions that led to its rejection also evoked a holiday from convention, repression, and fear of the exotic. That's why they kept coming before going back home with a lighter wallet, a full stomach, and the right to say "A good place to visit but. . . ."

I started out as confused as a visitor from Iowa when I was told, for example, that I would be a seventh grader at the local junior high school called Joan of Arc. I couldn't understand why I was being sent to a Catholic school. We were Jewish, though religion was hardly more than a cultural designation in my family; certainly not a way to pursue divine guidance, God's will, or even recent family history. I had enjoyed a childhood moment playing evil Persian Haman, the Hitler of his day, in a Sunday School Purim play but would a school named after a Roman Catholic saint who led France to defeat English armies in the fifteenth century before she was captured and burnt at the stake be the right one for me? I didn't know it at the time but, in fact, when the City built the school in 1940, the School Board probably named it in solidarity with the French, then facing a Nazi invasion and occupation.

This business of religion was confusing. There was the day that looking for nail clippers I opened a drawer in the table next to my parent's bed. A book with a plain brown wrapper of the sort that masked racy literature stared me in the face. Opening it, I discovered instead of pornography a tract by Mary Baker Eddy explaining something called Christian Science. I spent no time at all exploring its contents but the next day asked my mother what it meant. "Did she believe in Jesus?"

I remember distinctly that she chose her words carefully. Speaking at a deliberate pace, unusual for her, she answered something like this:

"There are times when to get through the day a grown up needs to be comforted." It would be years before I connected reading Christian Science—I don't think they ever attended a church service—with a need to find a cure for my father by invoking mind over matter.

At Joan of Arc, however, it wasn't Jesus but race, ethnicity, and disarray that I would face every day when I stepped off the packed Amsterdam Avenue bus at Ninety-Second Street. Here was the real beginning of an urban education in the imperatives of equality and diversity. The school was the setting for the initial stirrings of social change that would soon lead to the spread of black and brown New Yorkers from ghetto-like surroundings in central Harlem and the East Harlem Barrio throughout the boroughs and not only ultimately convert the New York public schools into majority minority settings but also dramatically change the shape of life in the City. All this was in the future but what I saw when I arrived was a school with a population of one-third blacks, one-third Puerto Ricans, and one-third "others"—meaning mostly Jews who couldn't afford private school and Irish and Italians from Columbus Avenue tenements who couldn't afford or had decided against a

Catholic education. Ira had offered to send me to one of
the elite private schools in Riverdale, Horace Mann, or
Fieldston, but I demurred. I gave him a phony reason—
they're probably snobbish, I claimed—but the issue for me
was cost. I just didn't think we could afford it. I'm sure in
retrospect this was correct but there is no way at the time I
could have actually known. I never told him or Alice of my
real reasons. I now understand the decision as marking
my arrival as a true parentified only child—a kid who often
unaware of why he is doing so identifies with adult concerns long before the actual arrival of adulthood.

Joan of Arc's eight-story, dun-colored building loomed
up like a high-rise prison or a custodial institution for
mental patients. The architecture sent a message of cold
and forbidding that had nothing to do with my sunny idea
of how a school should look. But we were welcomed every
morning by a cheery sounding principal with a name to
match, Dr. Stella Sweeting, over a public address system;
chimes introduced her daily upbeat report in every classroom. The inner life of the building, however, was as troublesome in its way as the institutional architecture of the
structure. In the days to come I concluded that the teachers were mostly smart and well prepared; it was clear they
were often on edge for reasons that weren't fully explained
by student behavior. They seemed apprehensive, unsure
what to expect from the strange and novel demographic
mix they've been handed. Prominent in my first day and

many days to follow was a random violence that hovered over the school day like a stationary cloudbank. On my first day, standing in a tight crowd of students forced to wait outside the school doors before entering, I was pushed from behind; then foolishly pushed back as I would have in Rockaway; punches were thrown; curses aired and returned to the speaker until we were separated by a teacher and hustled off to class as if it was all in a day's work. But I was a marked boy.

My move to the middle of Manhattan, to an ethnically divided public school that served a wide range of races and nationalities, children from both middle class and welfare-dependent families, to a Westside neighborhood that was layered with ample amounts of wealth, intelligence, isolated elderly, drug addiction, and erratic violence as well as pockets of poverty coincides with a shift in public attention across the country and a sense in the dominant culture that too many adolescents are lost, fearful, and unpredictable. The gang wars of the postwar period in New York City provided ample employment opportunities to dozens of journalists, academic sociologists, and social workers. The conventional wisdom most of them propounded, not necessarily wrong on that account, had it that predominantly racial and ethnic gang violence emerging in the 1950s lasted until it was ultimately moderated and diverted by the war in Vietnam and civil rights protests in the early 1960s. Thereafter, areas of Manhattan became the site of a

rapacious drug culture, first and foremost featuring widespread use of heroin and the robberies by addicts needed to
sustain it, eventually reemerging as lethal conflict between
competing drug networks.

Of course, as a junior high school student I wasn't in
touch with social theory or urban developments writ large;
I saw what I saw from the ground up. And what I observed
was a general fear from my fellow students that in a way
matched what was going on with the teachers, a latent
uncertainty, leading to a need to join together to keep safe
from frightening rumors of gangs, rumbles that were no
less scary because they might have taken place elsewhere in
the City or were just whispered about as likely to happen.
The key to belief in survival in such a universe was to pos-
sess a potent symbol—and the totem came to be an article of clothing, the slick satin jacket with a scripted gang
name. Social critics might be interested in the fact that these
were also the years that President Eisenhower's Secretary
of State John Foster Dulles popularized the deterrent value
of threatening massive nuclear retaliation. Without a satin
jacket, on the Westside you were "unaffiliated" that meant
unprotected and for that reason alone vulnerable; in short,
you had no deterrent capability.

Given the subsequent arrival of Leonard Bernstein and
Sondheim's *West Side Story* featuring warfare between
youth gangs called the Sharks and Jets, I still find it amazing
that I had sought protection with a small group of (mostly
Jewish) West siders in a club with a bright yellow jacket

embossed in blue script, unbelievably, with the name Sharks. The mystery deepened when I learned that the original plot of *West Side Story* had involved Jewish and Irish gangs with lovers crossing that ethnic line, before the show's creators woke up to the new working class whites versus Puerto Ricans Manhattan reality. The Jews and Irish were moving to Westchester or Long Island, whence I had come, if they could afford it. The change in the story line reflected this shift in Westside demographics.

Of course, the musical wasn't copying our name. We were a mild, middle class group of boys brought together by a need for physical protection—no one trusted the police to make a dent in random gang activity—but mostly we walked the streets, talked about girls, and, when we could, hang out late in the evening at a local restaurant on Eighty-Sixth Street and Broadway called the Tip Toe Inn that earlier in the night might have served dinner on starched white table cloths to our parents. We furtively smoked cigarettes while wandering the neighborhood, feeling relatively safe due to the magic of the satin security blanket. The truth is that most of the time prospective attackers didn't know how formidable was the array of fighters behind a jacket and so you might pass by a group with hostile intent untroubled if there was a fear of retaliation based on a fantasy of what could follow a foolish attack.

Later on such restraint disappeared, replaced by a tribal sense of my turf and not your turf, the proliferation of the homemade zip gun and other lethal weapons. There seemed

then a greater number of bad actors with so dim a view of
their future that there was no interest in measuring benefit
against costs before acting. In this new world if you were
in the wrong place with the wrong jacket, fear of retribu-
tion wouldn't protect you. One mode of action, however,
that bridged relatively, and I emphasize relatively, modest
levels of violence of my adolescence and the viciousness of
a decade or two later was the tactic of picking the youngest
or smallest gang member to push, punch, or even just taunt
the chosen victim who once having responded in kind was
mobbed by a whole cohort. If you recognized the tactic and
were cunning and quick enough to smile through it, even
smother the brat with a friendly move or two, you might
escape. As an innocent kid only familiar with the more
straightforward conflicts of an outer borough, in my first
Manhattan year I had to punch my way out of several such
encounters.

But by the late 1960s and early 1970s crime statistics
almost everywhere reflected a general rise in violence
among old and young alike. As I was practicing law, often
criminal law, during these years, I began to feel as if the
threats and fights that had been the daily experience of my
teenage peer group were quaint, different in kind, somehow
bounded by intelligible rules closer to the rough Depression experience of James T. Farrell's Irish-American tough
Studs Lonigan than the seemingly mindless acceptance of
violence that crowded my perception of what was happening

around me as I struggled to mount the law reform projects that were the bread and butter of my professional life.

During the Joan of Arc years, there were, however, two brutal incidents that took a toll on my body, threatened my future, but ironically implanted the illusion that I could, like the tribe of Manhattanites I had just joined, make my way in the world, except, of course, if whatever was mysteriously happening to my father also happened to me. At Joan of Arc boys were required to take a shop course (girls were sent off to a class called "Home Economics") that might be building wooden furniture, working with clay on an armature, or fabricating something out of metal. The idea was that the experience could translate into job opportunities later in life but if this was the motive it didn't appear much advanced by the resulting products, most of which were primitive, haphazard, and plainly ugly. Each of us worked on our own project at stone-topped laboratory tables, otherwise used by general science classes. At the table next to mine stood an awkwardly thin, six-foot Hispanic boy named Jose who had recently arrived in the City from San Juan or someplace like it in the Caribbean. He looked like a Giacometti statue, a kind of human string bean, as if his maker had left off before finishing the job. His English was hardly there; he rarely spoke and I had to explain the instructions from the teacher before he went to work on his chosen project, creating a weapon that looked in its early stages as if it would finally emerge as a

dagger or even a sword. Jose seemed amiable and he nodded his head thanks for my help like someone bobbing
for apples before he finally mumbled a gracias or two. The
teacher walked around offering suggestions, criticisms,
and at times actual help. I wondered what he would say
about Jose's weaponry but he passed us both by.

I was building a wooden box to organize the shoe polish
and brushes lying in disarray in my closet at home. I'd carefully cut the pieces with one of the saws hanging on a rack
near the teacher's desk and was trying to figure out how to
organize gluing them when I realized they just didn't fit. I'd
made a hash of the cutting. I wasn't looking at Jose at the next
table but studying the mess of raw lumber before me when
he called in his heavily accented English, "Heh, look at this."

He reached over to me with some object; my left hand
slid blindly toward him. I was wondering what to do with
the mess I'd made. My eyes were still on the pile of uneven
slabs on the table before me that I guessed I'd now have to
redo, when it struck.

It was overwhelming. The pain was all of me. I was nothing else.

I screamed.

Everyone turned. The teacher made a kind of moaning
sound and he moved toward us.

I looked down at the gash on my left hand and at Jose but
he was hollow, dull eyes staring straight ahead, with no evidence of recognition.

And then, and this is what made the event memorable—because physical pain disappears and becomes in time an idea—taught me something about myself it would take years to translate into awareness but which nevertheless, I believe, firmed into character instantly. I clutched the hand to my chest. Tried to shake off the tears. Turned and walked, then trotted, then ran, out of the classroom. Never beheld the teacher. Spoke to no one. Down the stairs I ran and out of the school onto Amsterdam Avenue.

The hell with the rules. The hell with teachers.

I hailed a passing yellow cab. Told the driver the address of our family doctor on East Seventy-Sixth Street. Closed my eyes and kept the hand close to my body, as if cradling an infant. Wept and whimpered at each traffic light. Paid the driver, with my right hand awkwardly pulling the bills from the few in the wallet I'd been given as a birthday present. Apologized I had no money for a real tip. Ran up the stairs and entered the office on the first floor of the brownstone. Crossed an empty waiting area. Pushed my hand toward the nurse at the reception. Let her take me into a treatment room. Cover the wound with a magic salve that turned the shooting spasms into dull discomfort, bad but not so bad I wasn't able to notice how pretty she was and how nice it felt when she had touched me.

"What happened?" were her first words.

"A soldering iron."

"How? Why?"

"No idea. No reason. Where is everybody?"

"Oh it's before office hours. I was just doing bills. You're lucky I was here."

Jose never returned to class. I never saw him again. The shop teacher failed to mention the incident. My parents were shocked and angry but at my insistence did nothing. My hand healed. Manhattan had forced me to take care of myself by making a decision. No one else was going to do it that was certain. I knew instinctively that there were people I encountered who would see what happened as a Puerto Rican problem. I turned this over my adolescent mind, deciding that no it was really a New York problem. The price of living in an unpredictable City, paradoxically a city of nomads, and that was all right because I had come to like the excitement, the prestige of being a tough New Yorker. I wasn't surprised, for example, when Ira told me our car had to be regularly moved from one side of the street to the other to avoid towing and I had to do it because he and my mother were both working. Fourteen, with no license, still no problem! I loved the responsibility and figured I could handle the risk. If a jagged mixture of hues and idioms, a burn or two, was the cost of freedom, of anonymity, of keeping the system off your back, apparently I was willing to pay.

The second happening was a greater test of my resolve, and my mother's too. Being more clever and farsighted than the Americans who foolishly lived on the other side of the

Hudson and beyond wasn't always enough. Sometimes without help you just couldn't take care of yourself. Maybe it takes a city, not a village, to raise the child.

Ever since my father hired a carpenter to nail a plywood backboard to the entryway of our Rockaway garage, I'd been dribbling a basketball, pretending my—then underhand—foul shot would decide the National Invitation Tournament championship at Madison Square Garden. In the era long before the dunk, my daydreams featured a carefully aimed (two-hand) set shot that would flow effortlessly through a swishing net.

Because I was tall and looked the part, a pickup team that played regular games in a neighborhood league found me as soon as we'd landed on the Westside. Late one afternoon, we were scheduled to play a team from a community center on their home court in a public school on 102nd Street, between Amsterdam and Columbus Avenues in a building that Robert Moses would one day tear down as part of his push for urban renewal. It turned out to be a rough game. These were scrappy kids from the streets near the center who were younger and smaller than we were. They quickly realized that the match was unfair. We belonged in different levels of the league but they had to try to win anyway and all they could do was be physical, commit fouls, and curse us out. It didn't affect the result, which was lopsided, but it justified us showing no mercy in running up the score. I was glad when it was over.

There was another game scheduled after ours; my team-mates sat themselves down in the stands to watch but I decided to catch the Broadway bus home. It was a big mistake. New York City public buildings of the era often featured heavy double doors at the street entrance matched, after a small foyer, by similar metal barriers on the inside. It was as if the architects had been warned that Genghis Kahn–like armed invaders from the steppes of Asia might seek to breach the community center perimeter and carry off the children. As I passed through the inner set of doors, gym bag on my shoulder, I was knocked unconscious by someone and something unknown. Whenever it was when I awoke, and it could have been five minutes or five hours so far as I knew, I was literally draped in the arms of a police officer, surrounded by my teammates and covered with blood.

Right away despite the blood and pain, I realized, this was payback for our game victory. The officer told me I'd been attacked with a lead pipe by someone who knew how to use it. I begged the cop to please take me home but he said, "I can't. I'm on duty."

Even with the blood dripping down my face and thunderclaps barging around inside my head, I knew there was something surreal about his response. He started writing in a notebook, eventually completely absolved himself of my fate, and passed me on to my teammates, none of whom were really close friends or even knew where I lived, to be taken home. Somehow they got me back to the apartment on Seventy-Ninth Street where they thought they would find parents to take over but, alas, they were out for dinner. There followed a series of scenes that I could only register between moans as I lay on my parent's double bed with ice on my nose and a towel covering my eyes.

I told my teammates they could leave but to their credit they wouldn't go. Still it was obvious they wanted out. What would they get when my parents finally came home? A hysterical mother? A furious father? They might be undeservedly blamed and what could they say knowing as little as I did. The oldest of us was merely fifteen. When my parents finally arrived, they found us in their bedroom, the boys were sitting on the floor, legs out, backs against a wall, sounding—I couldn't see them—as if they were about to be taken to the woodshed.

Astonishing us all, Alice took in the scene and immediately exclaimed as calmly as an emergency room veteran, "What the hell happened to you?"

Even covered with the ice-packed towel, blinded as I was, I could sense my teammates' relief. The boys left as soon as they could tell their story and decently depart. What followed was two weeks out of school, a face raw and swollen as If I'd just done a few rounds with the reigning middleweight champion, Sugar Ray Robinson, bloodshot eyes, a broken nose, and an end to that chapter in my basketball career. It was a long time before I was willing to admit how lucky I had been not to have suffered permanent injury, except for the broken nose, and I never really grasped—it being the denial capacity of youth—that I could have been killed. A few weeks after the event, a New York detective called my mother and me to his closet-like precinct office and embarrassingly revealed that through the neighborhood network he'd learned who had attacked me—an older brother of one of the players—but had insufficient evidence to prove it. The case would be closed.

It's only now, years after I deposed my last witness, argued my last case, that I can see how these incidents were threads that emerged in the fabric that I later wore in Court. Pundits and commentators can talk about litigation and its results but little really happens in court without a lawyer taking charge and pushing. Manhattan was telling me I had to think, to take charge, even when being beat down. No one else will do it for you! And there was one more event that sealed the deal. When my father died, someone had to tell his mother. When Alice looked away, I said I would do it. My cousin Stephen, a trained psychologist ten years older than I was, walked with me to the Broadway hotel where Gornie lived. When I delivered the news, I tried to be gentle but nothing could stem her grief, her screams that God was supposed to take her first. We stayed for a time trying to comfort her but then I decided to go. I had my own feelings to contend with. Gornie would have to be on her own. As we left her room, Steve pulled me to him, put his arms on my shoulders, and facing me said, "You showed incredible ego."

Confused and hurt, I whined "You mean I was selfish?"

"No, no, not at all," he quickly replied. "I mean you showed strength in doing something hard. In facing up to reality." Then he gave me a mini lecture on psychoanalytic theory that I little understood. What I did get though was a belief in my own powers to govern myself and to play such a self out in the world.

Robert

When people talk about the "real world," they are contrasting one set of affairs, maybe concrete and gritty, with another supposedly remote, abstract, perhaps privileged or academic. So the tough real world of Manhattan was the City, while the other boroughs were then just connected places. Our new surroundings were where the action was compared to the easygoing world of the quasi-suburb by the beach. Rockaway might suffer from common urban ills; it might be scary sometimes to ride my bike to school alone or for me to play basketball in a school yard too close to St. Francis de Sales but no drunks, gun violence, or even serious littering could possibly foul the sweet streets of a "Belle Harbor." Of course, this was pure fantasy, brought on by fears of racial and ethnic differences as well as a distorted sense of spatial relations. The cowardly metal pipe attack was in fact no nearer or farther from my new apartment home than the roughest neighborhood, one with its share of violence, domestic and otherwise, was from the small house on the quiet street from which I set out for school on my bike. But in the City you felt crowded in, trapped by compact space; the rich and the poor, mad and mild, sharing the same sidewalk. On Long Island, the miles might be the same but the threat appeared to rise elsewhere.

The real world had actually arrived for me in Rockaway after one of Alice's not so subtle finagles, probably instantly recognizable as such by an adult but obscure to her own son.

"Why not go over after school and play with him? You can watch Milton Berle. They have a TV."

"But he just lies in his chair."

"Robert just needs a friend to pep him up."

"But we aren't friends and he's a cripple."

"Gus will be so glad. She'll give you supper on Tuesday nights and you don't have to come home until after the Berle show is finished. I might even come over to watch."

As usual, she was the winner in these struggles.

Robert Wald was two years older. Despite his desperate physical condition, his mind was fully active; he spent his words freely on almost any topic. I thought he might have read even more books than my father. At least that had to be true about science at which Robert was a wiz. But not being able to move, what else could he do but read? His condition was never given a name by his mother but the symptoms were there to see and it was obvious nothing could be done about them. His chair was contoured so he could sit up partially with his thin legs extended but it barely supported his slumping body. The muscles were wasted or maybe they just didn't exist. He was a lump. A padded board was fitted behind his oversized head. Would it just flop backwards, I wondered, if the board was removed?

During the day Robert lived in this chair; every night Gus, a tiny woman with walnut-sized muscles and steel wool–like hair, pushed the chair to the next room and managed to move a totally helpless Robert into his bed. He pees in some kind of bottle that I think she has to hold but I've never seen him urinate. I'm afraid to ask how he shits. When he needs a bath, he is wheeled into a room in the back of the house that has nothing in it but a huge gray tin tank in the shape of a giant Y. The sides ping when I slap them. Here Gus drafts me to help lift Robert over the lip of the tank and cushion his drop into the shallow water. All the while he is barking orders, questioning the way his mother is moving him, and once at rest complains about the water temperature. The words Gus uses in response are as gentle as her touch when she lifts him. Robert keeps up his patter while she keeps up hers—a "yes, yes, yes" in response as if leaving the specifics of whatever it is he says in the air. I fall into this routine easily but I have to overcome a strange feeling that comes over me when I see his wisp of a penis. I think Robert knows that I look and must feel my curiosity as disgust but if so he never lets on.

My Tuesday visits become regular and after many months a commitment. Robert is caustic if I miss a week though he tries hard to hide the hurt. He takes it out on me in the talking game. The game is what we do; always the same, always different. We are the good guys outsmarting bad guys. He usually sets the scene—fighting Nazis or travelers on a spaceship or detectives on a boat to China, or exploring the Jungle in Brazil, or lost on the edge of the Sahara desert:

"There's a pool."

"You take the gun and stand guard."

"I'll fill the water bag."

"Be careful. It's dark but I think someone's coming."

"Only shoot if you have to."

We wrangle over the roles. I will be the detective who carries a gun. He will be the submarine captain or the counterspy. I will be an ordinary guy in the army or the air force pilot who hates the enemy.

Robert tries to be generous but he usually grabs the mastermind role and I know I have to let him have it. It's control for someone who otherwise has none. After sorting out the cast of characters we begin to fashion a story. It emerges from our talk in role and each player shifts its direction with his words, throwing his voice, adopting what we think are foreign accents, even while the other moves in a different mode entirely. Still the narrative takes shape, imposing its own discipline, bringing us a victim to rescue, evildoers to bomb or drown with our torpedoes, and, over time, girls who are deeply grateful, understanding we've saved them from evil or catastrophe.

I visit Robert almost every week for nearly two years except in the summer. It's impossible to forget about his condition but we settle into a routine. He knows more about me than anyone else except, of course, my parents but after the move to Manhattan I see him only once. It's a long subway and bus ride. I tell him about the City and Joan of Arc but he isn't really interested. And he doesn't want to play. He must be angry. He keeps his eyes on an egg salad sandwich that he can raise from the tray attached to his chair to his mouth. It's a tedious process reminding me of the pace of a rising drawbridge. Robert feels that I have abandoned him. He is sullen. Isn't sure how to deal with it. I am free not only to move about but also to make my fantasies real while he will always be stuck in his chair.

I am relieved that he hasn't suggested a talking game. I've now decided they are babyish. Robert is not curious about my new life but before I leave he looks at me directly for the first time and asks if I'll be coming again now that I live far away. I lie and say yes, sure, of course, but know that it isn't likely to happen. In fact, now that I have to cope with Manhattan, he passes easily from my consciousness until three years later. Alice tells me in a matter of fact way that he has died. "It was respiratory problems," she says as if it was long expected. "Gus and her husband will be moving to Manhattan to have a life at last."

"What did he have," I ask her, "and what caused it?"

"Gus never gave it a name. It's a blessing, he's gone," she adds.

Are these things passed down, I wonder, from father to son? But that's not a question I can ask. Years later, after I've learned that I'm actually not doomed by any inherited

genetic disorder, I do some research with the help of my
primary care doctor, Tom Delbanco. After listening to
his speculations, I decide Robert had a form of muscular
dystrophy called Duchenne's, named after its nineteenth-
century French neurologist discoverer. The disease is caused,
I learn, by a mutation in a gene that affects the X chromo-
some. While anyone can be victimized, the gene is usually
found in boys. I'm startled to find out it can be inherited
and wonder—without a shred of evidence to support it—
whether sensing this about Robert's condition powers my
own fears of harboring hidden damage.

In 2016, the Food and Drug Administration overruled
its own staffers and approved a controversial drug called
Exondys 51 that for the first time offered treatment to
Duchenne patients with one type of mutation that blocked
the capacity for normal muscular and motor functions.
Some medical researchers doubted the drug would work.
They pointed out the clinical trial included only a dozen
boys. They complained about the $300,000 annual price
tag, urging the drug company to refund the cost to patients
and insurers if the treatment failed. The controversy has
continued. A year later the *New York Times* reported families, patient advocates, and drug companies were still bat-
tling over the availability and cost (which could go as high as
$750,000 a year) of the drug whose value was still disputed.

I close my eyes and try to recapture the look of the boy
in the chair. I can't imagine anything other than an Act
of God changing his fate. But then there was his mother,

persevering without a shred of hope. A modern Sisyphus. A friend once backhandedly complimented me. He called me, "A master of lost causes." I wonder if early on I saw that in Gus. The thread running from my weekly playtimes with Robert to my later work at Columbia Law School isn't hard to follow. As a teacher and a writer I've always been able to create scenes, skits, and role-playing exercises. With my colleague and friend Philip Schrag, I will write a book about how to create simulations that are a way to train litigators for presentations to jurors and judges. I'm not much of a mimic but I can throw my voice into a dozen parts. Sometimes in class I force law students to deal with me as if I were a difficult and demanding client or I make them negotiate with an irrational adversary. When my voice goes gruff and aggressive, I am suddenly back over half a century playing an adventure game with Robert. The action there was in the dialogue and the voices that go with it. The voice did the work because it was the only tool Robert had available. Despite the fantasy, the emotions that came from the voices were real. The boy in the chair lived for this; the boy who went away inherited the method.

Ira

My father's given name was Isaac. He claimed he had no middle name. Like Alice, he was born late in his mother's childbearing years; like me, he had no siblings. When he was a teen, he insisted on being called Ira. Later he adopted the middle initial D, which his mother insisted stood for her maiden name.

Ira denied the D stood for anything. "I just thought," he said when I asked, "Ira D. sounded better; it helped me," he added, "in my business dealings." Later, I learned that at his birth my grandmother had, in fact, chosen her maiden name as his middle name. I decided that he abandoned Dreifuss for D to avoid its obvious Jewish association—the same reason he'd changed from Isaac—but was too embarrassed to admit it.

I was born when he was twenty-eight and he died nineteen years later when he was forty-seven. I never heard anyone call him anything but Ira and learned of his given name only after his death when I discovered a birth certificate, along with other secrets. The name change reflected a deep concern about anti-Semitism that followed him throughout his life, almost always just under the radar. In this, he was hardly alone. Adopting non-Jewish–sounding names was commonplace at the time, especially among second- or third-generation children like my father for whom the existence of a previous generation's immigration from Europe was hardly acknowledged by his parents. Alice had a male cousin born Goldberg who changed his name to Grayson when he became a traveling salesman. Certain *New York Times* reporters were famous at the time for using initials instead of Jewish-sounding first names. World-famous architect Frank Gehry was born Goldberg. Celebrated choreographer Jerome Robbins was born Rabinowitz. Growing up in New York City in the 1940s and 1950s, it was obvious that there were Jews who, whatever their inner doubts, never faltered in claiming their identity and their religious beliefs; just as many supplemented going secular by distancing themselves from any Jewish associations and by choosing gentile-sounding names. One could go on listing the famous name changers for days. There were others who simply ceased being Jewish to themselves and those around them. My friend Jacquie didn't learn her mother, who lost family in the holocaust, was Jewish until she was forty-nine. "She was scrupulously honest about everything," Jacquie said, "except that."

There have always been Jews whose primary identification is secular or cultural, who for a variety of reasons, often occupational, tried to manage their identity so as to control the way others saw them. Some had lost much of that identity but held on to pieces of it. As a child growing up in Chicago, my wife was supposed to bring an offering to a liberal Jewish congregation Sunday School to hang in the arbor observant Jews festoon with fruits and vegetables for the harvest time celebration called Succoth. After hearing the request her mother sent her off to school with a can of peaches. Despite such gaps in what this highly educated German-Jewish woman knew or wanted to remember about the accouterments of Judaism, she was clear that she was in fact a Jew. My father was in this camp but with one exception. He came to join the Anti-Defamation League (ADL), the decades-old Jewish organization that fought against bigotry. I grew up in a house full of books celebrating diversity and pamphlets condemning hate speech and the doings of the Ku Klux Klan.

Ironically, before his time with ADL when he would give occasional lectures to community groups, the 1930s resumes he sent out to prospective employers for jobs in advertising often included statements that he was a Protestant; my first shock in reading one of these documents in a moldy file he left behind wasn't so much that he'd changed his religion but the evidence that it was often the case then for applicants to indicate their faith on job applications. Even before 1965 when I filed the first employment discrimination case the NAACP Legal Defense Fund brought in federal court under the recently enacted antidiscrimination in employment provisions of Title VII of the Civil Rights Act, I would have thought it bizarre to find a job seeker for any but a job with a denomination-related institution trumpeting their religion on a resume but after doing the research I learned the practice was widespread. In my naïve belief I was, to put lipstick on a pig, just misinformed. In the Title VII case the defendant, an Eastern North Carolina A&P supermarket, folded immediately, offering a checkout job to the individual female plaintiff, the first black to get that job in her area. Though I never again litigated a Title VII employment discrimination case, I was proud that the more sophisticated specialists at LDF who came along later often used my legal papers as a model.

The years between my dad's Depression search for employment and his death in 1956 were full of ambivalence, mixed signals, instances of great progress, and hardly any. He started his search for work in New York but quickly realized that he'd have to have some actual job experience with some published ads to show before he could land the work he wanted on Madison Avenue. His first job for an Ohio department store lasted more than a year and ended, he thought, for budgetary reasons but then he and my mother moved to Boston where he'd gotten work creating the advertising for a now long-defunct regional railroad, the New York, New Haven and Hartford. He'd used the "Protestant" resume to get it and unsurprisingly it ended, or so he thought, when his boss discovered he was Jewish.

How discovered, I wondered, or was this just an excuse? His face contained no particularly Jewish stereotypical traits and his voice failed to betray his origins. The Meltsner name might sound Jewish to some, just another German-American name to others. In fact, a prominent German academic who once shared a lecture podium with me in Durban, South Africa, told me the name reflected an important job, that of converting barley to malt in the brewing of beer. Years later waiting to teach a class of earnest German university students about the sit-ins and freedom rides of the early 1960s I told this to my host, a professor at Berlin's Freie University, but he scoffed at the idea: "Most likely, your ancestors were workers in the smelting business; they probably did the dirty job of extracting metal from ore. Put an S in front of your last name and you'll get something in Yiddish suggestive of that awful work."

Whatever the truth, like his parents, Ira was born in the USA, in Manhattan. He attended Townsend Harris High School—the elite City public high school of the era—and graduated from New York University so if you were bent on keeping Jews out of your office, you could easily draw the inference that New York origins meant the applicant was possibly Jewish and conclude that there was something to worry about here. I was reminded how hard it was for Jews to break into the ad business by watching the extraordinarily popular 2001 television series *Mad Men*. Still, as Ira's credentials were available to the railroad before he was hired, I am left with another mystery. In my imaginary

conversation with my long dead father I ask him what happened and he says, "Actually when they thought they'd got
what creative ideas I had, I was disposable."

But, of course, this is really me the civil rights lawyer
talking. I am trained to search out plausible alternative
explanations for discrimination because in my legal world
that's the way decisions that look racially based are defended
by corporations and government actors. I suspect that, in
fact, leaving such matters a mystery was for Ira more comfortable than delving into the specifics of anti-Semitism
aimed at him. Yet as an active member of ADL he was
always quick to comment on any bigotry he saw that surfaced in the press and in this he made no distinction among
victims. In childhood, I ate dinner at a table where both my
parents could be expected to report sometimes with sad-
ness, sometimes with anger, stories of events that involved
abuse or discrimination on racial or religious grounds. This
may also partially explain the completely uncritical view
(which they shared) American Jews held of Franklin Del-
ano Roosevelt who was surely an improvement over any
other politician of the time but hardly earned the unques-
tioning loyalty, the worship and devotion, he received from
so many Jews and blacks. When I was eight, a radio program I was listening to in my room was interrupted by an
announcement of Roosevelt's death; I called downstairs to
tell my mother, hardly knowing what the announcement
meant. Her tears echoed through the house.

Middle class, religiously liberal, long-time citizen Jews of my parent's era desperately wanted to believe America was a new chapter in their lives. Almost to prove it, they willfully blinded themselves to aspects of their Jewish heritage, especially the experience of their families before they arrived in the United States during the 1870s and 1880s. The answer to questions about the immigrant generation and even the details of my deceased grandparents early life in this country was often an admission of total ignorance. Memories were erased, a classic reaction to trauma and, as my sister-in-law, the historian Gabriel Spiegel, reminds me, also characteristic of survivors of the Shoah. I only learned in my sixties from the researches of a relative so distant that I could never figure how to describe the connection, a California rabbi who had become the unofficial genealogist of five intertwined families, that the family was connected to a town in Lithuania that the Nazis turned into a killing ground called Rumshishok (or Rumšiškės).

As French psychoanalyst Nadine Fresco found when she interviewed the children of Holocaust survivors for her powerful 1984 article "Remembering the Unknown," some stories never got told. Silence ruled. Only years after the Holocaust did numbers of American Jews born in this country—somewhat like the searches of the generation of Germans who came of age after the Hitler era—seek to excavate the facts of ancestor life in Eastern Europe. I can conclude only that the events in Europe that brought my kin to the shores of America in the nineteenth century were so brutal that they were treated as catastrophic, and suppressed.

In my father's case being Jewish had little or nothing to do with communal tradition, ethnic heritage, or synagogue attendance. Rather he thought himself someone who was on his own with little or no family or community support. He was a risk-taker by necessity, not by choice. To get ahead, he would bargain with whomever had what he needed. So he assumed whatever posture served his ambitions and necessities. He had one foot inside and one outside the waters of the mainstream and somehow—I think it a New Yorker's trait—learned to smoothly slip in and out, to size up where he was and what was needed in any situation. A chameleon? No, that's too either–or. He compartmentalized a side of ethical humanism from business pragmatism and somehow kept both alive, even at work. This made him an exceptionally successful salesman. There was a deeper split here, however, between the public self and the private understanding that showed itself in his politics, which were far more radical than anyone around him. He always took the side of the underdog. Especially ethnics. He also regularly played long shots at the racetrack. But he rarely pushed his politics on others. That would have sacrificed his cover.

While my parents were alive, I never heard a mention of my great grandparents. It was as if they never were. I take that back: Alice referred to Ira's grandmother who apparently she'd met once as "Strict and religious. Very old country," but that was it. She spoke as if the woman was a creature from the dark past and a faraway land but I would learn from the Rabbi genealogist that she actually died in New York when I was four years old. Why did my parents treat her as if she didn't exist? Did she even know she had a great grandson? I could never find out.

Occasionally when I asked questions about history, often stimulated by news stories of the plight of European Jews, I was referred to my mother's sister, Frances, for an answer. She was a dozen or so years older than Alice and had in fact sponsored a refugee shortly after the end of World War II. Nevertheless, from her I acquired only a few stories that had the feeling of mythology but not much more. The best involved my mother's mother, Mollie Goldberg, who was described as so tough that she became, as I once wrote, New York City's first female private investigator, sniffing out fraudulent accident claims against transit companies with classic snooping techniques—changing disguises in taxi cabs while in mid chase, assuming fake identities, secretly charting claimants' behavioral patterns, and conducting rigorous research into the background of suspected malingerers. Frances told me, "Mollie was really very Sherlock Holmes like. She would report to the insurance company, 'I managed to spot this fellow with the supposed back condition. He was hard at work lifting bricks and mixing mortar.'"

Frances told me how her father, my maternal grandfather, who was called Jim, unapologetically took up with a teenager after Mollie died but details of the relationship, much less its etiology, were totally lacking. Cornered in her kitchen, even Frances, who was a dedicated and talented cook, could go just so far in tracking family history. She slapped her hands to shake off some flour and made it clear she wanted to get back to baking. I was left with a reinforced feeling that either I was descended from an incurious lot or life was degrading as well as impoverished in both the old country and the early years in America, so bad that, like warriors at last home from the front, even memories that could be passed down had to be drenched in some amnesia-laden liquid. Particularly strange was that the failure of these observant, intelligent family members to know more about the past than a few factual shards applied as much to their America-born parents as to the previous generations. The real lesson for me in this seek-and-hide set of experiences was an understanding that in families complex adaptations were the norm and that the only way to really figure them out was to break the code. I was so curious that it led me to my alternate career as a licensed family therapist. Unlike Tolstoy I found that all families, happy or unhappy, had secrets difficult to exhume.

My education in family cryptography did advance shortly after moving into the Seventy-Ninth Street apartment when Alice informed me that she had spoken to Rabbi Louis Newman at the Westside reform Congregation called

Rodeph Sholom. He had agreed that despite the lateness of the hour, I would be able to train for a bar mitzvah with Nathan Meltzoff, the long-serving temple cantor and coincidentally the man who conducted (unknown to him) the *second* marriage of my mother and father.

It turned out that Rodeph Sholom once had been governed by a group that included family members. When it was located on Lexington Avenue in East Sixties, her father Jim had been offered the job of sexton and funeral director. He was told it was a sure moneymaker, but he declined because "he wanted no part of dead bodies." Her uncle Jonas had taken the job to keep it in the family. I had never heard of any of this before but more importantly had no intention of learning Hebrew, going to Sunday School anymore and "becoming a man" before people I didn't know and a God I had never met.

To this she had two replies; the first was so outrageous, so totally ridiculous, that I still dine out on it over sixty-five years later: "Someday," she seriously intoned, "you might fall in love with a rabbi's daughter and her father won't let you marry her because you haven't done a bar mitzvah." This from a totally Americanized woman who might not even know what the word shtetl meant, a woman who because of family opposition had secretly married Ira before a Justice of the Peace in Connecticut, snuck back to New York, and even at the open ceremony two years later never told anyone but Frances that they had already married.

Though the deep story was still unknown to me, by this time I was much too smart about her ways to fall for this type of manipulation but I was also wise enough not to laugh in her face but to take what she said as if I thought it was serious. I told her instead I didn't believe in any religion:

"No bar mitzvah under any circumstances. This was America. If the rabbi's daughter loves me, she will just have suck it up and marry me, or else, well, I'll just have to survive without her."

This smarty-pants resolve lasted maybe two minutes by the clock. What did I really know at age twelve about "any circumstances," or my mother's specifically for that matter? All she had to do was unwrap her second reason to win the game. A year later, I dutifully read to the reform congregation the phonetic (even then I called it phony phonetics) Hebrew script from the Torah I had memorized with the aged cantor's help (I could not read a word of Hebrew), and drank champagne and smoked a cigar for the first time with my friends in the men's restroom of a catered space at the Hotel Alden on Central Park West and Eighty-Second Street, later covering the hotel's marble men's room floor with my vomit. Once restored to decent appearance, I carried home an array of presents ranging from a book commonly then given to bar mitzvah boys called *"Jews in Baseball"* to a few hundred dollars in cold cash. My attitude toward the event was truly profane as illustrated by the fact that I can remember all these years later what novels I read in my thirteenth year but not the portion of the Torah I rendered.

Alice's trump card had been a simple declaration that, "Your father would like it." This may have been intended as a commonplace, something meaning only what it narrowly said, but even then when actually knowing nothing of the facts I heard it differently as: "Your father needs to know you going to be a man because he might not be around forever." And so I went forward on this unspoken and unacknowledged assumption. It took a while to learn that one understands certain matters without being consciously aware of them.

There were, of course, other signs of Ira's fragility. The most vivid of the "Grow up as fast as you can" indicators was the assignment I have described given to me to move the family car to avoid New York City's alternate side of the street cleaning program. For those uninitiated the program—new then but now widely imitated—can be simply stated—two or three days a week for several hours all cars must be removed from one side of the street to enable street sweepers to do their job. Fail to remove your car and it will be towed to a City pound where you can retrieve it for a large towing charge (payment in cash only) plus a parking ticket. During these years my father worked a long day; my mother would often fill in as a temporary salesperson at Macy's department store on Thirty-Fourth Street where she had friends from college who had become buyers.

They made sure she was on call when there was need for a substitute.

In a City where a driver had to be eighteen and have insurance, where there were no learner's permits for the sixteen to eighteen cohort, fourteen-year-old me became the chosen car mover. For over three years several times a week I arranged to shift the Green Chrysler to spots safe from the tow truck. When none were available, I'd have to double park on the safe side of the street, do my homework sitting at the wheel, and wait for the all clear. The older I got, the more tempted I was to simply drive the car when I wanted to and eventually gave in, neglected to tell my parents, and on weekend nights drove with my friend George Sommerfeld to the Roosevelt or Yonkers harness racing tracks where we were regular visitors. I was never caught by the police but Alice soon figured it out. To my amazement, she didn't care. "You're a mature young man," she said. "I trust you." Here she was again urging me to grow up—fast.

Only later when my daughters began to take lessons for their driving tests did the madness of this arrangement hit me. New York may not be as much a challenge as New Delhi or Rome but even now I hold my breath in City traffic. And then I recalled that my mother had taught me to drive when I was eleven. She had taken me to the large but empty, out-of-season, public beach parking lot near where we had delivered sandwiches to the pillbox soldiers. After giving me some rudimentary instructions, she turned me loose in the vast lot. Surprisingly this worked. I decided she was a good teacher; I certainly was an eager student but the third and last time I was behind the wheel carving out lazy figure eights in the vast lot a police squad car drove into view. She told me to pull over quickly, snuggle, and pretend we were necking. The cop car passed us by.

My illegal driver years would come in handy. After I turned sixteen, I applied for a summer job as a busboy at a hotel on the shore of Long Island Sound in Westbrook, Connecticut, called Castlebrook Inn. I was ready to pretend to the boss I was an eighteen-year-old NYU college student but the issue didn't come up. Ben, the eccentric owner, favored blood red slacks, bright yellow shirts. He spent much of his time sampling every one of the brands of Scotch he served to his guests. He never asked my age but when I arrived for the summer season and presented myself to the office manager she had never heard of me. What's more, she offered, there were actually no more places for a busboy. After taking in my confusion she disappeared into a back room but after a few minutes returned. Was I, perhaps, experienced with cars?

A quick nod and I became the hotel's official (and illegal) driver, put in charge of a new Pontiac station wagon, told to pick up arriving guests at the Old Saybrook, Connecticut, railroad station, and ferry them to the Inn. I'd bring luggage from the car to their room and after asking if there was anything else they needed usually collected a tip. I was given a room in a ramshackle cottage near the beach that served as a dorm for employees, made friends with other

staff members—almost all authentic college students none
of whom came from New York and, therefore, didn't closely
question my phony NYU story—and went out after work
with waiters and busboys on nightly trips along the shore
looking for pizza, egg rolls, and beer. In the beginning I felt
privileged to go along on these jaunts. Making believe I was
a college boy, I talked a lot less than I was used to fearing
someone would discover my fraud but after a while I relaxed
and mostly tried to learn what it was like to go to college and
to date college-age women.

All went well until one day Ben told me he had fired his
handyman for drinking on the job, a trait I'd have thought
would have endeared him to the boss.

"You'll have to take over the daily run to the town dump,"
was his order; then he promptly disappeared.

The Inn produced an enormous amount of garbage and
trash. The cans, often stuffed with smelly lobster, mussel,
and clam shells, were loaded by kitchen workers every morning onto the back of a rusting gray Ford pickup truck. The
dump was located in a scrubby inland area a few miles away,
a typical New England landfill venue of the pre-recycling
era featuring dozens of scavenging herring gulls, piles of
brush, locals greeting acquaintances with the day's gossip,
and mounds of waste. The problem was I had never driven
a manual gearshift car, much less a truck, and because I
was not only illegal but also the supposedly experienced
Inn driver couldn't ask for help.

Fortunately, the luck that had gotten me a job held. The next day I waited until no one was close by and drove the pickup in first gear until I'd left the immediate area of the Inn. I pulled over and tried to shift into second and third but I had no experience dealing with a clutch. The grinding of the gears was nerve wracking. The truck bucked its way into second and somehow I made it along the main road to the dump turnoff. Once there I unloaded the cans and spent an hour practicing, bearing with the disapproving glances of coming and going town residents, until I could feel competent enough to return to the Inn. The next morning I expected the truck would be out of commission, its gears stripped clean, but somehow it had managed to survive my onslaught.

By my second summer at the Inn, I still wasn't old enough to have a license but was relieved of the need to drive when a busboy position opened up. The tips were better, and you could earn extra money running an evening bingo game for the patrons, though bringing dishes in and out of the kitchen meant dealing with fury of the head chef who treated waiters and the busing staff as the enemy. Either we wanted food before it was ready or, if there was a complaint from the dining room, had served it too slowly. The chef was short and hairy with gnomic looks that added to the power of his ferocity. He had the habit of cursing in Greek and brandishing a meat cleaver when the line sous chefs weren't producing fast enough.

One week in midsummer, he disappeared and the kitchen immediately calmed. I thought he'd quit or been fired but the following week he was back shouting at everyone who crossed his path. At one point, he muttered something to me and waved a six-inch cleaver in my direction as I emptied a tray at the dishwashing machine. I thought he must be losing it as he rarely even glanced in the direction of the machine. And he repeated the action with other busboys. Suddenly, a waiter told him off. They had words and I expected something unpleasant would happen soon that involved the cleaver but before it could on the very next day a late summer hurricane lashed the Connecticut shore, quickly flooding the Inn's dining room and kitchen as well as the approach road. The staff had to lead and at times carry guests across swirling waters to Ben's house on higher ground back from the Sound. Despite the turmoil I loved being part of the rescue. The angry water reminds me of wild surf pounding at the Rockaway jetties. To the dismay of the lifeguards, my friends and I would dash into the swell, dare the ocean to throw its force against us, and when it did get driven down into the sandy bottom of the sea only to emerge like heroes.

Anxiety

I came of age during a period popularly known as the age of anxiety, though the nervous and worried rhetoric that named it actually emerged earlier in the post–World War I period of the lost generation, round up of left wing dissidents, of dada, runaway inflation, emerging fascism, and a new world order. But after the end of World War II there was a resurgence: in 1947, W. H. Auden wrote a prize-winning, book-length poem of that name; Leonard Bernstein later turned the text into a symphony and Jerome Robbins into a ballet. The real war was over, but it had exposed how much worse things could be. George Kennan was predicting the grave difficulties posed by the coming conflict with the Soviet Union. In 1949, Stalin exploded his own bomb, ending the American monopoly on nuclear weapons and spreading fear that eventually it would be used to attack this country. I trace my own awareness of some unnamable darkness to remarks, asides, jokes, silences, and even sometimes explicit statements from parents who continued to tell of their suffering during the Great Depression years and how after being brought up in bourgeois security watched the businesses of their parents crumble and eventually disappear. Even as they modestly prospered, like so many Americans scraped their way back to a middle class way of life, purchased nice clothes, a new car, and trendy meals at Danny's Hideaway Eastside steakhouse where Ira was a regular, the possibility of another economic disaster was never far from their thoughts.

During the first years that I closely attended to events outside the family, the World War was ending but then came the knowledge from magazine images and shocked adults of the boxcars, the ovens, the starved bodies piled like human firewood behind barbed wire. Amorphous as it was, the thought came to me "Something should be done about this," and I have come to believe that, though the occasion and the object were different, my reaction had a lot to do with how I spent my working life. Nothing brings into play faster the usually abstract sense of justice than the specific experience of injustice.

Just when peace became familiar, the cold war came to replace the hot war. Soon there were graphic front-page newspaper drawings of how far an atomic or hydrogen bomb might wreak havoc. A general sense of anxiety mingled with the more specifics of fear. One is the beast in the jungle; the other the beast clawing at your door. The compelling, concentric circles in newspaper graphics spread out from central Manhattan, and quickly reached the part of the City where I lived. If a child missed the images charting potential radiation, all of us learned how to climb under desks to simulate protection from the fallout of a nuclear explosion. Many consequences flowed from this policy. First, we were taught to worry. Second, there were dim stirrings of interest in what government was all about. Third, it convicted the authorities of poor judgment, if not idiocy. Fourth, more significant to immature males flopping on the dirty schoolroom floors, it exposed what females wore under their skirts.

The greatest driver of anxiety in our household, however, was not a Depression hangover, international politics, the rage to punish domestic communists and their sympathizers, or even the Bomb but my father's bittersweet relationship with the company he worked for from the late 1930s until two years before his death in 1956. In one view this was a story of rags to riches. His career was going nowhere before he got this job. He started out a provisional salesman, selling the calendars, business gifts, novelties, and office desk items used by customers to make their brand remembered and, especially around Christmas, to keep the people they dealt with happy. He took to the work, he claimed, because he wasn't hawking hardware, but ideas. He may have only half believed it—I could never tell—but he had forcibly made himself over by internalizing the be-jolly, can-do, think-positively rhetoric of sales conference trainers. This was, after all, the era of Dale Carnegie and his enormously popular self-improvement bible, *How to Win Friends and Influence People*, which taught that you could transform yourself into a success, put troublesome emotions and interior doubts aside, and as Barbara Ehrenreich analyzed the phenomenon subject "one's inner life to relentless monitoring." At the other end of the social spectrum, but really on the same personal growth wavelength at this time, was the growing cultural presence of Alcoholics Anonymous and its Twelve-Step Program aimed at sobriety.

The company that employed Ira was called Brown & Bigelow. Home based in St. Paul, Minnesota, B&B promoted the items it manufactured and Ira sold as "Remembrance Advertising." The great enemy of the B&B sales force was the bottle of booze. "No one will remember who gave you the Scotch by February," salesmen would intone to prospective customers, "but this combination clock and butane lighter, this desk set in real cowhide, this stunning calendar showing mallards in flight, has your business name and number prominently displayed so when they need what you sell you're right in front of their eyes. It speaks of who you are as well as what you're selling." This was the key riff in a million sales calls.

Both Brown and Bigelow were dead by the time my father arrived at the company, the latter as a result of a bizarre North woods canoe accident; the business was now run by a larger-than-life, sometimes beneficent, sometimes merciless, autocrat and egomaniac named Charles Allen (Charley) Ward who was so enmeshed with Bigelow that he had been willed a third of his estate. The company story read like a movie script. If you were a B&B family, you knew it by heart, had to take it into account even if you were a thousand miles away from the factory and corporate offices in Minnesota. Charlie Ward bombarded his sales troops with adages like "When you stop being better you stop being good," with pictures of him displaying his diamond jewelry, ten-gallon hat, white suit, and brilliant tan. There were always holiday gifts, say of pewter kitchenware, for the missus or other reminders of Charley's largesse and most of all the embroidered tale of his redemption and success.

It began in Leavenworth, the formidable federal prison in Eastern Kansas, once the site of a fort that served as the jumping-off place for the Americans mobilizing to conquer the West. Herbert Bigelow, a respectable, conservative businessman was convinced, along with many others, of the immorality of 1913 federal income tax law, the first of its kind, to the point that he simply decided to ignore it. The government was looking for examples to prosecute and found one in the businessman; a court case sent him to prison for three years. While Bigelow was trying to grow his business, Ward had been living on the wild side. He'd been on his own since he was seventeen; if the dramatized accounts he put forth later can be trusted, and at least some of them are likely true, he had started by shining shoes but ended with gold rush dollars. In between he'd rode with Pancho Villa in Mexico and met Jack London in Alaska. He'd scored a small fortune selling animal hides from cattle killed during Villa's campaigns and then lost it all; he'd been a miner, a merchant seaman, a gambler, and finally a convicted drug dealer, sentenced (despite claiming he was framed) to ten years in Leavenworth.

According to a version of the Charley story, once in prison Ward had an epic conversion:

"Some silent power within his brain caused him to resolve to adapt himself to the prison rules and to become the most agreeable inmate in the prison. With this resolution, the entire tide of affairs of his life began to reverse. Charlie Ward had finally mastered his greatest enemy, himself."

Once redeemed, the story continues, his savior appeared in the form of Herbert Bigelow, just the sort of man whom prison inmates will make doing time a living hell unless he has protection. Ward took him under his wing and kept him safe. Bigelow was grateful, offered Ward money when he was paroled and ultimately a job when Bigelow was released—though Ward complained that he had to fight for it, as Bigelow initially wanted nothing more to do with him. Ward at first was given rough work at a rubber processing machine for twenty-five dollars a week. Within months, however, he'd made himself indispensible to Bigelow. Quickly promoted to foreman, by 1933 the ex-convict adventurer was made a vice president of a company then employing 400–500 workers. Later that year after Bigelow and a female companion drowned, the company board made Charlie Ward president.

By the time, my father came to work at B&B's Manhattan office Ward had turned the company into a profitable enterprise as well as a full corporate expression of his personality. Along the way he picked up a young wife, a pardon from President Roosevelt, a showplace farm in Indiana, a cattle ranch in the West, huge influence in Minnesota politics, and perhaps most remarkable of all a reputation for hiring hundreds of ex-offenders at the factory in St. Paul. Despite knowing that the psychoanalyst on whose couch I spent many tense but useful hours in my thirties would wonder if there was a connection, I am skeptical that growing up in the penumbra of Ward's history had anything to do with the fact that in the 1973 I wrote much of what became New York State's ex-offender antidiscrimination law.

Ward's empathy for men like him who had a run of bad luck or trouble with the law did not, however, extend to his sales force. Working on commission, a salesman would go without a paycheck if he didn't produce. If that didn't stoke enough worry, Ward's executives added to the pressure by setting unreasonably high monthly sales quotas. The search for customers was intense. My father brought stories to the dinner table of businessmen who listened enthusiastically to his ideas, took copious notes, called him back for clarification only to refuse in the end to buy; customers who arranged it so he couldn't get past receptionists to see them; purchasing agents who made it clear they required a kickback to do business; signed orders with explicit deadlines that the St. Paul factory agreed to and then missed resulting in canceled orders, bad feelings, and lost commissions.

At the same time seductive inducements were dangled before the men and their families—invitations to business meetings at well-appointed Florida resort hotels, promised bonuses for quota busters, and hints that children of favored employees might be invited to spend time at one of the cattle ranches owned by the big boss or his chief executives. Ira often talked as if these were commitments rather than conditioned on performance and I plainly wanted to believe him (especially the part about spending time on a Western ranch) but still I remember the edge of doubt that crept into his occasional rendition of a happy and prosperous future at B&B. Yet even as he grew concerned, my father was clearly getting on in the world. I could tell because the mail regularly included photographs of the big boss with a broad smile while he sat on his palomino as well as boxes of leather-bound notebooks, sleek memo pads, and something new called a ballpoint pen that came in such quantities that I could bring samples to school and use them to make new friends.

Ira overcame his initial reluctance to ask people to sign his order forms. He came to believe he was actually good at this work. He moved from depending on cold calls to prospects who had never heard of him to customers who would reorder every year by phone and ultimately to megadeals for company calendars arranged with high-level management—promotions for companies like the New York Central Railroad and City Services Oil Company, with professional athletes, signing one of the first black athletes to win an endorsement deal when he negotiated a contract with Jackie Robinson a year after he broke the baseball color line with the Brooklyn Dodgers. (He persuaded Robinson's advisors by arguing that white players earned extra money this way so why not Jackie; then he pushed the order through a skeptical St. Paul by arguing that a line drawing of Robinson in action would hang on the walls of colored barber shops and body shops across the country.)

While he set sales records and grew in confidence, made more money than ever before, allowing my mother to take part-time sales work at Macy's only when it pleased her, the undertow of worry never left him and never left us. Certainly the Depression memories didn't help and were reinforced by what was going on in society at large, like McCarthyism and the Cold War. Like most American liberals, even though not directly targeted, the Red Scare with its Truman-era loyalty oaths, congressional committee circuses, and naming names dramas was seen as a potential threat to their well-being. As memories of wartime unity dimmed, America was losing its sense of confidence; when who was a loyal citizen became an issue, many retreated into a search for private satisfactions. It was no accident that in 1948 Dale Carnegie turned his attention from the positive-thinking pitch of the thirties to a book called *How to Stop Worrying and Start Living: Time Tested Methods for Conquering Worry.*

As an only child without the annoying distraction of siblings I slowly began to translate my father's messages into

my own fantasies; while he was grappling with the daily
frustrations that went with earning a living by persuading potential customers the he had the right stuff to grow
their business, I was developing my amateur version of
Das Kapital (of course, long before I had ever heard of
Karl Marx). The class enemy soon identified itself as the
corporation—though it was some years before I general-
ized from B&B to doubts about the corporate form as such.
It presented you with a face like Charley Ward's that promised much but delivered uncertainly, ambivalently, and
unpredictably. And I had a thought that has stayed with me,
even though then poorly understood, that the liberalism I
saw in my country was not so deeply rooted that a halt to
economic success couldn't bring forth bigotry, strife, and
ultimately powerful antidemocratic forces.

Ira was eventually promoted from a high commission-
generating salesman to a salaried manager of the Manhattan office, the first Jewish manager in company history, but,
ironically, it brought him less peace (as well as less money).
Rather than struggling to meet the monthly quota expectations imposed on him from afar, he was now subject to
worry on account of the performance of some twenty-five
salesmen he hadn't himself hired and could only exhort.
He was well aware that few of his colleagues worked the
entire day calling on customers. He knew because he had
spent many an afternoon himself at Belmont or Jamaica
racetracks or slipping out to catch a Dodger's day game in
Flatbush at Ebbets Field. The work was too emotionally

taxing, the five boroughs too difficult to manage, the frigid gatekeepers too many to expect the men to spend the eight hours a day on the job—the time St. Paul factored into its quota projections. And why didn't the Midwestern executives with their rah-rah, rah-rah exhorting memos and unrealistic projected sales figures understand that in this business a good salesman was hawking a promotional concept, not taking orders for a concrete thing as in "How many boxes of widgets do you need this month?" The work was more art than science, the philosopher in him mused; you needed persistence but not time sheets. Free time, even watching the ponies or going to a ballgame or the theater, could grow the flowers of imagination, could nurture the engaging persona that made customers want to buy.

The successful salesman he had made himself by an act of will had taken seriously the spiel of the sales conference trainers, "When they say 'No,' you're half way there; all you need do now is shift them to a 'Yes.'" But somehow he had built a boundary between Mr. Outside and Mr. Inside. He adapted but only so far. Now he boldly told St. Paul to back off, cap their memos, and let him do what he was hired to do. It was for him both his undoing and his triumph; for me it was more proof that the relationship between corporation and corporate employee was untrustworthy and if you came too close to the corporate sun ultimately fatal. The stated rules were that this was business; if you sold goods and made money, you were a success. The reality was different. Outcomes like security in his job had as much to do with personality, interoffice jealousies, ethnic labels, and geography as his success in turning the office around. And because this was 1950s America, the time of *The Man in the Gray Flannel Suit*, the time of IBM worship, the greatest value of all was conformity. If B&B corporate decisions were sometimes predictable, the allocation of what you could truly rely upon was still random. Thus, a man's living and his family stability depended of what felt like a lottery. No wonder my father started taking me to Belmont Park when I was eleven. Neither of us was aware that I might take his lessons about the fickle world of the racetrack to apply more to the way I would view the American legal system than playing the horses.

In the short term, Ira won the war of the executive suite. He won on the numbers because his men, buoyed by the energetic postwar economy as well as his flexible leadership, beat even the outrageous quotas set in what Alice and I who had never been to Minnesota thought of as the frozen tundra of gopher land. He won with the men who, despite the case-hardening, cynical ways of those who had to grapple daily with the Manhattan sales grind, treated him with a grudging respect. When I was older, Herman Spatz, the senior salesman in the office, explained to me that because Ira was really one of them, he could govern without any of the usual backstabbing and the common lying about sales prospects that was endemic in the sales manager–salesmen relationship at B&B.

Herman was the same salesman who improbably persuaded Ira to suggest that I apply to Harvard College. "I sell to these guys." He confidently insisted, "The fix is in." I reluctantly agreed, knowing full well that my Stuyvesant High School grades and public school pedigree made acceptance impossible. I was baffled at the view of the academic world apparently held by these two grown-ups. Hadn't they heard of legacies for children of rich graduates and quotas for Jews? Later in life as a university dean, I would learn decisions over admissions were not for the faint of heart, or the ethically sensitive. But in my high school graduation year, Harvard College received twenty-one applications from Stuyvesant and accepted one. He was an outstanding lineman on our football team.

At first the accolades flowing from Ira's successful management of the Manhattan office were shared by the executives above him in the hierarchy—after all they had selected him—so much so that they asked him to take on one of the sickest territories in the country, the Newark franchise, where he could start anew in a sense by hiring whomever he wanted, training them with his own techniques, and deploying fresh troops across the fertile Jersey small business landscape. A New York cabby impressed my dad so much he offered him a job. He hired and trained my cousin Carol's husband Len Chase who despite having little experience soon set sales records before leaving to set up his own business in Connecticut. But such successes were also Ira's undoing. By being right he had made too many of executives fear he was a threat to take over *their* jobs. Whether it was that he won too much money at the nonstop bridge and gin rummy card games that filled the afterhours at the Minnesota sales meetings or on the overnight train that he and his managerial colleagues occasionally took West or because he rarely drank that was not only totally unheard of but also, well, someone might say, "Isn't that pansy like?" Or whether his notoriety was pinned to his ethnicity, allowing him to be cabined as too pushy or clever for the taste of the home office, or simply that having turned two offices around someone more malleable could now take over, but whatever the explanation it was plain that the powers that be were falling out of love.

Typically, the child's partial grasp of such matters while they are happening rarely comes directly from the spoken word. In this instance it was pieced together from the way Ira treated the shift in travel from the overnights on New York Central Railroad, which had been in fact his biggest customer, to Northwest Airlines. Standing behind the observation deck glass next to Alice while we saw him off at the Quonset hut terminal of the newly fashioned, then called Idlewild, airport in Queens was to watch a tall man with a usually straightened and open stance suddenly bent and tentative, looking as if he was mounting a scaffold not the stairway to a sleek new Boeing Stratocruiser. At the time, visible on posters throughout the City, pasted to billboards and subway walls, was the sample case–weighed down, hunched-over, dark shape of Lee J. Cobb playing Willy Loman in the first Broadway production of Arthur Miller's play *Death of a Salesman*. Despite his love of the theater, the pile of programs on the glassed living room coffee table announcing his playgoer credentials and family friendship with the legendary Broadway press agent, Sam Friedman, Ira made it abundantly clear he wasn't going to see the play. "I know too much about the New England territory," he added. Subject closed.

Women

My understanding of sexual matters accelerated at the same time that I learned that Ira's work was treacherous and the City a dangerous place; that the best course of protective action was to grow antennas, observational capacities to spot oncoming or even potential threats. As I walked the neighborhood streets or spent fifty minutes commuting each way by subway to Stuyvesant High School on Fifteenth Street, to an observer I may have looked like a typical student just intent on moving along to whatever goal he had in mind but, in fact, I was on alert, ready to defend myself—to throw up my hands and push away in an instant, as if soon expecting a blow or nasty intervention of some kind. As I came into sexual understanding or more precisely misunderstanding, apprehension of the troubling and unexpected City migrated to the world of female relationships.

Take my first crush. Barbara is viewed often in a schoolyard but never spoken to; no words are possible as none are known. I am an explorer arriving to discover the language of a new continent. She takes no notice of me. So I will provoke her, even torture her, by playing Pony Express. A boy grabs a bike, turns it in circles, and then with increasing speed dashes toward the brick wall of the school building, jumping off at the last minute, before impact. If the victim is the bike of another boy, retaliation is a rush to do the same to the aggressor's cycle if it can be had, very much an eye for an eye sort of thing, but if none can be easily seized a fight is likely. When I grab dark-haired (like my mother's!) Barbara's bike and play the game, the crash that comes doesn't evoke from her a startled first connection nor does it just dent a fender or burst a tire. In painful fact, the bike cracks in pieces. Rim and spokes bend. Fork separates from wheel. Frame splits in two.

She weeps. Unbelievingly faced with damage beyond my imagining, I turn red with shame. This first learning is of how sexual failure destroys composure, and then threatens the self. Carrying the unwieldy pieces ten feet behind Barbara as she cries her way home, I decide I never want to see her again; that I will have to be more careful in the future with girls. I have no recollection of making amends.

But there is little occasion in the near term to apply any wisdom that might have flowed from such a regrettable outcome. My initial exposure to things sexual is to female anatomy alone, a richness of images flooding my home and thus my mind from the sexually suggestive visual depictions of B&B pinup calendar art. It should be clear that most of these images are seductive and suggestive; that they bear the same relationship to later-day pornography with its love of the exposed genitalia, huffing and puffing masturbation, anal intercourse, and *Kama Sutra* positions that a leer stands to an assault. Even *Playboy, Penthouse,* and *Hustler* are in the future. No one has even dreamed of Internet porn much less underwear as clothing, sexting, and going to the "slut pages." Only rarely do the artists of the 1940s and 1950s go in for full nudity; they never show the beaver and bush like the rarely seen shady periodicals secretly held behind the counter of stores selling magazines, cigarettes, and even egg creams that seem to lurk on every corner of the City.

The girls painted by the most famous of the artists, Peruvian-born Alberto Vargas, were familiar to anyone who had seen the painted fuselage of a World War II warplane. Vargas was but the best known of a stable of artists who produced images of models, showgirls, and movie stars with breasts leaning out from bathing suits, cat costumes, cowgirl vests, lacy brassieres, and evening dresses. Marilyn Monroe was one of future Hollywood stars whose career prospects mightily improved after her pinup gave our service men something to come home victorious for. Vargas was the king and B&B aggressively marketed his top heavy "Vargas Girls," using images that led the US Post Office to try to put *Esquire* magazine out of business— unsuccessfully as it turned out, when the Supreme Court in a unanimous 1946 decision ruled that the post office was without statutory authority to revoke a periodical's second class mail permit on the basis of material that might be suggestive but was not obscene.

This was the legacy I carried into actual relations with young women as I emerged from the cocoon spun by an attractive mother who was not clear about the allure of her body, who had a physically failing husband and but a single male child. Then too many looks at the graphic images of women exposing their nudity through peekaboo clothing, the sources of masturbation on calendars, and a deck of cards with fifty-two Vargas Girls cavorting as close by as a peak into my father's sample case. Certainly all this was reenforced by a culture that advertised and worshiped the sexual while at the same time hushing up the details, one that held lust as well as premarital sex as improper, if not unnatural. And worse the message was that the way a male viewer came to a female was only physical. No wonder I had no idea how to speak to girls.

The adolescent confusions that followed were complicated by becoming a reader at the same time I was suffering in and with the flesh. In 2008, I was asked along with many other Cambridge, Massachusetts, writers to contribute an essay to a volume celebrating the inauguration of the City's sleek new main library building. It was an opportunity for me to revisit the St. Agnes Branch of the New York Public Library on Amsterdam Avenue where I had spent many hours hiding out from the strangeness of Manhattan, its 1950s gang culture, and the feelings of morbid isolation of the newly arrived. The branch was unrecognizable, having been gentrified by a generous benefactor, but I took a seat, closed my eyes, and settled into my memories.

At St. Agnes I discovered a haven, a conflict-free zone where I felt able to choose any book on the shelves, where I was left alone to read what I wanted to read, and, thereby, as I understood it, was treated as an adult. At first, I viewed the array of books without preconceptions or goals. Books had always been around the house; my parents were readers. But most of my early reading was school-related, though I was a keen follower of baseball stories written by my hero John R. Tunis about a fictional version of the Brooklyn Dodgers. A staple of my literary exposure at the time were the sports pages Ira brought home nightly. He was a great lover of newspapers; buying the local paper was the first thing he did, he told me, when he arrived in a new town. I knew of Grantland Rice and Jimmy Cannon before Hemingway and Fitzgerald.

At St. Agnes the books were there to be opened and closed, read to the end, sampled or discarded, felt deeply or thought unintelligible. I started my investigations with the letter A but soon realized that to make progress I had to learn how to graze. To this day, I keep my bookcase arranged in random fashion, indulging in the conceit that my unconscious will help me choose the book I need to have at that moment. I'd like to think that in the months I hid out at the library before feeling secure enough to go out and about in the City I discovered the great books and fell in love with great literature but the truth lies elsewhere. I read and read all right—to the detriment of what homework I was supposed to be doing—but at first the books, with one exception, were what might be described as "Delinq. Lit." These were stories of urban street gangs, of their crimes, rivalries, and cruelties to women. The most famous of these was Irving Shulman's 1947 *The Amboy Dukes*, the tattered paperback version of which was also being passed from one sweaty teenager hand to another often with "the hot parts" underlined. The Dukes appear in so many memoirs and recollections of the time that its author deserves recognition of the sort usually extended only to high-toned literary figures.

Shulman set out all the elements of the American Dream's counterlife. Adults with little economic mobility have lost their children to a youth culture of deadly neighborhoods, brutal sex, ethnic hatred, thievery, and violence. The Dukes hoodlums were urban Jews, though in later editions they were what one reviewer called "Goyized." The setting was wartime Brooklyn. It was later matched in tone by Willard Motley's Chicago version, *Knock on any Door*, whose young hero Nick Romano is a Catholic altar boy whose criminal career is epitomized by a quote surely better known than the book (often wrongly attributed to James Dean) that expressed the mood of these adolescents perfectly: "Live fast, die young and leave a good looking corpse."

It's easy at this distance to put down these books for their trashy melodrama, exaggerated picture of the lower depths, their morality tale endings but when first encountered I gobbled them up, following both authors long enough to acquire more of their work, *Cry Tough* by Shulman and *We*

Fished All Night by Motley. I think the attraction went beyond the surface titillations to the presence for a coming-of-age young city person of a hostile or at best indifferent urban environment that was resisted and pushed back against, even if the push was often deviant, even criminal. The characters in these books were always opportunistic. They took their own forked path. This is what you will face, the buried message suggested, if you don't make it in the life of the squares. While the low life had its thrills, it was obviously a dead end. So most kids read these books to imagine what it was like living free of restraint and then after a while they'd go back to studying for their tests. The real delinquents probably never knew they existed.

Before I moved up from juveniles betraying their parents' middle class hopes with reefers, gang fights, promiscuity, and a lookout for remunerative crimes, I discovered another retreat from the fear of the unknown streets in Metropolitan Museum's Egyptian collection. Visitors to the Museum today will find it difficult to believe that during 1950s not only were weekday afternoons admission free but the place also was as empty as a mausoleum. I wandered the rooms, fascinated to see the caskets that had been excavated from tombs but looked almost new, the models of ancient boats and gardens, and the beauty of jewelry thousands of years old. Even without knowing anything of the details of the culture, I tried to feel proud at where I was spending my time but deep down I knew I was hiding out, not ready to face the City.

My months of self-imposed isolation, after school alternation between the Met and St. Agnes, ultimately drew me toward page turners with glittery themes among the affluent and notable. The first of these books was *Never Love a Stranger* by Harold Robbins. It contained elements that the author would rework in over twenty novels in which as his obituary put it, "women were beautiful, wealthy and wanton," and men either had clawed their way to power or were rich, randy, and unscrupulous and usually "possessed of all the restraint of college freshman." His plots were slick, sexy in a mechanical way, full of "heavy breathing," and the perfect supplier of vicarious experience to a boy who wanted to skip adolescence and immediately acquire the sex, money, and mastery that all adults seemed really to want despite their denials and the obvious banality of their daily lives. Why else would Robbins sell an estimated 750 million copies in 40 countries?

My discovery of Philip Wylie in the St. Agnes shelves marked a small step toward greater maturity. In Robbins most everything was explicit, orgasms were complete, power unrestrained. In Wylie's *Opus 21* the women offered themselves but the eponymous protagonist preferred talking while he waited over a tense weekend to find out if he had throat cancer. Wylie had a varied career. He had been a government official, a successful science fiction author, as well as a novelist of manners but he was famous most for *Generation of Vipers*, a vehicle for his vicious screed against

middle class American mothers, forever labeled the deni-
zens of "Momism":

"She smokes thirty cigarettes a day chews gum, and con-
sumes tons of bonbons and petit fours. . . . She plays bridge
with the stupid voracity of a hammerhead shark, which cannot see what it is trying to gobble but never stops snapping its
jaws and roiling the waves with its tail. . . . She drinks mod-
erately, which is to say, two or three cocktails before dinner
every night and a brandy and a couple of highballs after-
ward. . . . But it is her man who worries about where to acquire
the money while she worries only about how to spend it. . . ."

Wylie called mom "a human calamity" but claimed he
was truly surprised and then regretful when after this caricature he was called a women hater, "a high-scoring world
class misogynist," because he claimed he was actually a
great lover of the female sex. A reaction, if he really believed
it, that tells you all you need to know about what it meant to
grow up as an urban male in these years. If this wasn't confusing enough, there was the wildly different greatly respectful way my father treated my mother. He never spoke a harsh
word to her in my presence. If I ever got past the impact of
these introductions to how a man might understand his
dealing with women, it surely is due to his modeling and the
kindness, not to mention patient instruction, of the women
in my life.

Around this time passing afternoons in her Southside
Chicago backyard tree house my wife-to-be was reading

E. E. Cummings and Edna St. Vincent Millay and then when she moved to Massachusetts as a teenager memorizing the best lines from Edgar Lee Masters' *Spoon River Anthology*, Gerard Manley Hopkins, and John Donne. Was I bent by my very different reading list? You bet. How did I escape perversion—if I did? The answer is real, as opposed to virtual, women who (mostly gently) brought me up. But it took a while to get the message, a lot of better books, a marvelous liberal arts education, and an older woman, Rita, my first girlfriend at Oberlin College, to take the first steps toward being someone like my father, or what I thought was like my father because, of course, in time I came to realize that while I knew a great deal about his virtues I knew precious little about his vices except his two- to three-pack-a-day romance with Parliament cigarettes.

But before Rita and her successors, I was bedeviled by teenage identity issues. They may have been characteristic of the times but in my case multiplied by never being quite sure of my place in a group. It was a long time before I realized it has something to do with being an only child, one treated too early like a would-be adult. In adolescence, I spent much time with myself, even when I was physically with others. I wore a mask but believed I did it lightly. People will take me as I appeared, I hoped; they won't care enough to ask what's going on underneath. The challenge of the mask is remembering when you are wearing it and separating the masked man if you can from who you think you really are. Not something I could do just by closing my

eyes, cogitating over my fate like a Rodin figure. At least
this was impossible while hormones raged and virginity
was felt not as a stage of life but as a failure. While I moved
through these days, every other teenager I knew was going
through their own version—their own version of what is
essentially madness.

I wanted to be sociable, to overcome this sense of sepa-
ration, but it was hard work and it proved much harder
with the girls who came my way in adolescence. To escape
from the burden of introspection, I tried to make my time
with neighborhood friends as active as possible. I covered
doubts about myself and fears of the future by cramming
as much as I could into the day. I played too much poker,
losing my allowance more often than I want to remember.
I led my friends to the racetrack, where my father's tutelage
has made me comfortable. Whenever a group formed, I
urged us to play stickball in the park bordering the Museum
of Natural History at Seventy-Ninth Street and Columbus
Avenue on a short field, now obliterated by upscale land-
scaping and soon to disappear totally—like so much of the
City I grew up in—by a Museum addition. Or we would
bike into Central Park to play on what we called Eagle Hill,
part of a woody area of the park known as The Ramble, a
famous venue, of course, for cruising gays, a circumstance
of which we were oblivious.

Standing together on Broadway outside of Schrafft's restaurant at Eighty-Third Street where during the day my
mother may have had a ladies lunch we talked to girls from

the nearby apartment houses on West End Avenue and debated their looks and reputation after they left. Gene often shared wisdom about girls from his older brother, who was in college and according to Gene "a big stud" who is totally comfortable with females. We listened carefully but it was hard to believe we will get such an easy place with women. Most of the boys on the block are on the loose; though they know they have futures, their shape is still obscure. That women will be a big part of it is known but deflected, oblique, askew. I'm amazed when I learn that they all want to be older fast too.

The Village

A place unlike anywhere else. If it were a book then definitely escapist literature.

I hoped high school would save me from what seemed hopeless confusion but it didn't; I know quickly it can't because it's all boys. Still the location changes my life. Because of the crush of students, Stuyvesant schedules upper class students from early in the morning until midday. Eventually released every day into the Manhattan streets and close to an hour by subway from home but also a few minutes to Greenwich Village, I spend many afternoons in Washington Square Park watching the outdoor chess players and chatting up teenage girls, most of whom are cutting classes; a few are runaways, or claim they are. I sneak into New York University buildings to use the bathrooms after doing what little homework I can manage in the libraries. When I have the money, I nurse a soft drink, sit, and read at a back table at the Cafe Rienzi on MacDougal Street, sneaking looks at the work shirts, beards, leotards, and peasant skirts of the coffee drinkers. No one bothers me.

In the beginning I take advantage of being a kid to whom no one pays much attention. The Village in those days was, of course, no longer like a real country place but the contrast was striking between its low-rise buildings, Italian bakeries and restaurants, and raffish street life with the stolid apartment blocks, the straight lines, and the many congregating elderly of the Westside. As I grew older and bolder, the simmering local scene came to a rolling boil. I began to grab every opportunity to mix in with its places and people. This is a time in Village history when bands of roaming teens arrive on weekend nights from other parts of the City. They come to sample a place they know only as myth. Easy to join with them, no questions asked. Sometimes there will be a connection to a party or a spontaneous get together at the apartment of some nameless person where booze and music, sometimes pot, flow. These gatherings just seem to happen; after they were over it is hard to remember the names, the addresses, or even the faces. The takeaway is a vague feeling that I am an adult, an assurance that I can navigate and feel comfortable in this City that is, of course, the most important place in the world. What counts is what its people say, what appears on its stages and in newspapers. All else is marginal. Period.

To a certain knowing New Yorker all you have to do to evoke this time is to list the names, places, and anecdotes— Woody Allen (as a comic not a filmmaker), the Five Spot,

Frank O'Hara, *Le Figaro*, Miles Davis, the Village Vanguard and the Village Gate, Norman Mailer, The Bitter End, the Judson Church, John Lee Hooker, the Living Theatre, Nat Hentoff, and Charles Mingus. Dylan Thomas was there, famously drinking himself to death at the White Horse. Artists like Jackson Pollack and Willem de Kooning were brawling at the Cedar Street Tavern, which wasn't located on Cedar Street. The beatnik rebellion against 1950s blah was big news but Kerouac, Ginsberg, Corso, and the others at first seemed to spend more time in San Francisco or Morocco than in New York though you could hardly avoid hearing about them in the coffee houses or following their doings in the *Village Voice*, a paper everybody seemed to read. Folk music was enjoying its golden moment before the rock revolution overwhelmed it. Everyone knew of Pete Seeger and the Weavers. Joan Baez and Bob Dylan were emerging. A new coffee house seemed to open up every month. They featured folk singers many of whom got their start at the Monday open mike night at Gerde's Folk City. Beat writers would read and collect what they could by passing the hat. Women prisoners, many of them prostitutes, were held in the since destroyed, high-rise House of Detention off Sixth Avenue. Many a night pimps, mommas, and boyfriends would stand across the street at the head of an alley called Patchen Place, where E. E. Cummings lived; they'd hold loudly shouted conversations with women confined high above them about bail money, child care, and court cases. The off-Broadway theater scene left the shadows.

A few years later in 1959, Julian Beck and Judith Malina brought Jack Gelber's gripping play about the drug culture, *The Connection*, to their Living Theatre. It probably was the first encounter for many in the white middle class audience with heroin. Seeing it from the cheapest seat solidified my embrace of the theater.

I took a first date to a West Village coffee house. While we were getting to know each other, a young Negro poet began to read a bitter poem about race. In the 1950s the Village scene was still dominated by whites so hearing Le Roi Jones, later Amiri Baraka, was an event. Jones would soon dump his white wife and write a searing play where a white tease provokes and finally stabs a black man to death. That night he gave the young white audience a taste of the black nationalism that would become his trademark but this was pre–civil rights movement, at least as far as whites were concerned. His appearance in the cafe was notable simply because he was there. The racial movement from Harlem South that I'd first observed at Joan of Arc hadn't yet conquered the Village but along with Gay Liberation a little later, it would soon.

The Bohemian past of the Village had given birth to a dazzling cultural display of art, literature, comedy, theater, and music. The quality of the performers and their work was not, however, foremost in my mind. I just knew that I want to be part of the scene, to be able to retail the encounters and the stories, to be able to claim what was happening in the Village was my own, even though I was only an observer and didn't have the money needed to see or hear what was happening in most of the scene. Still in the Village I found it easy to connect with the people around me, especially girls, though I never made any close friends during these forays. Far better I thought then was the ability to join others for a night even if I might not see them again for weeks, or ever. As a result, I was confident that as soon as I emerged from the subway at West Fourth Street or Sheridan Square I'd connect with something good.

In the Village I was on my own; because so much was happening around me, I didn't think I needed friends but I have a different life in my Westside neighborhood where I started to hang out with a group of older boys. I listened to their talk about girls, assuming they knew things I didn't. We moved around the neighborhood in a pack without a purpose unless just not sitting at home was enough of one. Sometimes though we'd go to clubs on the lower Eastside like Eddie Condon's to hear Dixieland Jazz. I was underage but carding was rare and seemed unknown to the people who ran the Stuyvesant Casino on Second Avenue where we sat with a dozen others at round tables, served generous pitchers of frothy beer by beefy waitress wearing dirndls while horn players with names like "Wild Bill" and "Kid" and a group called "The Tailgaters" blasted away. It was a gathering of young people from all over the City but you stayed with your own group. The music was thunderous so there was little talk; instead we would drink more than we could hold; often one of us puked near the subway on the way home.

Alice had little to do with her relatives except sister Frances but she has a favorite from the side of the family she rarely saw and almost never mentions except to complain that despite having plenty of money they failed to help out her father when his business crashed. He ran the Banner Messenger Service, delivering packages, documents, and other items thought to be essential to business from one Manhattan address to another. At his Forty-Third Street office, a one-floor walk-up that is now a tall impersonal tower, overweight and gruff, shirttails out, Irving sat before a bank of phones orchestrating his "boys" as they traveled the City. Before I was sixteen Alice contacted him and as a result he offered me an off-the-books job. Suddenly, not only on my own in New York but traversing the City with a legitimate purpose, I was earning money that I can lose at the racetrack or poker table. And I am learning the Manhattan geography in a way that I will never forget. The imprint of buildings, the layout of streets and subways will stay with me long after, in true NYC fashion, the developers wrecking ball has done its work. Fifty or more years later, formally an exile, I can easily bore a companion by noting what was "over there" before what has now replaced it—or even replaced what had replaced it.

While I was testing my newfound Manhattan freedom, I kept an eye out for the parental reaction. I had no curfew. Brief answers to where I was the night before don't elicit much scrutiny. There is very little questioning. The message I take from them is that whatever I do is ok but, of course, they have no idea what it is I do. The history here is long. At eleven they had let me take the bus from Rockaway across the Marine Parkway Bridge to Brooklyn, and then the subway to Union Square in Manhattan to see my Uncle Mike's brother, a dentist who charges us family rates. Then a couple of years after we move, when I'm fourteen, I'm sent to Miami by myself over Christmas vacations on the Atlantic Coast Railroad to visit Delphine Harris, a Rockaway realtor who is Alice's surrogate mother. Retired to a North Miami Beach bungalow with her even more ancient husband, Delphine smothers me with hugs and cooks a mean spaghetti with meat sauce but deep in her eighties she has no idea what oversight I require. Let loose, I learn that if I'm careful, I can get served at Saxony Hotel bar at night after spending my days at Tropical Park betting on the horses.

Because I am now a veteran Manhattan traveler, I discover Fifty-Second Street, then the jazz center of the City if not the world. Near Seventh Avenue it's one long line of brownstones leased to jazz clubs. Each one has a bouncer but by careful study I can latch on to a group of college kids, slip into the bar, and make a beer last for an hour. The music is more challenging than Stuyvesant Casino Dixieland and I have trouble understanding where the melody has gone. This is the Bebop era; at first, I have no guide. I hear about a disc jockey named Symphony Sid who is all over the radio dial. While he is white, he seems to know what he's talking about. He loves Dizzy Gillespie but I struggle to figure out what the beboppers are trying to say.

My musical taste had been honed on the conventional Tin Pan Alley songs, by the musical scores my parents bring home from their Broadway musical escapades, popular offerings from shows like South Pacific and Carousel, or standards rendered by Sinatra and singers like Margaret Whiting whose version of Rodgers and Hammerstein's "It Might As Well Be Spring" from the 1945 movie *State Fair* radio disc jockey Martin Bloch plays again and again on his popular program *Make Believe Ballroom.*

At first, I feel I'm being exposed to music that requires a translator when I listen to Gillespie, Charlie Parker, or Lester Young on local late night radio. Their names are passed around by white kids to prove they are hip but I'm hearing Esperanto or Sanskrit. I need a translator. And then on a day when I've crossed and recrossed the City delivering package after package, it comes to me. This music is a city rhythm and the City is New York. I try to hear the blues in it but if it's there I can't find them. I think Gillespie is the tip of a spear, an avatar of a black culture I hardly know exists. In just a few years all this will also change.

My forays to Fifty-Second Street and to the Village taught me I could survive on my own, and not be swallowed up by the complexity and scope of a City that effectively—as if by whim—created and destroyed identities, the way it dealt with buildings, overnight. I was able to make my own choices, find people to talk to, and explore a physical life unimpeded on a broad canvas not just in the slender confines of an outer borough. Or so I tried to convince myself. Only rarely did I allow the thought that I was lonely; that I had no idea where I was going, how I would live my life, and who I would live it with. There is, in fact, a troubling adolescent lesson built into this Manhattan childhood. The names, the glamour, the competition to be recognized all fuel an ambition but not a path to get there. And how could I find one because as of yet I have no goal, no mission other than to escape from the feeling of failure that comes from knowing you want something even if what you want is indistinct—over the horizon—and fear you won't get it or even deserve it.

After the intensity of these years, my connection to the downtown scene is marginal, if persistent enough, to remind me how much the place once mattered to me. Years later there was Angela Davis held for extradition at the Eighth Street Women's House of Detention after her arrest as an accessory to California murders but later acquitted in no small part because of my colleague and close friend Margaret Burnham. One night Allen Ginsberg took time off from a coffee house reading to spend a couple of hours in the bourgeois surroundings of my Riverside Drive apartment trying to persuade me to bring a legal challenge to the constitutionality of federal laws criminalizing drug possession; I took his proposal to my boss who quickly decided that such a case had zero chance of succeeding. When NYU Law School hired me to evaluate one of its legal programs, I was given a room in a Morton Street building that to my amazement looked across to a large apartment building located on the exact site—in 1910—of my grandfather Charles Meltsner's dry goods store. My closest friend Harry Subin taught at the NYU Law School for over thirty years. We usually had our pasta at his favorite Italian restaurant on Sullivan Street where they greeted him as *professore*, which didn't stop him from wondering if the mafia owned a piece of the action. It was at another Village eatery that Bruce Simon, a prominent union labor lawyer, told me his clients had warned him never to sit with his back to the door in mob territory.

In 1967, I was a small investor in the theatrical success d'scandal, Barbara Garson's *MacBird!*, playing at Art D'Lugoff's Village Gate on Bleeker Street, the only theater that would house it. Audiences howled at the parody that had an LBJ-Macbeth character, brilliantly rendered by a young Stacy Keach, knocking off a JFK-Duncan figure and then getting his due from Macduff, called in the play Robert O'Dunc, for brother Robert Kennedy. The play ran almost a year in the Village and then in Los Angeles. Everything about it—bloodying Johnson for his Vietnam escalation, making fodder out of the Kennedy Assassination, the zest of the countercultural audience—was a reminder that the Eisenhower years, the time when I first wandered into the Village as an innocent kid looking for experience, adventure, and sex, were long gone. Dead in fact.

After a *MacBird!* performance, I walked down McDougal Street. At the corner of Bleeker was the San Remo Café

where I'd first noted the vitality of the area's gay culture—
though gay wasn't the word used then. The Italian-owned
bar looked on its last legs and would close soon but a decade
earlier it attracted hip writers and painters like Jackson
Pollak, Jack Kerouac, and Gore Vidal not that I ever recognized them there. On one warm, airless Manhattan night,
I remember the crowd of men, so many wearing what
seemed a uniform of brightly colored button down shirts
and crisp chino slacks. I was struck by how trim were the
bodies. Facial hair was not yet in fashion. It was, I thought,
like a visit to a foreign country. I'd stood at the crowded bar
nursing a beer, allowing the chatter of the men to surround
me. Stonewall was two years away; AIDS on the dark side
of the moon.

Zabar's

When I first moved to the Westside at age twelve, Zabar's was a small grocery store, smaller than the Asian markets that are found all over Manhattan today, and not upscale at all. I remember buying sour pickles from one of the barrels lining the center aisle that contained various "raw" products. The place appeared to be a typical small family business; if it had a good reputation, it was only in the immediate neighborhood. Time passed. Zabar's expanded and expanded again and again. It birthed pretentious satellites and became a reference point in fiction and folklore. Bagels and coffee are now delivered worldwide. Shopping there on visits to the City is for me an exercise in nostalgia.

Some years back Heli Meltsner bought a food processer—at a time when they were not well known—made by the Japanese company Sanyo. Zabar's was by then a thriving institution that employed hundreds, especially favoring Dominicans. It took up much of a block on Broadway with an entrance and exit beloved of panhandlers. Especially on weekends it was as crowded as a rush-hour subway car. One day the tiny plastic gizmo that connects the bowl of the food processer with the source of power snapped. It was the typical modern problem—a broken, unrepairable piece of plastic that could be produced for maybe two cents rendering a sophisticated piece of equipment totally useless. Unwilling to toss the machine in the garbage, I wandered into the store to see if there was anything that could be done but in truth I couldn't imagine a fix. Adhesives just don't do it with plastic.

Standing by the door was the Mr. Zabar of my childhood, dressed in a white smock, carefully watching over his domain—the masses buying their sliced lox and Nova, white fish, gourmet cheese, and bagels. Despite now ruling a food empire, he looked much the way he had when I first bought sour pickles from him.

I approached and explained my problem. Zabar heard me out and said not a word but led me to a scuffed worktable in a corner near the exit. He opened a drawer filled with scattered pens, paperclips, assorted scraps of paper, rubber bands, and from a corner near the back, invisible to the naked eye, he extracted the sliver of plastic—a perfect replacement for the broken piece. He handed it to me, still wordless, and then seemingly dismissing me from his mind's eye turned again to watch customers passing through the checkout aisles. Plainly I was no longer in his consciousness but a few hours later the Sanyo was back in business.

The Way Forward

Growing up in the City finally filled me with what I thought was manly, clever experience. I now felt at home and for a while that was enough. Eventually though, mostly in those empty times when there was nothing to distract or divert me, I had to face that experience without purpose is deadly. Manhattan was good for distraction and diversion but there was just too much noise to let me figure out a future. I decided to leave it and Oberlin, Ohio, an almost total unknown, was certainly getting away from it. With very little idea of what direction my life would or should take when I entered the college in 1954; to the extent there were thoughts of the future I just blindly assumed I'd have to end up doing something like my father. This left me sad but also elated when anything new came my way, as when Barbara Seaman, who would become a controversial feminist activist and author, took me under her wing and encouraged my writing.

Ira had been replaced as a manager and offered his old sales job but he decided to leave B&B and start his own company—a decision he wouldn't have made if he'd known the true state of his health. He planned selling pretty much the same sort of items that B&B offered, mostly to a back-list of former customers. The summer after high school and before I was to leave for Ohio, I suggested he let me try to do some selling on my own. I asked for the work not out of any expected pleasure from doing it but because of the same only child identification with a parent that had led me to find a way to reject his offer of a costly private high school education. It was clear that by leaving his job and starting a company our small family needed money. I felt I should do my part but while I was aware of my motive somehow kept it out of my mind most of the time.

Despite some hesitation, he gave me a sample case, an order book, a list of contacts, and the keys to his car. "Give it a try," was all he said.

After some initial difficulties with New Jersey's multiple highways and confusing townscape geography, I found my way to many small manufacturing plants, car dealerships, and insurance broker offices that crop up all over the Central and Northern part of the state, politely introduced myself to receptionists and secretaries, and waited until I was told that the man on Ira's list I'd come to see was too busy or wasn't interested or would be happy to talk to me if I made an appointment for the following week. There were a few exceptions, usually men who had bought from Ira before, but even they weren't particularly friendly, acting more as if they were disappointed that they were greeting a seventeen-year-old kid instead of seeing him.

I could tell from the cold initial greetings that no order would be forthcoming but most of the time went through a sales pitch I'd gleaned from listening to my father over the years. He had always taught that the first reaction was usually negative, even hostile. Sometimes the customers listened, allowing me to run out of steam before declining to buy. I remember one fatherly, pot-bellied, chain-smoking owner of an insurance agency who asked lots of questions and admired some samples. Here I was sure was my first sale but he was interrupted by a phone call and waved me off. Sometimes customers halted my patter early on to dismiss me, saying they weren't interested or that the items in question weren't right for their business. It was a crushing experience.

I lasted three days, grateful that Ira never commented on my failure. He took back the car keys and gave me a quick hug. There was no effort to pass on feedback that would help me learn to be a better salesman. In fact, it was pretty clear he didn't want me to be a better salesman or any kind of salesman. He'd calculated the message would be delivered by the rejections he plainly expected: the typical American belief that the son had to exceed the father. I was allowed to lick my wounds and forget. He was, I think, able to confirm his sense that I was to go in a very different direction in life than his, not that he ever conveyed what that course might entail.

A clue about that direction did come from college football. He was a fan not a player but loved the game; early on
he took me to see Columbia play Cornell at the University's
athletic complex called Baker Field on the tip of Northern
Manhattan. It was clear we were there to root for The Big
Red of Cornell, not the Lions of Columbia. The whys of this
were never explained. Ira did favor a black Cornell running
back, in an era where there were few African Americans
on Ivy League teams, named Hillary Chollet, and would
follow his all-American college career closely. Chollet was
a mixed-race creole from New Orleans who had been initially recruited by Louisiana State University but dropped
when the school was informed of his race. He ended up at
Cornell where he was an outstanding basketball as well as
football player. Ira had plainly adopted him as the favorite
of his fandom. Once we even traveled to Philadelphia to
see Chollet play in the annual game between Cornell and
traditional rival Penn. Perhaps taking me to football games
was his way of bringing me closer to the kind of American
success story he saw in my future. The game allowed us to
spend hard-to-come-by father–son time together but it
also linked to an elite Ivy League culture. Not apparently
the sort of experience he'd had at New York University.

When finally I applied to colleges, Cornell was initially
my first choice. I knew little about it except that friends of
friends said it was great academically but very large and
that upstate New York had a lousy climate. Someone passed
on that it had a very high suicide rate, information that I

found bizarre, with students regularly jumping down a nearby gorge to their deaths. In 1954, I was accepted with a scholarship but I decided not to attend when Jerry, my closest summer camp friend, sold me on Oberlin College. It was smaller, and, though rural Ohio seemed exotic, it also appeared less scary than Cornell. But the crucial fact in my choice was that it promised an experience farther away from the City and from New Yorkers. I needed distance from where I was raised if I was going to figure out who I was.

One day in September my parents took me to Grand Central Station where I boarded an overnight train to Chicago that stopped in the then auto manufacturing city of Lorain, Ohio. There I found a cab that took me to Oberlin, a town much smaller than I could believe with a tiny downtown, a single traffic light, a collection of nineteenth-century college buildings, and a dormitory room in a structure of seeming cardboard walls hastily thrown up during World War II to serve as the residence for ninety-day wonders, a fast track naval officer training program. Federal Hall, as it was called, was still there a decade later.

In the three years I spent at Oberlin before I graduated, I prospered, though it was awhile before I got over using a defense of big city, New York worldliness and superiority whenever I felt insecure about my intelligence or social skills. I met friends who would remain close for life but also an openness and kindness from the majority of Midwestern student body that was totally unfamiliar as well as an institutional prudery about the physical life of young men and women that I found destructive. One couple married without the permission of the college; the woman but not the man was expelled. Though one of the first, if not *the* first, coeducational college, school officials balanced political liberalism with restrictive social policies as if serpents from the Garden of Eden were lurking in the Ohio brush. But the teachers were marvelous, by and large dedicated more to their work with students than achieving notoriety in the wider professional world. I learned how bad my writing was and how I could try to correct it. Free of the distractions of Manhattan, I was forced to dive deeply into my courses.

Most importantly, I encountered a teacher who modeled what suddenly I knew I wanted to be. Robert Tufts had been a speech writer for Adlai Stevenson's 1952 campaign for the presidency but the story that brought me to his class in government and later any others I could find was that he had been forced out of the State Department policy planning group along with a number of others for liberal positions that at the time included a campaign by some Republicans to claim that State Department diplomats were soft on communism, responsible for what was called Losing China in 1949 to Mao Zedong. Tufts could have been bitter but far from spreading cynicism he drove home a clear message that good could be done, change was possible, and it might be accomplished by enlightened government policy. He was a liberal democrat to the core and had a trait that to the extent I took it in would save me untold grief—he could be bold, even passionate, but no matter the storm he radiated calm.

At the same time there were other powerful government and history teachers at Oberlin. Tom LeDuc was a follower of maverick scholar William Appleman Williams of Wisconsin who taught that American foreign policy despite its veneer could be out and out imperialist. He thought our economic expansionist aims played a role in creating the cold war and documented how we could be as violent as other nations in defending our perceived interests. Robert Fletcher was an eccentric, white-haired miniature of a man whose major work was a history of the college but he taught an implicit lesson that I digested but didn't fully understand until the penny dropped later when I finally figured out that my primary intellectual orientation involved connecting the unconnected. Fletcher did it, as I once wrote, most powerfully by the way he gave final exams. Despite our pleas, he would tell us nothing in advance but walk into the classroom at the assigned time and write a word or phrase on the blackboard, and then disappear. When confronted with "Fences" or "Wilkie" or "Bankers," we had been warned by previous students that Fletcher wanted us to take what he had given us and relate it to the dynamics of periodic social change. So, for example, "Fences" became an opportunity to write about the settlement of the West, the tension between Indian tribes, the agrarian farmers who need to protect their crops, and the cattle ranchers committed to an open range. My favorite Fletcher story was about the female student who had gotten an A by describing that as part of the 1940 election campaign when she was three her father had taken her to a parade at which Wendell Wilkie, the Republican candidate, marched, and held her on his shoulders so she could see him pass by.

The historian who made the most lasting impression was a tall and thin, hawk-like Englishman named Barry McGill. How he had landed in Northern Ohio was unclear but the feeling among his students was that he brought an exotic rigor to his classes in world history. Arrogant, demanding, and often supercilious, he held our rapt attention, providing support for the notion that teaching excellence had nothing to do with sweetness, light, and good guys. His history course moved so fast that a class wit remarked, "If you blink you might miss half a century," but somewhere after the Reformation and before the Enlightenment amid the ghastly seventeenth-century turmoil of Europe, McGill slowed the march of (mostly Western) history to ask if we believed it was possible for the present world to have a religious war.

The first student to respond drew the obvious parallel between religious conflict and the competing Cold War ideologies of the United States and Soviet Union. McGill waved off the comment with a "Yes, yes, of course," and peered down at us from his great height looking for more. By religion, he meant religion, not political ideology; he was asking about warfare over the ways of different Gods. As a freshman I usually laid low in this class but in the silence that followed I found myself wading in, speaking with a certainty based on no prior knowledge, study, or reflection: "No one believes in religion that intensely anymore," I expounded, though generously admitting it was a big talking point for some. "Maybe war for oil or to keep hearts and minds from communism but war for religion. Not likely. We're past that."

McGill didn't argue with me, but he gave me a studied look that said, "I know something you don't." Weeks later out of the blue he invited me to his office, handed me a book, and dismissing me brusquely declaimed, "This will help you understand that events have many causes." I can't remember the book but whatever it was a professor calling me out this way was magical. The encounter came back to me when the events leading up to and after 9/11 proved how wrong I had been about religious wars. But long before then it had helped seal my skepticism about certainties, my own as well as others. I found particular sensitivity to use of the word "must," a favorite of editorial staffs, columnists, and opinion piece bloggers. It's well to reserve a portion of doubt for even the most heartfelt of our beliefs, a principle that on occasion causes me grief in my own classes because I will take a stance against the grain of what most of the students believe, even if it's not something I adhere to myself. I tell myself this is a valuable tactic to challenge students' given assumptions, and so it is, but it probably also reflects a certain oppositional tendency that has never left me. Nevertheless, when even before 9/11 it became clear that in parts of the world religious divisions were sparking surreptitious bombings and violent confrontations, I was pleased to note how my history professor's forty-plus-year-old question, not my abrupt answer, had proved a lasting learning experience.

The Odd Beginnings
of a Career

How I got to the Yale Law School wasn't calculated to nurture belief in the higher purposes of the law. Erwin Griswold was then a towering figure in the legal world. The former dean of the Harvard Law School and a future solicitor general of the United States, he was known as a demanding leader, a man with strong opinions and such total self-confidence in whatever direction he decided to take that he could terrify faculty colleagues. As solicitor general he argued more than a hundred cases before the Supreme Court, including a losing effort on the part of the Nixon Administration to keep the Pentagon Papers from publication. When at Harvard, he published an influential book defending the use of the Fifth Amendment at a time when Senator Joseph McCarthy was attacking use of the constitutional safeguard but he also infamously asked female students, "Why are you at Harvard Law School, taking the place of a man?"

My interest in Griswold derived from the fact he was a loyal alumnus of Oberlin, having graduated from the college in 1925. A full tuition scholarship—then worth $1,000 a year—had been set up in his name for one Oberlin student a year to attend Harvard Law School. One of my best friends, Stan Fisher, and I had applied. We both needed the money but it was no surprise when the committee selected Stan for the award and named me only runner up. He had a sharp mind and a much better academic record, not to mention a wonderfully droll sense of humor. Our mutual friend Harry Subin hadn't applied for the scholarship—on his college application he had listed his father's occupation as "financier" or "investor." The three of us planned to room together at Harvard if I was able to come up with the tuition but Harry and I really wanted to go to the Yale Law School, which had the reputation at the time of turning out more lawyers who held interesting public service jobs than Harvard. We conspired to persuade Stan to call Yale, tell them about his Harvard award, and modestly suggest Yale might match it. He agreed.

Not only did Jack Tate, the Yale associate dean, offer Stan the same money as Harvard immediately after hearing that he had won the Griswold, but also when the award then passed to me I took a deep breath, called Dean Tate, and amazingly succeeded with the same pitch. Harry, Stan, and I would all graduate from Yale, later practice and teach criminal law, and stay close as a group until Harry's untimely death in 2011.

Many years later after serving as a Columbia faculty member and a visiting professor at Harvard, I understood why Jack Tate had acted quickly and decisively. At one Columbia faculty meeting in the early 1970s, the intense debate was over which of the four highly qualified young candidates for appointment the school should go after vigorously. They were all exceptional, former clerks for Supreme Court Justices, with brilliant careers likely ahead of them. They'd interviewed at Harvard and Yale as well; we were told that Columbia had to act quickly before they accepted offers elsewhere. I was junior faculty, seated next to a senior colleague, a large man with a walrus mustache who said not a word as different speakers droned on listing the virtues of their favorites and slyly suggesting the limitations of the other candidates. My colleague seemed uninterested, his eyes focused on the text before him; he paged back and forth between two thick, bound collections of law review articles.

A divided faculty finally voted on whom the dean should make the first offer. But then procedural objections were raised; so even though the meeting time had expired, another vote was taken. Then more talk. Well into the second hour of the meeting the selection was finally settled; the dean and faculty rose, chairs scraped, we all took our first steps toward the door of room when a sudden crash echoed through the room like a bomb exploding. My next-seat colleague has taken both heavy volumes and thrown them down hard on the table. Startled, everyone turned toward him.

"Beat Harvard," he shouted.

While rarely acknowledged, the rivalry between Ivy League schools for promising students, prestigious faculty hires, and national recognition has never abated. Jack Tate immediately recognized an opportunity to "Beat Harvard," but not so far as I know did anyone in Cambridge take notice.

As a student at the Yale Law School, I came quickly to understand the first year of law school is where you learned to analyze formal expressions of legal doctrine— the famous goal of "thinking like a lawyer"—but if you grasp the process, or think you do, I decided the remaining two years were just cumulative, with very little additional payoff. Once I (foolishly) felt that I had acquired this skill, school seemed a lot less interesting. Most of my fellow students were aiming for jobs with large law firms where they will be doing work on commercial projects of interest to corporate clients. With memories of my father's tangles with B&B, and my admiration for the kind of work Robert Tufts did, I had little interest in such a career, even though I would eventually learn that financial savvy is just, if not more, as important in fighting the battles I wanted to fight as knowing how to litigate human rights issues. Here again I operated on misperceptions and false assumptions just like my belief that I understood all I needed to know about legal analysis.

And there was another factor at play. At Oberlin, I'd been exposed to the riches of a far-ranging intellectual life in a monastic, if secular, environment. While I loathed being marooned in a Northern Ohio small town so much that I graduated in three years, I eagerly embraced the college's message that study of ideas for their own sake was a worthy endeavor. The power of this value in the college helped explain why so many of its alumni attended graduate school and eventually took teaching positions. Law school was quite different in this respect. Here intellectual firepower was usually directed toward pragmatic ends; you used ideas and smarts to advance a client's goals, which I learned are mostly the goals of corporations when you work for the kind of firms most Yale Law graduates would join. Usually overlooked in the way law was taught—even at a progressive place like Yale—was how a client's true interests often transcended a narrow victory but rather implicated a just legal system.

Whether it was these forces or simply the sum of too many years of schooling, my attention soon waned. I almost dropped out for a time like Stan who studied and worked in Europe until he returned to a career track a year or so later but instead of leaving I just spent more and more time away from New Haven in Manhattan reading nineteenth-century English novels and visiting old haunts. I dated a lovely woman who I knew from college. She had emigrated to the United States from Lithuania after the war, hiding for part of it in a convent. Her father had been an official in the Lithuanian government that Stalin quickly dismembered; after arresting him he was sent to Siberia and never heard of again.

She was then going to the Columbia School of Journalism. The summer before we'd hitchhiked across France and Spain—I stood out of sight only emerging to view after truck drivers pulled over when they saw her arm go up. We spent some time in the Basque country, and then took in the Prado, a bullfight, and Cicottes, a famous bar with Hemingway associations; after Madrid we were floored by the Gaudi architecture in Barcelona, ending up in Marseilles where we planned to part. But first she insisted I go to a hospital emergency room to deal with a case of impetigo I'd contracted from a rusty razor blade. With her excellent French she persuaded the doctors to take care of me right away. Within minutes I was surrounded by a team of white-coated medical people chattering away in a language I did not at the time know. But I felt instantly that I was being treated with love.

I wondered did I have the most important and challenging infection they had ever seen? I was given antibiotics. Nurses carefully scrubbed away the red sores and crusts covering my face. Later in the day, I was released but told sternly to regularly cleanse the sores. The nurses handed over a wine bottle full of an evil-looking purple liquid I was to use along with a bag of cotton swabs. We had very little money but when I tried to pay the doctors told us there was no charge. They merely said something that translated as "This is France. Thank you America."

She and I decided the way we were treated had a lot to do with being Americans at a time when memories of wartime alliances were still fresh. To meet her in Paris to start the trip I had hitched by myself from London to the Channel ferry at Dover. Looking a bit like a vagrant who needed decent clothes and a haircut, I was nevertheless picked up by drivers minutes after throwing out a hand that held a sign reading "American student"—one Englishman insisted I come home with him to meet his mother, who then prepared a classic English tea.

Carrying my swabs and disinfectant, we parted at the Marseilles train station. I had no idea whether we had a future but I knew enough to know that I wasn't ready to lose her. So a year later I chose only courses that could be collapsed into a few days of the week, drove fast to the City on the Merritt Parkway, forgetting about school by the time I reached Westchester County.

One other law student had a schedule like mine. Cynthia was a year ahead of me, married to an editor at *Esquire* magazine. I drove her to the City every Wednesday or Thursday evening. One day she invited me upstairs to her brownstone apartment for a drink. Her husband wasn't home but there was a typewriter and a manuscript sitting on a living room table next to it. When I asked, Cynthia told me a little about his work. There was a chair in front of the typewriter and I imagined myself seated, pouring out articles that would be published with my name appearing as author. I asked myself, isn't this the life I really want? Reflecting on this anti–law school experience, I wondered what I'd be letting myself in for when I graduated. I realized I wasn't sure where I'd fit in as a lawyer but it was suddenly clear that I had to write, though I had no clue about what. That I had almost no money and had never published anything but political columns in the Oberlin newspaper didn't seem to matter.

Then something happened that brought me closer to that typewriter. A law student a year ahead of me, Victor Navasky, had started a political satire magazine at the law school in 1957. Announcing his stand against the dullness and banality of 1950s, Navasky calls his "leisurely" (published whenever) quarterly *Monocle*. Why? Because "In the land of the blind the one-eyed is king." It was a classic little magazine—though Victor hoped it would become the American version of British *Punch* and the French *Le Canard Enchaîné*—with a first press run of 500. The times seemed ripe for the brand of witty, clever-writing Victor teased out from a talented group of writers. Many of them will make their mark in the years ahead—Calvin Trillin, Dan Wakefield, Michael Harrington, Kurt Vonnegut Jr., and David Broder to name just a few. He had a knack for wooing well-known others who would offer to contribute— celebrated law professor Charles L. Black who wrote under a pseudonym, playwright George Axelrod, conservative icon William Buckley Jr., and *L'il Abner* cartoonist Al Capp.

On graduating, Victor ignored the practice of law, took a job writing speeches for "Soapy" Williams, then the Governor of Michigan, a possible presidential candidate, and made me *Monocle*'s Associate Publisher (and later a director) basically running the business side of the magazine for my last year in New Haven. *Monocle* will never succeed as he hoped to become a regular monthly with a national following but it makes an immediate mark in the magazine world with articles reprinted or excerpted in *Harper's*, the *New Republic*, the *New York Herald Tribune*, and *The Best of Science Fiction*, among a long list of others. I even get to make a cameo appearance telling the *Monocle* story on NBC television's "In Person." I was hooked. In the years that follow Victor will write powerful books, one about Robert F. Kennedy's Justice Department, another on the witch hunts of the 1950s, while becoming the longtime editor and then publisher of the venerable left journal, *The Nation*.

In late 1962, when he calls on me again, I am litigating the most important cases of my life at the height of the pre–Civil Rights Act years and waiting for the birth of our first child. But New York is in the middle of a destructive newspaper strike that lasts almost four months, seriously damaging the City's press. Victor reacts immediately, calling on the talented group of young writers he has nurtured at *Monocle* as well as newcomers he's joined to an informal network to produce in a week or so hilarious parodies of two of the papers (and their prominent columnists) closed by the strikers, the *New York Post* and *New York Daily News*. Victor had the goods to make a splash but he needed financial support to get the *New York Pest* and the *New York Dally News* printed and out to the City's hundreds of newsstands. My job is to mediate the deal with the main financial backer; it turns into a cliffhanger. Victor is at the printer's somewhere in the suburbs. The backer sits across a desk from me in Manhattan. Phone calls back and forth turn nasty as the backer asserts what Victor thinks are new conditions. But at the very last moment before the press run has to be canceled, they find a way to agree, though both are unhappy.

At graduation, I decide I want to work for the American Civil Liberties Union but a stronger wish is avoid the law school to practice assembly line entirely, see more of the world, and try to earn some money by freelance writing. I take the New York State bar exam but before the results are in board an Italian Liner bound for Venice with stops at Gibraltar, Genoa, Naples, and Patras in Greece as it makes its way up the Adriatic. The ticket is for the lowest class and it is cheap. Though I'm still not a published writer, with Victor's example in front of me, I plan to finance my way around the world by selling articles about whatever crosses my path. I have almost no knowledge about how this is done. Fortunately, my friend Elsa runs an agency that represents journalists and places their articles; generously she makes out a press card in my name.

I'm on the lookout for stories as I spend a week in Venice, and then time in Zagreb and Athens. But it's getting colder by the day and I haven't written a thing. No wonder, as a would-be journalist, I'm half-baked: I haven't given much thought to what makes a good and readable story. When I've stayed as long as I can at the Athens Youth Hostel, I write Stan Fisher who is still on a leave of absence from the law school. He is doing farm work on a kibbutz in Northern Israel while he studies Hebrew. He tells me the kibbutz people say I can join him if I'll work for my room and board.

My best friend from the youth hostel is a leather-jacketed, tattooed biker who has driven across Europe for months, stopping where he wants, for as long as he wants. I persuade him to take me to Piraeus on the back of his motorcycle. We arrive in time for dinner but my boat doesn't leave until 7 a.m. After Souvlaki and Hummus, he decides to find a brothel; when I tell him I'm not going to join him, he gets permission from the madam for me to wait for him on her covered porch, and disappears. I fall asleep and almost miss my boat but he hasn't reappeared. I never see him again.

What it Was Like before *Roe v. Wade*

I can recall the second-floor back bedroom in the New Haven house where I lived for the 1958–59 academic year. Despite the gap of years, the Bishop Street address seems embossed on my brain. I can remember even the chipped enamel on the stovetop where I cooked absurdly heavy on the carb meals for my three housemates. But my memory of what finally happened has always been shaded by doubt. It could be because the two of us were always improbable lovers. Or it could be because of the abortion.

I don't forget her strength and her body. She was magnificently thin but hard skinned, full of sinew, and almost as tall as I was. I'd never talked to, much less been intimate with, a woman who looked like this before. Her hair was naturally dull blonde. The rest of her as close to pure white as you can get without being albino. Standing together before a mirror, the contrast made me look darker and more compact than I was. I've lived a life filled with women who made their own way while holding men to their promises. I think she was the first but if not she certainly set the standard. As I would find out, she knew who she was and what she wanted.

We started talking idly at some university eating place. A science graduate student, she came across as reserved but determined. Physics was the family business. I told her I just knew the Nobel would come someday and she smiled as if to say, "That's a good line."

She asked a lot about how lawyers thought. What was their "epistemology?" I told her that so far as I could tell lawyers just worked. Whatever their worldview, their thoughts usually served the work. There was no epistemology I could name, though maybe those of my professors who had never actually practiced had one.

She must have thought that answer was more smart than superficially clever because we ended up in my bedroom. We kept at it for months, usually late at night after our studies. It was a time when graduate students took classes seriously. I was always prepared to be questioned in class, even if I didn't fully understand the case that was up for discussion. I would have been embarrassed otherwise. She was intense about science but I knew enough never to ask her to explain what would have been beyond me. Our sex was new to me. It was like a good workout. We were compatible because without ever talking about it we knew that along with some intelligent conversation about this or that the sex circled us. We probably had no future. Wanted none;

just whatever it was we were doing then. There were no judgments. We were helping each other. "Friends with benefits"
wouldn't be named for decades but I suspect that's what
it was.

But here's where my doubts surface: What birth control
were we using? Was one of us overeager or did a diaphragm
or condom malfunction? I know we fell over each other with
"You're not to blame" assurances but what were the facts?
Could there have been a suppressed desire to do something
that would make us more than happy partners? Or a way
to get out from under the coming of adulthood, responsibilities prefigured by endless grad school reading assignments, or was it just a way to put aside the need always to
be thinking.

At first, we were together in what to do—isolated and
stuck but nevertheless teammates. This was the age of
abortion repression and we came together against it. Once
involved, you learned the demand for the procedure far
outstripped the supply of providers. The affluent and well
connected had private hospitals; everybody else had to
scramble. Lurid tales of coat hanger and back-alley deaths
were in the air. Abortion hadn't been much of a concern
for the criminal law until the middle of the nineteenth
century when, according to the essayist Roger Rosenblatt,
the organized medical profession used antiabortion politics to reverse loss of patients to "midwives, homeopaths,
folk healers, or poorly educated doctors." The infamous
antiobscenity federal Comstock laws included provisions

criminalizing birth control. By 1900, abortion was illegal everywhere in the United States even though it had been acceptable before quickening at common law. There was a sordid history of cops coercing women who had fetuses aborted with threats of exposure if they failed to reveal the identity of their abortionist as well as of women dying from botched clandestine procedures inflicted by the incompetent, or themselves.

For most of this history, the organized medical profession abetted the prosecution and sided against the women. As one might expect, mortality was greater among black women than among white. In the 1930s hospitals decided to create committees that would have to approve before a medically necessary abortion could take place. Doctors failing to use the committee process were in trouble but so were those who did use it as they were often refused approval even when they were sure their patients had powerful medical reasons to terminate a pregnancy. After World War II, however, an increasing number of doctors rebelled against these efforts to thwart their medical judgment, especially when the life or health of a woman was at risk, though the real shift in medical opinion would not take place until a few years later when birth defects were linked to the drug thalidomide and to rubella, German measles in pregnant women.

We were unaware of most of this but it wouldn't have mattered if we'd known. All we did know was that what had to be done had to be done secretly and quietly. Statistics suggested that one of four American women would have an abortion by the age of forty-five and that there were perhaps up to a million illegal abortions a year, but very few women talked about having one publicly and information about our predicament was scanty. Still as the novelist Marge Piercy would put it, "whether abortion is legal or illegal, large numbers of women will resort to it."

We never questioned the necessity. Both of us said we wanted children someday but knew we might be ready for careers but not to be parents and despite a great deal of satisfaction with each other marriage was never discussed, even to reject. I don't think adoption ever crossed our minds. Neither of us wanted family involved. I didn't want anyone involved, though I knew that was impossible.

We weren't students of the reproductive rights world but weren't totally ignorant either. There was no question of "funny" remedies like jumping jacks or herbals or pills that were supposed to clean her out. We had a kind of baseline of common sense that could only have come from some foundation of being good kids who despite having fumbled here were averse to ruination risks. So we decided the best course was to talk to as many peers as we could who might have had a similar problem or know someone who did. To avoid revealing too much, we could say we had a friend in trouble, though it was doubtful anyone would believe us. The response to this was universal: there were doctors out there who defied the law, some out of principle, others because the money was really good. The challenge was finding someone who was careful and safe.

We both had heard of the Pennsylvanian—I made him into a Quaker but in fact he was an atheist, a Republican, and a Rotarian—who in a small, coal-country town near Pottsville had safely taken care of thousands of women in need, charging them almost nothing. He was described as a saintly, principled figure. He would be our savior. Through one of her college friends we were able to get what we thought was Dr. Spencer's phone number but despite repeated attempts to call no one ever picked up. Then we heard news dashing our hopes—he had closed down for a while because of a prosecution. Later I learned a woman had died of a heart attack on his operating table while under anesthesia; he'd been indicted for manslaughter as well as illegal abortion. Though it was clear that he'd done the abortion, the death had nothing to do with it. Spencer was so respected in his town that in 1959 the jury of a neighboring county acquitted him after only a few hours of deliberations.

I knew from a close friend's experience that there were places in Cuba, still under the rule of the dictator Batista, where abortions could be had but neither of us felt confident enough about the Caribbean to pursue the idea. Traveling to the islands also meant money we did not have. Neither of us had much in the bank after paying for room, board, and tuition but I was sure we'd have enough if we could find someone nearby, if just barely.

While we despaired and dithered over where next to seek advice, what we needed was right in front of us but we never saw it. A group of women's advocates, parenthood planners, medical doctors, and Yale Law professors had been trying for well over a decade to have Connecticut's 1879 ban on the sale of contraceptives set aside. The first major case involved doctors who had married patients who it was alleged would suffer significant harm if pregnant. Later married women themselves were brought in as plaintiffs to remedy defects that had led the Supreme Court to reject the first appeal. A second case foundered over the lack of enforcement of the statute. While abortion was never mentioned, the deeper issue of whether women could control their own bodies was obviously in the background. These folks would have known where we could get a safe abortion.

The activists had been as unsuccessful in the Connecticut legislature as in the federal courts but because the legal cases had been turned away for technical reasons, they were gathering support for another try. One of my only seven female classmates, married to another law student, had been recruited as a plaintiff in one of the cases that was then moving through the lower courts but she and her husband had used pseudonyms. I knew nothing of her involvement.

Leading the charge, however, was my torts professor, Fowler Harper, a strong civil libertarian, author of a leading treatise in his field of tort law but a rather disorganized teacher who filled the empty narrative space in his classes with colorful stories. He was often lampooned by classmates for reaching down to his belt with two hands to pull up his pants over a sufficient belly without missing a beat as he made a point about a legal doctrine. An engaging, friendly figure who was plainly very intelligent but, alas, just not a very compelling teacher; I often felt he wanted to be anywhere but in our classroom. Of course, with this attitude it was no surprise that I'd deservedly gotten a C on his final exam.

More to the point, Harper never mentioned to the class his role in the family planning movement. I never put him together with the vague news that there was constitutional litigation over the statute emerging out of New Haven. After the 1961 defeat in one of the cases on the ground that the statute had never been enforced, the activists tried a new tack. Eventually it would prove successful. They opened a clinic in New Haven that dispensed birth control information and paraphernalia. It took until 1965 but the Supreme Court finally agreed to reach the merits of the dispute. In *Griswold v. Connecticut*, the Justices by a vote of 7-2 declared the state law invalid because it invaded the privacy rights of married couples. Griswold was roundly criticized for finding a right to privacy, not explicitly mentioned in the Constitution, in the margins, or penumbras, as Justice

Douglas called them, of several of the Bill of Rights but his approach survived, becoming the essential bridge to *Roe v. Wade* in 1973 and the decisions that followed it invalidating efforts to criminalize abortion.

I can't say connecting with Professor Harper, or my first amendment law teacher, Tom Emerson, as tightly wrapped as Harper, was random, who would end up arguing Griswold before the Supreme Court after Harper's death, or Mrs. Griswold who gave the case its name because she ran the Planned Parenthood clinic that the state thought had violated the statute would have led us to a safe and less stressful end to the pregnancy. It was certainly true of the times, however, that connections of this sort allowed many university women to avoid the clandestine and troublesome episodes that would be our fate.

It started with a blessed phone number passed on by someone who I can't remember, which yielded a location on a quiet street, the name of which I cannot recall either, in a leafy Brooklyn neighborhood. She was told to come alone for a preliminary examination but, of course, I went too, waited down the street, watching first from a doorway and then making an effort to look casual, reading a paperback novel while sitting on the stoop of a brownstone house on the same street for half an hour. I was too nervous to take in more than a page.

When she came out, we walked to the subway in silence—was the stop one of those streets like Baltic Avenue memorialized by Monopoly? Were we in Fort Greene or Park

Slope or perhaps near the site of the soon to be demolished
Ebbets Field, the only part of the borough I knew well? I
can't say. The area was a maze. I agreed with Thomas Wolfe,
"Only the Dead Know Brooklyn."

While the subway train rumbled over the bridge to Manhattan, she finally spoke. She told me the date and that it
would cost $500.

"We'll split it," she added quickly.

"No," I said firmly. "It's my responsibility. I'll find it."

"We did this together. We'll both pay."

Silence. I remember the silence but not in the end how
much I did pay. Whatever it was, it came from my previous summer earnings as an insurance adjuster for accident
cases in the Catskills. The price meant we were at the high
end. Decades later legal abortions cost less. We were, of
course, paying for the risk.

When a few days later she started preparing to leave for
the appointment, we had our first and only fight. She prohibited me from coming. "I'll take the subway there; a
cab back," she insisted. "You can pay for the cab." Deeply
relieved, of course, but feeling my manliness was questioned
I balked.

"I'll go and lurk."

"Go ahead," she replied, "but I'm doing this alone." She
wasn't angry, she was just adamant; after enough time and
argument passed to feel I had recovered my dignity I con-
ceded. There was something of the mix of stubbornness
and certainty that reminded me of my mother. I wish I'd

been able to voice that it was her body so she got to decide but if I had the thought it was buried under the weight of anxiety and the power of her resolve.

I would wait for her in the apartment of good friends, out of school, slightly older, a commercial artist and his British wife. I loved them both, mostly because she was kind and beautiful, and read the right novels and he was living proof you could be yourself but still earn a living in New York. They offered to go away for the weekend, leaving their place to us in one of those nondescript 1920s Westside buildings on Ninety-Sixth Street.

When she arrived hours later, she was a mess: she sought to lean on me and was dead weight; from the door, we staggered together to get her to the bed. She was short on details. A woman helped him, was really all that was said about the thing itself. She'd had a shot of something but didn't elaborate. There were some pills to avoid infection, maybe penicillin. Was it dilation and curettage or some other method? She waved the question away. "I'll take my painkiller and sleep." I sat in a chair while she collapsed on the bed, attentive and useless. She would moan and then whisper apologies. The pain was hard, she finally admitted.

When I saw the blood, I shriveled, defeated by fear. Imagining dreadful scenarios. I felt cold but she felt colder, laying out under a sheet like a bird—white as a swan—writhing in a snare. After a while she let me sit on the bed next to her and gently rub her back. She stifled a few tears. It went on that way for the rest of the day. The blood stopped, as she predicted it would. The pain became a dull ache that she said later hung around for only a few days. I brought in Chinese food that she poked at and then threw up what little she'd swallowed.

We slept like two spoons set in a drawer. Late the next day I drove her back to a dorm in New Haven. Over the months we eased away from each other gently and then totally lost touch. Until I started teaching criminal law the memories disappeared but over time occasional associations gathered the story together, though the gaps are still large.

If she reads this, I wonder what her version would be. I'd certainly want to know but I can't find her on a college alumni site, on Facebook, or on social media. There is no obituary so I can hold out a slight hope. I so much want to check the facts. And did she have a good life?

In 1970, Governor Nelson Rockefeller signed a bill legalizing abortion in New York State. Two years later he vetoed a move by Republican legislators to repeal the new law. Shortly thereafter, the Supreme Court decided *Roe v. Wade*, though it settled little; unlike many other once-controversial High Court rulings, the abortion issue has remained contested for many years. From the beginning of 2011 to August 2015, according to the Guttmacher Institute, states enacted 287 new legal restrictions on access to abortion care. The following year, however, the Supreme Court decided that at least in Texas requirements that clinics providing abortion meet restrictive regulations governing doctor hospital

admitting privileges and certain surgical-center requirements placed a substantial obstacle in the path of women
seeking a previability abortion and thus constituted an
undue burden that violated the Constitution. But plenty of
the 287 restrictions are still in force.

It is ironic that despite there now being a constitutional
right, it's probably harder for some women to arrange an
abortion than it was for us over fifty years ago. In South
Dakota, for example, the only clinic is over 300 miles from
one major population center; like thirteen other states South
Dakota requires two clinic visits before the procedure can
take place. Five states have only one clinic; an estimated
twenty-one have extensive and burdensome regulations that
result in restricted access. Abortion remains a powerful
emotional issue for many Americans and the impact of its
political dimensions dwarfs the legalities. After the 2016
election it is anyone's guess whether the law will return to
what it was when we had to violate it.

Archeology in an Ancient Land

Months after graduating from law school and still unpublished I found myself working at an archeological site overlooking the turquoise of the salt-laced Dead Sea near the Kibbutz Ein Gedi—an oasis with streams and waterfalls famous as the supposed locale of the biblical *Song of Songs*. The country nearby was so rough, so parched and desolate, that our modest pay was called "shoe money," the price of a new pair of new boots. We volunteer diggers were bivouacked atop a dry canyon ironically called the Nahal-Hever (brook of the friend) a few miles from Israel border with Jordan to search for traces of a 135 AD encampment of Jewish rebels, loyal to the revolutionary leader and "president of Israel," Shimeon Bar-Kokhba, who were hiding in a deep cave 100 meters below the barren cliffs from the Roman army. Later the site was given the name the Cave of the Letters because of the discovery in its deepest recesses of ancient parchment documents. So far the expedition, led by archeologist (and former general) Yigael Yadin, has been a surprising success. One night he displays for the group some of the items found in the bat-infested, three-chambered cave—an ancient property deed, bronze keys, a brass mirror, Bar-Kokhba–issued coins, jewelry with semiprecious stones like carnelian, agate, and amethyst, shallow bowls called patera, seeds kept recognizable after almost 2,000 years by the dryness of the climate, and a net used to snare birds that were a source of food for the inhabitants trapped in the cave. One of the letters calls for help to fend off the "gentiles," as the Romans were called. Nearby is the Cave of Horrors where a cache of the skulls and bones of the Jewish rebels were found.

One day my wife-to-be and I are given the task of reconfiguring the housing pattern of the Roman siege camp constructed on the top of a cliff located high above our archeological site. We have met in the back of an open truck in an army convoy taking us from the dull and dirty desert town of Beersheba—now four times bigger with art galleries, schools, a theater scene, a cleaned-up river, and parks—to the site of the dig. Aside from an immediate physical attraction, we are drawn together by finding how similar a place we are in our lives. For both of us this is a year to sort out a future. Without knowing what she wanted to do next after graduating from Swarthmore College, Heli returned to Israel where she had visited before as a tourist thinking she might take courses for a master's degree in Middle Eastern studies but soon decided she needed a total break from school. She patched together a series of part-time jobs that left her free to travel and meet people who interested her—teaching modern dance at a private ballet school, English to uninterested North African immigrants who wanted to become farmers and young girls from Jerusalem's orthodox quarter, the Mea Shearim. The announcement that Yadin was seeking volunteers to go to the Dead Sea caves hinted at an adventure that captured her imagination. Neither of us, of course, had the slightest training in archeology.

Working under the cloudless sky and a blazing desert sun we were trying to figure out where the Roman soldiers placed their tent foundations, lookouts, and fire pits while they starved out the Jewish rebels hiding in the caves below. We were confronted by a chaos of stones but fortunately Yadin had ordered a series of aerial photographs that show the outlines of the camp's plan. The Romans chose the site, as he later wrote, because it was "ideally suited from a military point of view," providing "maximum coverage of the paths leading to, and from, the cave below." This was a choice that ultimately proved deadly to the rebels holding out in the cave.

Moving heavy stones spread across top of the cliff to their original places was taxing and tedious; they were so heavy that we had to face each other while using all four hands to do the lifting. It's in a glorious spot but there is no shade to protect us. When we need to rest, Heli magically produces a pack of American cigarettes; we take our break sitting on the walls we have proudly raised, smoking and staring at the ash red, lifeless Moab mountains in Jordan across the shimmering waters of the landlocked Dead Sea.

As there is no peace at the time between Israel and Jordan, an Israeli army unit has come with us to set up camp, bringing the food and water, tents for sleeping, a generator to light the cave, and a metal detector. The army is here for our security. The concern is over saboteurs crossing the border at night and even of disruption caused by Israeli soldiers who regularly dare each other to cross in the other direction for a surreptitious visit to the mysterious ancient stone city of Petra.

One evening Bruno, the Army unit's bushy-haired highest-ranking sergeant, tells me it's my night to share guard duty with a recruit. True, I have a rifle range familiarity with weapons but not with anything as powerful as an Uzi. Or as heavy. He quickly shows me how to disengage the safeties and explains the blowback action. I hardly take in what he is saying, remembering that I am "unfit for military service" but following him to my assigned post I suddenly think of a case I read in law school. Someone who has lost his US citizenship because he joined a foreign army was appealing to the Supreme Court. How did it come out? I can't recall but I tell myself that such a rule can't apply to one night guarding an archeological dig campsite. Still I am a reluctant warrior. Bruno senses my hesitation but ignores it. He describes the camp's perimeter I must patrol and walks me away from our tents to his dust-covered Jeep, reaches in the backseat, and without looking at me hands over the magazine.

"What," I stumble, "do I do with it?"

In reply, he used a Hebrew expression I have never heard and from his tone didn't want translated. Without looking at me, he explained again how the weapon worked, and then turned away. After a few steps he looked back and still moving away in his sabra-inflected English said, "Why not get your picture taken?"

Today Ein Gedi brings in loads of tourists to see its nature theme park. For about seven US dollars you can jump in the natural pools, search for desert animals like the ibex, and visit the souvenir shop.

During nine months in Israel I picked grapefruits and carried bawling chickens to the place where they were slaughtered and plucked, learned a few Hebrew expressions but not much more, and proofread copy at then liberal *Jerusalem Post*, the country's English language paper, until the editor hired his girlfriend for my job. On Easter weekend, I finally made my first sale. Posing as a Christian pilgrim, I crossed the divided City at the Mandelbaum Gate, the checkpoint near the Western edge of the Old City then in Jordanian hands. After finding the Wailing Wall in a rabbit warren of back streets some children playing in the dust—as I emerged, a bearded stranger— ran away as if they'd seen Satan. Later in the day, I photographed a loud but orderly street demonstration of young men in support of Egyptian president Gamal Abdel Nasser and sold the image, as well as a brief report, to the *Post* for the equivalent of ten dollars.

I'd gone to Israel because the weather was changing as winter came on in Greece; Stan was already there studying Hebrew. His kibbutz, Beit HaShittah, was located in Northern Israel, in the fertile Jezreel Valley, across from the ridge line of Mount Gilboa—a place rich in biblical history as where King Saul and his sons fell in war against the Philistines. Ethnic or religious feeling had nothing to do with my ending up in Israel, though everyone I met assumed I was on some sort of pilgrimage and it was awkward to explain otherwise.

Yet I soon became fascinated by Israeli society. In 1961 it was a young and progressive country, dominated by Europeans whose memory of the Holocaust was fresh. Many of those I met had a story to tell of how and when they survived and reached Israel. Despite being surrounded by hostile nations, the country seemed surprisingly secure, though it was recognized that the question of war was when, not if. The brutal violence between Arab and Jew, the murders and village destruction, that followed the 1947 United Nations vote legitimizing a Jewish state was rarely discussed. In my presence, at least, the Israelis I came to know were more interested in their internal politics; a comment I heard more than once was "two Jews, three political parties." It was easy to approach or be approached by almost anyone who crossed my path. I met a fighter pilot, a university lecturer in geography; recent immigrants from Eastern Europe. Yuval and Rina Levy, a lawyer and his wife I'd known in New Haven, put me up in their hilltop villa across from a clutch of noisy peacocks whenever I was in Haifa. I had an affair with an impossibly beautiful Romanian immigrant and made friends with British Jews who were called "Anglo-saxeem" by the Israelis. I partied with sabras and recent arrivals and for a time forgot where I'd come from.

In Tel Aviv especially there were many who wanted to be in America instead of in Israel. They would ask me the price of goods, whether I had a TV, and the brand of the family refrigerator. Others took an entirely different view of the world: I must immigrate. One pitch was the country needs you for the fights ahead; the other was more aggressive: "Just you wait," one newcomer from Poland angrily insisted. "Wake up. A Hitler will come to America too. Only in Israel can a Jew be free." I listened politely to such exhortations but said little in response; behind my silence was an understanding that raised in relative safety and comfort, I had no standing to disagree. In my mind, however, I fended off such claims with an inner narrative of US liberal constitutionalism, surprisingly far from home nurturing the civil rights lawyer identity that I would soon claim. I generally felt envied and was usually treated with great courtesy and respect—in both cases much more than I deserved. It dawned on me that symbolically I was a representative of a country that was both an essential financial and a political support for the embattled and isolated new state as well as a sought-after refuge, in the imagination if not the reality, from the stress of living surrounded by mortal enemies.

I was treated so well—for reasons that had nothing to do with anything I'd actually done—that for a very brief moment I thought I should stay and see where I'd fit in but it was truly a brief moment. I was secular; Israel was plainly never going to be totally so even though half the people I met were atheists. I had invested much in learning my country's language, history, and folkways. In contrast, I knew only a scattering of Hebrew sentences. In Israel I'd have to start from scratch but even though I could learn the language I now had a profession and a love of what I thought of as progressive, if difficult, American politics that could hardly be replicated anywhere else. I never seriously considered remaining but did allow myself to have a few conversations about it with Israelis I met as I traveled. Perhaps it was recognition of the difficulties the country would face or maybe just a way to ease various social situations. At any rate, I was running out of money. It was time for me to go home and face the world of work.

Israeli novelist Amos Oz recalled the words of his Aunt Sonia on her arrival in Israeli from Europe in 1938: "I went up on deck [and] there was the city of Tel Aviv. . . . I can't describe how all at once the joy rose up in my throat; suddenly all I wanted to do was shout and sing, This is mine! . . . I'd never experienced such a strong feeling before in my life, of belonging, of ownership." The joy she experienced in joining a humane, open society, despite the dangerous threat of Arab enemies, had not dissipated by my time in Israel but following two wars and the seizure of territory ultimately occupied by hundreds of thousands of settlers Israeli society became a place unrecognizably different in its attitude toward its neighbors and any potential peace process.

I knew I would never have a feeling like Sonia's about Israel but I'd had a similar experience in 1958 when passing into New York harbor. I stood by the rail of a converted Victory Ship owned by the Holland America Line along with hundreds of other student travelers returning from Europe and saw the Statute of Liberty for the first time from the sea.

Coming to the Law

The geography of hell is still in the process of being mapped.

(Novelist Wright Morris reviewing
Ralph Ellison's *Invisible Man* (1952))

I've spent every one of the fifty-five plus years since I returned from kicking around Europe and the Middle East in the belly of the legal beast. Not what I planned, even though I was eager to sue those I regarded as the enemies of the fair, the just, and the different. Nevertheless, you'd think given the length and variety of my tour of duty I'd be confident about the values of my profession. You might expect I knew fully well why I went to law school and became an attorney and teacher. If you met me at a dinner or a party or a professional seminar, you'd probably think that here was a guy who could *at least* tell you clearly how much of what lawyers and courts do is worthy of respect, how well law schools are meeting their responsibilities, and why the Supreme Court decides the cases the way it does.

You might also conclude I was satisfied with my career, one that played a role in the gestation of all sorts of progressive change and was pleased with the results. As to each of these matters I'd have a lot of positive things to say. I can and will, for example, go on at length about how radically different things are for the people LDF represented. Nevertheless, it's just as certain that the more you probed, the more you'd find me uncertain, ambivalent, tentative, and unwilling to claim hopeful societal outcomes.

A favorite story of mine tells of a Jewish mother and her son who lived in Poland as the Nazis drew near in the late 1930s. Shortly before the actual invasion a gentile couple offered to hide them in an attic room from the advancing Germans. The son refused this invitation because he couldn't imagine being cooped up with his mother. A few months later the son was given the opportunity to escape alone from Poland to America. Again he declined the offer. He could not imagine leaving his mother behind. This is the kind of ambivalent devotion I feel about my work. I am very much the part of what vexes me.

My feelings are matched by almost everyone I know who was there then and is still alive and kicking. And it was the way we looked at things even before the election of Donald J. Trump. For every bow toward pride there is a "maybe", a "but", or an "on the other hand." By this point, some of what you've heard from me might strike you as carping. Or

cynical. Or you might conclude, as did the South African
Nobel Prize novelist and political activist, Nadine Gordi-
mer, while we once dined in a fancy Manhattan restaurant
that when it comes to human rights most legal activity is a
waste of time, money, and energy.

I would have agreed with Nadine if she'd talked of only
modest results but the brush she used was broad. She
was a political activist in a place where at the time of our
conversation white racial dominance talk of incremental change through litigation bordered on the unreal. She
believed the people had to rise up. Ironically, I'd been introduced to Nadine by Felicia Kentridge, a South African
lawyer who was the daughter of one of the country's first
women attorneys and the wife of Sydney Kentridge, a bar-
rister of international reputation who had represented Nelson Mandela and conducted the inquest that revealed the
police had killed charismatic antiapartheid activist Steve
Biko. Felicia was the moving force behind the 1979 creation of the Legal Resource Center, a public interest law firm
modeled on the NAACP Legal Defense Fund; she persuaded the Carnegie Foundation to send me to Johannes-
burg to help set it up. Along with a Foundation executive
named David Hood, Felicia was convinced, and she was
proven right, that litigation against the apartheid state
would never bring it down but it would serve to establish a
legal culture that might help plant a constitutionally based
rule of law when the racially based system of privilege and
disparagement inevitably began to collapse. In 1997, the

Kentridge–Hood view proved correct when South Africa adopted one of the most human rights–friendly constitutions in the world.

Despite this work and dozens of other examples, it's hard for me to admit how conflicted I am about the value of the reform movements I was part of, even though for myself if I had the chance I'd do very little differently. I was handed the great gift of close friends, exceptional colleagues, and work that advanced human dignity. I can count a long list of supposed victories. But it turns out I expected too much. One of the side effects of the kind of law I did was that there is on the whole a buried assumption that events can be influenced. I thought our vision of a just society was around the corner and instead today it seems far, far away.

I don't think I was ever blind to the barriers. New York City taught me a lot about obstacles because from an early age I felt survival in the City required overcoming them but the institutions of the law have only partially responded to change and that tends to apply also to the subject of the laws. To be sure there have been massive improvements in the status of minorities and a sensitivity to intolerance and inequality but it's undeniable that what amounts to an American caste system is still alive and well. I no longer believe, if I ever did, that progress is inevitable. Our LDF client, Martin Luther King Jr. famously said, "The arc of the moral universe is long, but it bends towards justice" but if so the speed of the arc's rise is most deliberate, perhaps tediously so, even if it isn't, as Ta-Nehisi Coates has it, "bent towards chaos." On the other hand, one of the characteristics of today's world that I most dislike is the difficulty we have of truly celebrating our blessings and the many lives that have turned out for the better. To pick one of the reasons just as an example, Malcolm X turned to the Nation of Islam out of a quarrel with the support of white supremacy he found in the worshippers of a Christian God. A good many denominations, though certainly not all, have turned away from that history.

It may be better to be poor today than a hundred years ago but if so it's just barely. You can point to better medical care, more available "things," and a safety net that is an improvement over the almshouses and farms my wife documented in her book, *The Poorhouses of Massachusetts*, where she charts how venerable institutions were designed and operated in Commonwealth from its founding until the past century. But contemporary expectations for the basics of decent life are totally different than in the nineteenth century. The nation's safety net, moreover, is famously leaky, torn by omissions, lack of funding for subsidized housing, and bureaucratic catch 22s that take away support when a poor person makes some slight headway toward a better job with a slightly higher wage. Transcending even the barren and deprived life of many of the poor is a widespread public attitude, abetted by some politicians and a complacent mainstream media, that the poor are lazy, uninterested in a better life, and simply unwilling to put in the hard work that promises success to true believers of the American dream. In recent years the forces that dominate government policies ignore the fact that most of the poor are children or elderly or caretakers of others who can't make do on their own or the physically or mentally disabled. There is widespread denial that absent aggressive government intervention it takes inherited social and economic capital to rise above the systemic barriers faced by the poor. At a lecture I attended recently a woman who called herself an exception because she had just won a city-wide lottery that placed her and her son in supported housing challenged the audience by asking for a show of hands:

"How many of you received help from family or friends to buy your first apartment or house?"

The few hands that were not raised belonged to upper middle class and affluent white listeners. And how could it be any different when the African American family members who might have contributed inherited capital to their children or grandchildren earned about half on average of white counterparts? In 1940, only about 12% of blacks aged twenty-five to twenty-nine had completed high school. There is no end to statistics that point in the same direction. It's not, however, that there haven't been massive changes in the economic prospects available to an emerging African American middle class but these significant advances fail to completely displace the legacy of past stigmatization and mistreatment.

Sometimes I am overwhelmed by the disparities experienced by minorities and the poor following implementation of fair on their face policies that look neutral but don't turn out that way. I wrote once about the different rates paid by blacks and whites for the same life insurance policies and car purchases. Recently I came across an investigation by the *USA Today* revealing that in the past seventeen years blacks had been killed in a disproportionate rate as a result of police car chases, nearly double what would be expected based on a percentage of the population. Everyone has heard of Driving While Black but this was something new—Car Chased While Black. In 2016, a police chief who was the president of a 23,000-member police management organization issued a formal apology "for the actions of the past and the role of our profession has played in society's historical mistreatment of communities of color" but such concessions are rare. Then there is the 1976 Supreme Court case that required proof of animus—despite the prevalence of implicit, unconscious, unacknowledged bias—before the Constitution's Equal Protection guarantee can be applied.

When major scandals in the national government are uncovered, the culprits are usually brought to justice because of the cover-up, not so much because of the nefarious events themselves. When it comes to the way race influences decision making, from voters to Supreme Court Justices, the cover-up is basically denial of the role race has played. The varieties of this denial are many but the most prominent one is the belief that if there is no discernable individual bias there is no depravation.

Between 2011 and 2015 fair-housing testers visited 2,300 housing foreclosure sites in 38 metropolitan areas. They discovered that Fannie Mae, the quasi-governmental lending agency that was supposed to oversee them, had allowed houses in minority neighborhoods to deteriorate at a far greater rate than those in working and middle class white areas. Such structures were to cite one example five times more likely to have unrepaired broken windows. Fannie Mae denied the allegations, subject of an ongoing federal lawsuit, but tellingly in a statement to the press revealed it had now hired local contractors to make maintenance changes to hide visible signs of blight.

The glass may be half full or half empty for you but for me it's contents are murky. As a result, I'm in the middle, which happens to be the title of a political column I coauthored for my college newspaper. In most of those essays, my best friend coauthor and I found that politicians danced toward safety, even cowardice, but also noticed that from time to time it was necessary for them to turn toward higher aspirations. Occasionally, they acted accordingly. I was even then pulled in two directions. Certainly the former is all around us but has the latter survived? I'm not sure. It's just hard to decide on any particular day whether to feel pessimistic or optimistic or even to escape the dilemma by claiming impotence.

All I know is that there is more work to be done. These days I think we get the policies we deserve and so see the frustrations in larger type but in a funny way, one I didn't predict, I want to get even busier and do more. Here is some of the evidence that brought me to this point. My testimony.

TM

In the summer of 1961 when I came home from Europe and the Middle East, I knew very little about the NAACP Legal Defense Fund. Indeed I wrongly thought it part of the National Association for the Advancement of Colored People, an understandable confusion given their joint origins and 1950s divorce that continues with many to this day. The two organizations had actually been separated when powerful Southern Senators gearing up their fight against integration complained to the Internal Revenue Service that they had interlocking board of directors. Of course, I knew Thurgood Marshall was the civil rights leader who had been the leading advocate in the 1954 cases ending enforced segregation of the public schools but other than that he was a shadowy figure, a name recognized, but not a man known. It was more or less like an East Coast baseball fan aware that someone playing for a team in California hit a lot of home runs. I knew very little about the man's history, personality, or likely future. Of Jack Greenberg, Marshall's second in command, an officer in World War II and a Columbia Law graduate who would be my boss for almost ten years I knew nothing.

I'd come home without much to show except some rejection slips as a freelance writer but I'd seen a lot of the world, survived periods of relative isolation, and existed on very little money in foreign countries. I had a greater confidence in myself. A month after returning, Heli and I married and rented an apartment in Manhattan after I decided not to pursue a couple of federal government jobs. I was most serious about the Civil Rights Division of the Department of Justice but a senior lawyer there told me to be careful, warning me that it was far from clear that the Kennedy Administration would endorse vigorous enforcement of federal law. Away for almost a year, I hadn't given much thought to practicing law but after the McCarthy era had always dreamed of working for the New York office of the American Civil Liberties Union. I decided to apply there but I clearly was out of touch. I was told, "The ACLU already has *a* lawyer."

Only serendipity can explain how I came to be hired by Marshall and Greenberg. It began with my mother-in-law suggesting I talk to some of her well-placed friends about my career plans, which led eventually to an interview with a friend of one of them—Ed Lucas, a New York lawyer who worked for the American Jewish Committee mostly writing legal briefs on religious freedom issues. Lucas, whose son Tony would write, *Common Ground: A Turbulent Decade in the Lives of Three American Families*, one of the greatest

American books on race, gave me the impression that the kind of civil liberties work I'd aspired to do ever since watching the televised hearing in which Joseph Welch demolished Senator McCarthy was really not all that satisfying. It wasn't clear why he thought so but he gave the appearance of a man who life had treated badly. Lucas did say the pay was lousy in good guy law and he had few ideas for me to better my job prospects. As I was leaving his office—literally half out the door—a last minute aside made all the difference.

"Thurgood Marshall is looking for someone," he murmured. "Give him a call."

It turned out that one of the then six LDF lawyers, Norman Amaker, had been called up from the reserves by President Kennedy as part of cold war maneuvering and ordered off to Berlin for a year. There was an open spot on the staff. My call led to an interview with Greenberg, a recommendation from my constitutional law professor Alexander M. Bickel and a job offer from Marshall at a salary of $6,000 a year. As I have written elsewhere, I never thought I'd be paid so much to start—in those days Wall Street firm starting salaries weren't that much higher—and foolishly offered to take less. Greenberg whose salary at the time was only $17,000 gently admonished—"never, never" take less money for doing good. (Some stories, like this one, are so good you keep telling them.)

I soon found out that Marshall, while still deeply involved in key decisions at LDF, was engaged in a delicate set of negotiations with the Kennedy Administration over a federal judgeship, one of the first to be offered to an African American—then, of course, described everywhere as "Negroes." Bobby Kennedy, the attorney general, only later to become a great friend of civil rights, took a hard line at first because he was worried about hostility from Southern democrats whose support his brother needed to push through a challenging legislative program. RFK offered Marshall a district court judgeship.

TM declined, insisting on an appointment to the Court of Appeals. "My boiling point is too low for the trial court," was his argument for a seat on a higher court: "I'd blow my stack and then get reversed." The Kennedys tried to play hardball but Marshall was adamant, a position that stiffened the spine of everyone who learned about it. Kennedy dithered until one of the few highly placed black Democratic Party operatives intervened, insisting that Thurgood Marshall was "Mr. Civil Rights" for the many minority voters who had put JFK over the electoral threshold and, therefore, he deserved an appeals court appointment. At the time, gossip had it that President Kennedy assured Marshall's confirmation by agreeing to nominate Harold Cox, a racist crony of Senate Judiciary Committee Chair Senator James Eastland of Mississippi, as well as J. Robert Elliot, a Georgia segregationist to the federal bench. Marshall got what he wanted, important for both him and the Civil Rights Movement because it sent a message to the country that changes would be forthcoming. His confirmation still took months. Cox predictably proved a great embarrassment. To the dismay of both Kennedys, he rejected every significant civil rights claim that came before him, sometimes with racist language comparing blacks to animals.

I was happy for my boss but, initially, felt a personal loss. Except for being in the audience of a network radio program for kids hosted by Babe Ruth and getting to shake the hand of Jackie Robinson outside the Dodger's clubhouse when Ira closed his calendar deal, I'd never been so close to a historic figure before. He was a large man with an even larger personality who seemed to dominate every room he entered. In the months before he took the bench I'd been able to hear what he had to say about some of his great cases, watch the way he dealt with people, and consume some of his endless supply of stories and jokes.

Marshall would soon begin a judicial career that would eventually make him the first black member of the Supreme Court. Despite an acrimonious 1967 Senate Judiciary Committee hearing where Southern Senators tried to bait him into a misstep by treating reports of his sardonic humor as if they were antiwhite statements, he was confirmed with only one dissenting vote. But his 1961 move to the Court of Appeals immediately raised the question of succession at LDF. Founded as an office that was merely part of the NAACP in the 1930s by legendary black lawyer, Harvard Law School graduate Charles Hamilton Houston, under Marshall LDF had orchestrated a train of successful precedents that led it to be recognized as the legal arm of the civil rights movement. Though there was no candidate to succeed him with Marshall's stature and name recognition, Robert Carter, then the general counsel of the NAACP, had played a key role in the Brown cases and he was well known among civil rights insiders. Backed by a compliant board of directors, the choice, however, was Marshall's to make; instead of Carter he selected Greenberg, a white man, a total surprise to almost everyone except those of us on the staff who knew that Greenberg for some time had been running the day-to-day affairs of organization while Marshall devoted himself to rallying the black community and enjoying the accolades that came with being the lead lawyer in Brown.

The few who complained about selection of a white man to succeed Marshall are often quoted when the matter is recalled but they were a small minority. Jim Hicks, a columnist for New York's leading black paper, the *Amsterdam News*, mildly questioned Greenberg's appointment and the following year journalist Louis Lomax thought that the black man in the street would resent anyone who wasn't black in power at LDF. Sadly, when Greenberg died at ninety-two in 2016, his *New York Times* obituary implied there had been significant dissent from Marshall's decision but, in fact, there was little negative comment from the African American press. Greenberg had argued one of the *Brown v. Board of Education* cases and the lawyers in the South with whom LDF worked closely knew him well. They supported

Marshall's choice even if they were surprised that Bob Carter hadn't gotten the job. Some gripes from NAACP board members had more to do with their desire to reassert control over LDF than real opposition to Greenberg.

Carter, however, felt he should have been chosen and was deeply disappointed. His hurt was understandable. He had been second in command at LDF before Marshall arranged to move him from LDF to the post of NAACP general counsel where he had an impressive title but little staff and money. Carter also had seniority over Greenberg; during the run-up to *Brown*, he had played far more of a leadership role. When TM was absent, as he was when investigating the atrocious treatment of Negro soldiers serving under general Douglas MacArthur in Asia, Carter was the acting head of the organization. And of course he was black. Five years later appointment of a white man to head LDF would have created a heated controversy. In 1961, the issue hardly surfaced.

The problem for Bob Carter was that he had an increasingly acrimonious relationship with Marshall. In his 1998 biography, *Thurgood Marshall: American Revolutionary*, Juan Williams summarized the 1950s Marshall–Carter ego battle that emerged from his researches: "Marshall saw Carter as a first-rate legal mind who handled the office's affairs expertly. But Marshall also saw Carter had come to resent him. Carter complained to Board members that Marshall often behaved like a prima donna. He wanted all the public attention, he made all the speeches, and he got all the credit, while day-to-day issues and concerns fell on Carter's desk."

There was serious mistrust between Marshall and Carter but as potential leaders of LDF there was little apparent difference between Carter and Greenberg. Carter later became a federal judge, and Greenberg, after heading LDF for some twenty-five years, became the dean of Columbia College and later a Columbia law professor. I never worked with Carter but many lawyers thought both men were superb tacticians who also saw the larger picture of how litigation, protest demonstrations, and politics intersected. Both had the stamina required for social reform lawyering and they knew well the players in the small but intense world of civil rights activists. Neither of them was warm and cuddly but both were honest and fair-minded.

The larger question is whether the resolution of the succession changed civil rights history. Any answer is, of course, speculative. They both shared similar formative experiences as part of the legal team Marshall assembled to challenge segregation. They were products of a civil rights culture that trusted test case class action litigation would bring progress; they both managed staff lawyers and lawsuits in a traditional top-down way. LDF had years of courtroom success under Greenberg but that hardly proves Carter's record would have been less impressive. If there was one place where Carter might have provided different leadership, it was to push LDF to greater emphasis on attacking lack of black educational achievement in northern school systems. As a close friend of Derrick Bell, an LDF staff member in the early 1960s who later became the first tenured black Harvard law professor and a powerful foe of LDF's emphasis on desegregation cases, Carter might have been more likely than Greenberg to seek educational equity and local control instead of integration as a remedy for discrimination in educational opportunity.

But his memoir, *A Matter of Law*, makes clear that Carter was no separatist: "While integration did not necessarily ensure quality education," he wrote, "the integrated school was the indispensable first step towards providing equal education for black children and the best education for all children."

Ultimately, leadership succession at LDF had more to do with personality than with policy—Marshall's as well as Greenberg's and Carter's. To my surprise, the enduring lesson is much what I thought it was as a young lawyer watching it happen. Do not assume, I concluded then, that those doing good deeds are necessarily kinder and gentler human beings, more sensitive to others or less manipulative, than those in the business or political world. Power politics are not alien to the world of high ideals; indeed, given the strength of the forces arrayed against them, a good case can be made that public interest lawyers have to be even more tough-minded than their adversaries. At any rate, it's a trait all three men shared. Another version can be found reflected in the well-know one liner oft attributed to Henry

Kissinger as well as a host of others to the effect that *"Academic politics are so vicious precisely because the stakes are so small."* Issue-focused observers like to think policy debates are divorced from the personalities of the individuals supporting and opposing them but all too often this is wishful if not magical thinking.

In my early days at the Legal Defense Fund before the passage of the 1964 Civil Rights Act my work involved flying South at least once—often more than once—a month to appear in court or to work with local African American lawyers and their clients in planning and prosecuting anti-segregation lawsuits targeting racially exclusive schools, hospitals, and a variety of public facilities from golf courses to fast food restaurants located on government property. When I started working for LDF, our offices were on the seventeenth floor of the since torn down 10 Columbus Circle office tower. Because of the reluctance of many Manhattan building owners to rent to LDF, Thurgood Marshall needed the political influence of Hulan Jack, the black Manhattan Borough President, to obtain the space from power broker Robert Moses, who then controlled the property. Later we moved to larger quarters on two higher floors, but in 1961 six staff attorneys, their secretaries, and support staff worked in tight space. At first, I shared a tiny windowless office with Derrick Bell and Norman Amaker, for the few weeks before Norman was shipped off to Berlin. The library was small and the copy room only slightly bigger than a broom closet. Intrastaff memos weren't necessary.

All you need to do to communicate with the rest of the staff was to hold a loud conversation in the central hallway.

The only exception to our cramped quarters was Thurgood Marshall's office, which, while hardly palatial, offered some privacy when the boss was out. There was a seating area with several comfortable chairs but the room was dominated by his classy, if scuffed, seven-foot-long, art deco, wooden Stow & Davis desk. In contrast, every other desk on the seventeenth floor was standard-issue metallic plainly bought in gross at some office supply company. From the windows behind Thurgood Marshall's desk was a glorious view of Columbus Circle and beyond it Central Park but the desk looked inward to the seating area where I often went to write briefs and motions on yellow legal pads when he was traveling and the room was empty.

Then there were the times, late in the afternoons of demanding work days, when his office became a place to unwind, to hear a great storyteller's gravelly voiced tales of dangerous lawyering in the segregated South including some where he was told to get out of town or else, his commonly off-color jokes, and worldly comments on the issues and the leading personalities of the day. George Stevens Jr.'s 2008 one-man play *Thurgood* faithfully evokes the Marshall of moments; when I saw it performed recently by Johnny Lee Davenport, I felt TM had returned from the grave.

Thurgood Marshall loved a good drink and he would pull a bottle of whiskey from the bottom left desk drawer, fill a glass, and push the bottle toward you. Then he'd lean back in his chair, put his feet up on the desk, and hold forth. Because for much of this time he was waiting on what became an appointment to the Court of Appeals and busily preparing for a confirmation hearing where he would face off against Senator Eastland, these were not rigorous work sessions. There was certainly shoptalk but it was talk of the sort that might take place at a water cooler or a neighborhood bar after work. These were moments a young lawyer wanted and needed. A relaxed, totally unpretentious, but larger-than-life boss talking openly of his youth in Baltimore, great cases he'd known, his favorite lawyer tactics, and a gallery of heroes and villains. Thurgood Marshall not only was a great storyteller, but while he was telling the story, it was part of his genius he made you feel, whatever the story, that it was meant for you.

Jim

Beginning a career in the presence of Thurgood Marshall taught me I had to learn the history of black America. Even though I had studied history in college, to say my knowledge was deficient would be a gross understatement. And I was hardly alone. If it wasn't so sad, I would have laughed at President Trump's apparent ignorance when he made a black history month remark about famous antislave activist and lecturer Frederick Douglass who he said "is an example of somebody who's done an amazing job and is getting recognized more and more. . . ." Douglas died in 1895.

Bizarre, but in a way understandable. Commonly assigned textbooks for both high school and college courses said almost nothing about the great migration from the South or the shape of black life in the twentieth century. Even the reality of slavery and the rise of Jim Crow were only marginally covered. If you knew anything about peonage, lynching, or the creation of the NAACP, the information probably didn't come from anything that happened in a classroom. And of course the schoolroom was but a small part of a national landscape where, as Michael Eric Dyson put it, "one of the greatest privileges of whiteness is not to see color, not to see race, and not to pay a price for ignoring it. . . ."

After my interview with Greenberg, I devoured everything I could find. Sociologist E. Franklin Frazier, historian and activist W. E. B. Dubois, numerous pamphlets on race published by the United Nations, and W. J. Cash's *The Mind of the South*, a book that prepared me for what I would face when I traveled across the region. Greenberg had himself written a book called *Race Relations and American Law* driving home how little attention even my fancy Yale legal education had shown for civil rights law.

But it was my new colleague James M. Nabrit III who helped me shed the rust accumulated in a year abroad and made me into a civil rights lawyer. Before he got ahold of me all I had was motivation and the dim remnants of three years of law school classes. Jim did his mentoring quietly and by indirection, always implying that whatever he suggested was really up to me to accept or reject, that no matter how much green he saw, I was still in charge. Never a lecture or an order but a conversation between equals— which of course we both knew was totally untrue. By his nurturing my sense of evolving professionalism, I was able to see how scared I was, fearful not only that I didn't know enough but also that I would never know enough to do the work at the level it demanded. Until he pointed the way out of the woods, I felt I had to cross a land that was mined with unknown rules, inflexible deadlines, and treacherous analytics. Part of the problem was that the fear had to be buried. Young lawyers too often believe they can't admit how little control they feel without suffering career consequences. Fifty plus years later, this phenomenon has little changed.

Jim was older; he'd served two years in the service stationed in Paris doing intelligence work for the US Army, and loved it. I had the feeling that if it weren't for his pedigree, which no one could match, he would never have returned from France. But he was born to lawyering; his father was one of the *Brown v. Board of Education* lawyers, later the dean of the Howard University Law School and then the president of the whole University. Ted Shaw, a one-time LDF Director-Counsel, called him civil rights "royalty." Jim was sent to fine schools where there were few of his color, which was so light that another might have tried to pass but he also grew up in the society of his dad's colleagues. When he wasn't off at prep school in Vermont or studying at Bates College in Maine, he was the kid in the background when Spotswood Robinson, Louis Redding, Clarence Mitchell, or Oliver Hill came to call. It embarrasses me how today few know of these names or what they did.

Jim's work habits, however, were ridiculous. He might barge into my office to explain his latest system for picking racetrack winners through his well-used off-track betting account; then without missing a beat he'd unroll a set of City maps to show why a complex pupil assignment plan in Denver was a way to keep the schools segregated. He might remain closed in his office for days organizing his underwater photography from the Caribbean or practicing magic tricks but how then, I wondered, did the brief get written, case advice get sent around, edits be found on the top of my desk?

"Well, I find the time at night," he admitted, "because I've gone lunar."

Jim had the most talented secretary in the place, a very large woman named Doris Hendricks who sometimes carried his words to me—"Mr. Nabrit would like you to. . . ." When she came to my office, you could tell she felt she was passing on gospel. In the years when I intensely disliked air travel, fearing every flight South would end up in flames, he talked me through the turbulence, passing on new Thurgood Marshall stories or alluding to the sexual escapades of lawyers we both knew. He kept his voice low, slowly drawing out each story as if to keep me distracted while bumpy Delta flights carried us to and from New Orleans or when we suffered through scary air bump drops on one of the last DC-3 flights scheduled by a major airline as it churned its miserable way to Southside Virginia. In ten years the only times I heard him raise his voice in anger was when he called out a few federal judges for being phony "statesmen," by which he meant they had been giving segregators more time than he thought they deserved to comply with the law.

One night I was sitting with him, a gin and tonic in my hand, on the terrace of his high-rise Park Row apartment in lower Manhattan. His wife Jackie, the sweetest and most conventional woman I knew, was in the kitchen with my wife making dinner. Jimmy who was also gadget crazy focused his high-powered binoculars on a tenement room a quarter of a mile away in Chinatown watching Asian men gathered around a table: he was sure it was a gambling den and for some reason was obsessed with trying to figure out the game they were playing from across three Manhattan streets. Earlier in the day, I saw him studying a *How to Do It* book on blackjack card counting; a few months later he told me he had unsuccessfully tried his luck at an Atlantic City casino but, at least, the House hadn't figured out what he was doing.

There was something endearing but also instructive about how many sides of the man emerged when he wasn't locked into his role of civil rights legal expert. Jim argued before the Supreme Court a dozen times but what really got him going was his home-grown system for predicting which Justice would end up writing the majority opinion in argued cases. For some reason he never converted his statistical method into an office pool. After computers became common, Jim put aside most of his hobbies and avocations; totally absorbed, he was anointed the office go-to techie.

I second chaired some of my first trials with him but after LDF let me work on my own; our collaboration was mostly writing appeal case briefs together. Along with our colleague Melvyn Zarr, we filed an influential friend of the court brief in the famous case of *Loving v. Virginia* but my favorite of his many adventures in litigation involved one of the most shocking cases of police overreaching in American history. Jim persuaded the federal courts to stop dragnet, warrantless, searches of the homes of hundreds of innocent African Americans in Baltimore, Maryland. The cops didn't have any evidence of probable cause to intrude. They were simply looking for two black criminals and in their eyes this justified barging into home after home. The case is forgotten today, though it fits right into the narrative of Black Lives Matter. Challenging abuse has to be a constant because power has a short memory and the rule of law is fragile. In May 2017, for example, the ACLU filed a lawsuit backed by video evidence detailing how Madison County, Mississippi, police conducted numerous warrantless home invasions, "jump-out" tactics that targeted young black men walking down the street and roadblocks in black neighborhoods. A recent Department of Justice report suggests Baltimore police still do everything they can to avoid rules protecting privacy supposedly enshrined in the Fourth Amendment to the Constitution. No way law enforcement would have so behaved in the white community.

The last time we talked Jackie had died; Jim was in a Maryland retirement facility. At first, he seemed interested when I suggested a trip to the Pimlico racecourse but soon diverted the conversation to his latest at home betting system; finally, he admitted that he didn't get out very often. Like old times, he launched into a story about the extracurricular doings of someone we both worked with but he could hardly get to the punch line; he laughed so much at his own telling. It was a friendly laugh that pulled you in, embraced you, the same way it did fifty years earlier when he was explaining a winning strategy in some aspect of a tough test case. Jim died from lung cancer at eighty in 2013, decades after he stopped smoking the filtered King Sano cigarettes he was known for. He would be followed in death three years later by Jack Greenberg, leaving me the only LDF lawyer from 1961, the only one hired by Thurgood Marshall, still alive. When I wandered the Columbia campus after Jack's memorial service, I felt that I was now the sole keeper of those early days' memories.

Americus

Anthony Trollope once wrote that "the legal profession does not concern itself with morality" and there is truth to the observation at least so far as it applies to judges resting their decisions on explicit moral principles. In the law reviews and blogs, constitutional scholars debate preferences for formalism versus pragmatism, originalism, or a living Constitution. There are, however, times where unfairness and legality clash, and right triumphs. This may have been the case more often during the civil rights era than during any other time in American history. In 1963, I represented four young civil rights workers, three whites and one black, who along with a group of local young people peacefully marched down a main city street in Americus, Georgia (a city once represented in the state legislature by Jimmy Carter of nearby Plains), to protest segregation—blacks had to sit in the balcony—in a local movie theater. The case was notable because the prosecutor brought a charge of "insurrection" against the four, a capital crime that allowed the state to hold them without bail for months. He was candid about his motives: "We were in hopes that by holding these men, we would be able to talk to their lawyers and talk to their people and convince them that this type of activity . . . is not the right way to go about it." As absurd as it was for the state to charge the group with a capital crime, the prosecution would go forward while the four remained in jail.

Regardless of the situation, it is usually impossible to persuade a federal court to halt an ongoing state criminal prosecution. For technical reasons our plea to do so came before a three-judge federal court, one of whose members was J. Robert Elliott, a jurist committed to segregation, but the panel was dominated by Elbert Parr Tuttle, the chief judge of the region's federal Court of Appeals. He swiftly granted an injunction forbidding the prosecution. The prosecutor later admitted that he had brought the charges to intimidate even though he knew that the Georgia insurrection statute had been held unconstitutional in 1937.

Judge Tuttle had a reputation for not tolerating the use of state power to sabotage efforts to end segregation. Watching him grant my motion in the Americus four case made a deep impression on me. It drove home again what had overcome me as I took up the work—I had a purpose in life, a reason to be larger than seeking my own pleasures. And it led me to an unusual thought—at least for a lawyer responding to a judicial order. My reaction was aesthetic. Judge Tuttle had done something of beauty. He had fulfilled the promise of the law to remedy gross injustice. The state prosecutor and the community he represented acted on an abiding belief that they had an unlimited power and sufficient virtue to oppress their opponents, who happened to be their neighbors. Judge Tuttle cut through the tissue of legal argument to a place where fairness reigned. He chose to use his discretion to offer protection but he couldn't have done it without an underlying sense of justice in his own person and also found in the values of the larger community. In this case, whether you call it empathy, a sense of communal value, or—as John Rawls might say—to identify with another's fate—the deeper foundation for his action was in an unwillingness to tolerate injustice when he had the authority to do so, and perhaps that's why I saw it as beauty.

In 2017, when Donald Trump nominated appeals judge Neil Gorsuch to the Supreme Court, he said that the judge "understands the role of judges is to interpret the law, not impose their own policy preferences, priorities, or ideologies." Trump hardly invented this deceptive way of talking about the art of judging. Famously, Chief Justice Roberts defined the judicial role as that of an umpire calling balls and strikes and "not to pitch and bat," a formulation that is doubly deceptive because it wrongly assumes a rigidly determined strike zone and, more significantly, suggests judging is a robotic activity.

Politicians and would-be jurists of all stripes promote this narrative, one that conveys to the public the misleading impression that what courts tend to do is a mechanical implementation of decisions made elsewhere by elected representatives or their administrative appointees. Some judicial decisions fit this mold but more, certainly when the application of important constitutional and statutory generalities is at stake, require judges to use their discretion, which boils down to results that flow from their politics, value preferences, previous experience, as well as individual professional judgment. In the Americus case, Judge Tuttle followed his own "policy preferences" but he also drew upon a generally accepted sense of fairness. He could have decided to deny relief to the rights workers. There were precedents for and against. He simply chose justice as he saw it. That same discretion can be used for ill but that was not the case here.

Tales of Reform—Failure

In 1961, the same year I was hired by Marshall, a twenty-nine-year-old editor at *Boy's Life* magazine, named Herb Sturz, needed a small amount of seed money, amazingly only $500, to explore creating a foundation that would "address the hopes and challenges confronting American youth." It wasn't a large amount but he didn't have it. An associate of University of Chicago President Robert Hutchins suggested Sturz ask for help from Louis Schweitzer, a wealthy businessman and philanthropist. Schweitzer quickly wrote a check thinking of it pretty much as a donation. He'd certainly never see the young man again and when Sturz tried to pay back the unused portion of the loan, he expressed astonishment: According to Sam Roberts' 2009 biography of Sturz (*A Kind of Genius*), "Schweitzer was stunned. No one had ever sought to return money to him before."

He told Sturz, "I assumed you were just coming back to ask for more." A close friendship followed that resulted in a new career for Sturz as director of the organization

Schweitzer funded, ultimately called the Vera Institute for Justice. It would become the most effective engine for criminal justice reform in New York City history.

Schweitzer hired Sturz on the basis of what looked like a tale concocted by a Hollywood screenwriter, even though it was true. A second story about how Vera became a force for social change was as startling. After hearing from a friend that there were 1,000 young New Yorkers held in jail pending a trial simply because they were too poor to find bail money, Schweitzer was appalled. With Sturz's help, the two visited Brooklyn and Manhattan jails to confirm what the eccentric businessman had been told. They "were shocked by the Dickensian squalor: the filth, the stench, the overcrowding and the pervasive sense of despair and degradation among people whom the system assumed were innocent."

The result of the visit, a product of Schweitzer's money and vision and Sturz leadership, was ultimately the Manhattan Bail Project, an innovative way of dealing with pretrial release that would have a national reach. Half a century later Vera would still be trying to change the way criminal courts treated arrested individuals but it had also expanded its work, issuing a series of influential reports on the operation of the courts, setting up the Wildcat Service Company to hire unemployed ex-offenders and ex-addicts in a subsidized transitional work program that aimed to reduce recidivism and welfare dependence, and over the years spinning off numerous startups including the Legal Action Center, organized to fight discrimination against people with histories of addiction, HIV/AIDS, or criminal records, and a messenger service to employ men considered unemployable elsewhere who had criminal records, or a history of drug or alcohol abuse.

The approach of the Manhattan Bail Project was to encourage pretrial release on a promise to return or on bail terms an individual could meet. The method employed was straightforward—provide judges with reliable information about background, employment, and community ties of an accused that strongly suggested a return to face charges. Before the project was made an official part of the court process, judges in Manhattan (as in most places) reflexively set a monetary amount as a condition for release in even minor cases. There was little serious consideration of whether an accused was likely to return—the legal standard governing terms of release under state law—and so the release decision was really left to a bail bondsmen, an agent of a private insurance company, who would determine if an accused had the financial resources to get out of jail.

On its face such a system discriminated against the poor. It also led to unnecessary and costly detention in jail facilities that rarely provided even the modest social or rehabilitative services available in prison. Violent and drug crime is often a public health problem that cannot be successfully treated only by lockups. A bitter saying went around in the 1960s that unfortunately still is true today: "When a man is sentenced to prison and is transferred from a local jail his standard of living immediately rises." Moreover, arrestees who couldn't make bail risked losing jobs and, even worse, research conducted by pioneering bail reform scholar Caleb Foote made clear that a person detained was more likely to be convicted and more harshly sentenced than if released.

By putting information before judges suggesting an accused was a good candidate to return to court, the Bail Project approach thus gave the judges a justification for setting conditions that maximized release. The original focus on the extent to which people are "held in jail simply because they are too poor to pay what it costs to get out," as Nicholas Turner, the current Vera President put it, along with similar initiatives in cities such as Philadelphia and Washington, DC, proved a powerful incentive to 1960s reformers. Robert F. Kennedy, then the US attorney general, became a bail reformer. In 1964, Vera and the Department of Justice held a National Conference to launch "a concerted national effort to deal with the inadequacy and injustice of present administration of the bail system." A year earlier Kennedy had instructed all US attorneys to recommend release on recognizance "in every practical case" but if the cases I handled were any indication the standard was not always implemented in a way that had the transformative effect the attorney general seemingly intended.

My close friend and law school roommate Harry Subin, then a DOJ lawyer, also concluded in a pioneering 1966 study of the District of Columbia Court of General Sessions—the initial entry point to the DC judicial system for criminal cases—that bail was generally set with little information about the accused. Instead it was based primarily on the offense charged as well as on race, age, and even physical appearance. Scant effort was made to release defendants on a promise to return; there was little recognition that even small bail amounts for the poor in misdemeanor cases would lead to detention. The District had just established a bail agency on the New York model; Harry detailed the resources that would be required to assure it would be able to bring facts before those making bail decisions. Research like this influenced mainstreaming of the reform issue at the bail conference. In 1966, President Johnson signed into law the Bail Reform Act, providing for release without financial condition in all federal cases unless the magistrate or judge determined "that defendants will not appear as required." A year later, the National Crime Commission appointed by Johnson called for state legislatures to study and adopt changes to the money bail system; over forty complied by adopting some version of the 1966 Act.

Following the Manhattan Bail Project approach, the underlying purpose of most 1960s bail reform was to defeat knee-jerk bail setting based on the offense initially charged, a charge that was also often subsequently reduced while the bail amount might remain constant. Success of the reforms was real but it was also limited. Rural and other areas without resources to assemble data about community ties continued to resort to reflexive monetary bail setting. The commercial bond industry remained in use. Judges did not always change ingrained habits to follow bail project recommendations. In more serious cases it was obvious that despite the general legal understanding that in non-capital cases an accused had a right to a bail amount that was not excessive to protect the presumption of innocence, setting bail amounts at a level meant to keep defendants in custody was widespread.

The root of the problem was best explained by Patricia Wald, a pioneering woman lawyer whose career took her to the chief judgeship of Court of Appeals for the District of Columbia, often described as the nation's second high-est court. Wald actually began as a bail reformer working with the Kennedy Justice Department's point man, her Yale Law School classmate Dan Fried. She concluded there were two entwined narratives at play; the first emerged from the reform projects, from Kennedy's desire to press an initiative seen favorable to minority communities, and finally from the analysis of criminal justice professionals and consultants. This profile depicted a low-income accused with a range of community ties who would return to court, be unlikely to offend while the case was pending, would probably end up charged with a less serious offense and who might even be acquitted or have the case dismissed.

But those who opposed widespread release on recogni-zance or other nonmonetary alternatives—many prosecu-tors, the bonding companies, and politicians ripening "soft on crime" campaigns—saw a different type of offender: someone with multiple arrests who was a good candidate to recidivate, even commit crimes while on bond, maybe even rob to get funds to pay for a better lawyer; someone who might return to court when required but was also a danger to the community. Of course, both types could be found enmeshed in the criminal justice system.

At the height of the civil rights movement, with greater understanding of and empathy for the plight of black Americans growing as segregation came under fierce attack, many were willing to see an accused as someone who was worthy of individual attention and presumed innocent. The 1966 Act itself emerged from a Congress that was engaged in crafting and programs like Medicare, Medicaid, Head Start for preschool children, Community Action programs for neighborhood betterment, Legal Services for the Poor, and other initiatives. This was an era when even a segregationist like North Carolina Senator (and former judge) Sam Ervin could be a soldier in the bail reform movement. He introduced the legislation that became the 1966 Act, though he took the position that the Eighth Amendment did not confer an absolute right to bail so that the "dangerous" could be detained.

It was certain, however, that more muscular intervention would be required to change ingrained reliance on the criminal charge in the money bail, bondsmen-dominated, system. To make sure that such reform principles became the law across the land required a constitutional decision adopting some version of an Eighth Amendment right to bail by the US Supreme Court but there were both doctrinal and practical problems in even contemplating such a move. Foremost was that the Amendment prohibited "excessive" bail but failed to define what excessive actually meant or even indicate there was a constitutional right to release. The scanty history from the constitutional debates was not revealing.

Caleb Foote believed that despite the "puzzling" language of the Eighth Amendment, bail was "excessive" if it was set at a higher figure than necessary for release. Foote reconstructed the history the Framers likely relied upon as a way of making sense of the bail clause but he admitted that eighteenth-century law was complicated. It was possible from his analysis to conclude that the technicalities were little understood. He did point out that the First Judiciary Act and several pre-1791 state constitutions provided for an absolute right to release in noncapital cases and he also relied on a recent Supreme Court case, *Griffin v. Illinois*, that held a state could not condition a poor person's criminal appeal on the payment of a fee. Foote contended that the bail language of the Eighth Amendment must be given an interpretation in line with *Griffin* by requiring that any detention of an accused who would be released but for financial circumstances violated the Equal Protection Clause of the Fourteenth Amendment.

Anthony Amsterdam was a colleague of Foote's at the University of Pennsylvania and was totally familiar with his work. When the Ford Foundation made its first grant to LDF in 1965 to set up an office bringing cases to end discrimination against the poor, Jack Greenberg assigned me leadership of the criminal law side of the program. Now that the money that could pay for litigation was available, I asked Tony to help find a way to mount a constitutional challenge to depriving the presumed innocent of their liberty just because they were poor. The state, on the other hand, had a weighty interest in assuring that an accused did not avoid returning to court. The Bail Reform Act tried to balance the two considerations by enumerating conditions other than detention that might reduce the possibility of flight, including restricting travel, associations, and residence; finding an organization that would supervise the accused; and setting financial conditions like paying a small percentage of a bail amount that the individual could meet.

Tony and I decided to try to get a case to the Supreme Court that would once and for all clarify the meaning of the Bail Clause. In a way this was a frolic: we were both overwhelmed with other responsibilities including the growing responsibility of our capital case docket that was about to include any inmate white or black who sought our services. But something about the subject—a constitutional provision that was largely ignored and what my law school colleague Ron Goldfarb had called a system of "ransom" in a book by that name—drove us on.

We took the position that when there was a likelihood of appearance and the existence of nonfinancial release conditions, it would be "excessive" for a court to detain an accused by setting a higher bail amount than could be met.

Additionally, we contended that any detention that was due to poverty amounted to punishing someone without trial in a way that prejudiced the opportunity to mount a defense. There was scant Supreme Court precedent on these questions, though a 1952 case upheld the attorney general's authority to detain an alien while deciding about deportation. The Justices there had thrown cold water on an Eighth Amendment right to bail but even the challenge of distinguishing that case from ours paled before the practicalities of getting a bail case to the Court before it became moot.

It usually takes years to move a case through the lower courts to the point where a request for high court review is possible. In short, we needed a client who was in jail because he couldn't make bail but who looked like he would not abscond. And he had to be detained for the duration; the minute the client accepted a plea bargain or was found guilty or had his case dismissed, the controversy would be over. We couldn't, of course, ask a client to stay in jail when he could get out by pleading just so we could get to the Supreme Court. Nor could we control the docket of a trial court; if the judge wanted to go ahead with a trial, we could not stop it. The route that offered even a glimmer of hope was to prepare virtually all court documents needed for the state courts in advance, filling in facts as we learned them, and making constitutionally based motions in all courts up the appellate ladder for accelerated treatment on the ground that every day our client spent in jail was a day that could not be recovered should he ultimately prevail. Then we had to find a litigant willing to let us try this approach.

Tony and I drafted the papers; then we let our plan be known to public defender organizations, and waited.

And waited.

My first call several months later was from a New York legal aid lawyer who represented a man charged with molesting his girlfriend's young child. When I took my draft legal papers to LDF secretaries on duty one evening, they were reluctant even to type them given the description of the crime. This was a wake-up call—if these facts put the two women off, this client wasn't the right person to front what would be a difficult test case. We decided to keep looking.

It took even more months before we got lucky. I was contacted by Harold Rothwax, the legal director of Mobilization for Youth (MFY), the leading antipoverty organization on the City's lower Eastside. A member of his staff was representing an MFY employee who'd been charged with being member of a group of six that had supposedly assaulted a plainclothes officer when he tried to arrest a friend for a drug offense. Bail had been initially set at what he thought was the absurd amount of $25,000. Would we take the case?

Harold would later be my colleague at Columbia Law School for a short time until he was made a Criminal Court judge by Mayor John Lindsay. To the shock of many of his former associates, he was so rough on defendants and on unprepared lawyers that he earned the nickname "The

Prince of Darkness." Hal would often invite me to sit on the bench next to him while he processed arraignment cases at lightning speed, offering leniency for a guilty plea if the defendant immediately agreed along with a pointed threat that the next offer would not be so generous. But the bail case was before his transformation. He insisted there was no way the client, Antonio Gonzalez, could make bail even though he wasn't a flight risk. He was only nineteen, an American citizen, with no criminal record and had lived with his father, brother, and sister in Manhattan for the past two years.

Gonzalez could be the client we were waiting for but we had to explain to him that he would have to stay in jail for a short period even if we could lower the bail amount. He readily agreed because he was willing to help change the law; we moved immediately to fill in the blanks on our previously prepared legal papers with his particulars. On October 20, 1967, we lost a motion to require his release we had filed with the trial court that Gonzalez would come before if he were indicted for a felony.

Three days later—with bail reduced to a $1,000 but still Gonzalez told us beyond his reach—we went before the State's intermediate appellate court, the Appellate Division, and presented our constitutional claims. That court did us the favor of a prompt dismissal and we moved on quickly to the State's highest court, the Court of Appeals in Albany. Martin Spiegel, Gonzalez's trial counsel, argued the case on October 31, 1967. On December 7 we got the decision we expected holding that the bail was reasonable even though it resulted in jailing our client simply because he couldn't pay. The court was unanimous. While the opinion pointed out that the present bail system was "subject to abuse," the judges took the position that changing the system was up to the state legislature.

The case had moved through the court system in record time. Now we had a shot at seeking review in the US Supreme Court, our goal all along. We filed a petition for review promptly and just as promptly it was denied, a moral victory of a sort being that Justice William O. Douglas registered a dissent. He would have heard the case.

Antonio Gonzalez had been willing to remain in jail to help us make a constitutional point that if successful might have affected thousands so I was pleased when the charges against him were ultimately dismissed but he was not our last attempt to force the courts to contend with incarcerating the poor. Later in the year I tried a similar tactic on behalf of a Chicago gang member hit with high bail in a case where there was little proof of other than his membership in a gang. The result was depressing. My motion for release on nonfinancial terms was met with disbelief by one of Mayor Richard Daley's handpicked Chicago judges. He quickly turned hostile, interrogating my client in the hope of showing I had suborned perjury. When that didn't work, he rejected all our arguments out of hand and issued a warning: "You better be careful counselor before you bring any more frivolous motions again to my courtroom."

When I moved on to federal court, the response was just as hostile. One of the few black judges on the federal bench asked me why I had come all the way to Chicago when "we have plenty of good lawyers here." With a rhetorical flourish he asked, "Are you an outside agitator?" I wanted to quip, "Only in Arkansas and Georgia" (where in fact the same charge had been leveled) but kept my mouth shut. He then dismissed the challenge to the money bail system without a written opinion. The case never went any farther.

In 1984, when Congress passed a new bail statute, there was a sense that across the nation practices had reverted to pre-1960 levels. The new law added preventive detention to the mix of options available to the federal courts and it too was imitated by many states. Thus, a bail setter would be told to aim at release on nonfinancial terms but was also authorized to deny release if there was clear and convincing evidence of potential danger to the community. The Supreme Court approved the practice in the 1987 Salerno case. It was a decision that the Court reached out to make, there being a strong argument that Salerno and his codefendant were actually no longer subject to detention.

Preventive detention has surface attractions. In theory it applies without monetary discrimination but instead measures what may be legitimate fears of continued criminal conduct. In practice, however, it has a serious negative impact. Even accepting there are appropriate cases for immediate detention, predictions of danger to the community are often barely credible. They are hunches based on the charged crime. The decision to detain takes place before a judge or magistrate who has limited information and so relies on prosecution representations. To be sure there is a refreshing candor in denying any opportunity for release in certain cases. After all, judges have always found ways to reach the same result even before it was authorized by setting a high bail figure—one that the press would dutifully report—but despite the new law, judges continued to set money bail amounts in cases where release seemed appropriate as well as when they just didn't want to be bothered holding a "dangerousness" hearing. Such a result is the worst of both worlds.

At about this time bail reform began to unravel in most places that did not have Manhattan Project–style agencies in the courthouse. Herb Sturz was still at it. He was a master at working out advantageous relationships with police, prosecutors, and court officials but his influence outside of the City and the District of Columbia was patchy. Reflecting the New York City's long-term relationship with Vera, the pretrial system worked well for many—68% waited for trial at home but national figures told a different story. Despite pockets of reform, release on recognizance was provided for only 23% of all felony defendants. Four out of five releases involved money bail and amounts required almost doubled between 1992 and 2009 as mass incarceration moved into high gear. "Money and ability to pay," one study concluded, "is still the most important factor in determining whether a defendant will be released." Most bail decisions, as a commentator put it, are still driven "largely by guesswork."

Today, there are pockets of real progress and signs of a movement to once more challenge overdetention, but in many places the bail system still looks remarkably like the way it appeared to Louis Schweitzer, Herb Sturz, Robert F. Kennedy, Patricia Wald, and to Tony Amsterdam and me in the 1960s. On any day there are probably half a million pretrial detainees held in the nation's 3,000 or so jails. Increasingly, the jailed are the mentally ill, homeless, deviant, and addicted. Few are offered the social services that might treat or at least stabilize their situation. Instead the police, the courts, and the criminal law constitute not only the front line of the societal response but also in too many cases the only line.

A portion of the detained have been incarcerated for nonpayment of fines, police booking fees, court costs, and probation and parole user fees because they are broke. These practices, aimed at bolstering municipal budgets, hark back to debtor's prisons prohibited in this country well over a hundred years ago. President Obama observed that Ferguson, Missouri, "used its justice system as a cash register, imposing steep fines . . . including $301 for jaywalking and $531 for untended lawns." Nonpayment of these fines could lead to jail, though the Supreme Court has made clear that incarceration can be used to collect criminal justice debt only when a person has the ability to pay but refuses to do so. In a 1970 case brought by LDF lawyer Stanley Bass called *Williams v. Illinois*, the Supreme Court ruled that extending a maximum prison term because a person is too poor to pay violates the Constitution. The following year the Court ruled that lower courts cannot automatically convert a poor person's unpaid fines into a jail sentence. Finally in 1983, it decided that lower courts cannot revoke probation for failure to pay a fine without first inquiring into a person's ability to pay and considering adequate alternatives to imprisonment.

These rulings establish at least a constitutional right to a judicial inquiry into ability to pay. Nevertheless, detention for debt continued unabated. Elected lower court judges fail to make serious inquiries into ability to pay before ordering jail. A public defender in Illinois recently observed a judge who asked people who came before him if they smoked. If the person was a smoker, the judge found willful nonpayment and ordered jail without any further inquiry. This focus on tobacco may be unique but the general practice of which it is a type is not.

The counterattack on reform actually began almost before the ink had dried on the 1966 federal Act. With 1960s civil disturbances crowding the public mind and crime rates beginning to rise, Republican politicians ushered in tough on crime arguments that were enhanced by Richard Nixon's campaign for the presidency. Recent disclosures confirm the racial subtext of the wide variety of Nixon initiatives that focused not on poverty but on crime. "As urban disorder escalated," Elizabeth Hinton wrote in her definitive study of the period, *From the War on Poverty to the War on Crime*, "the overall focus of domestic policy shifted even further from fighting poverty to controlling its violent symptoms." Administration advisors saw the threat of crime as emanating from black youth in urban neighborhoods. Increased federal crime control funds incentivized arrest patterns by the use of primitive computer programs that targeted both neighborhoods and particular individuals. At the same time the government announced the War on Drugs, resulting in bringing to the justice system thousands of first-time offenders and addicts. Thus was born the initial steps toward the incarceration of over two million Americans. In such an environment bail reform withered.

A report by Dan Baum in *Harper's Magazine* quoted John Ehrlichman, who served as domestic policy chief for Nixon, as saying that the drug war was a ploy to undermine Nixon's political opposition. Baum reported that in 1994 when he was writing a book about the politics of drug prohibition, he asked Ehrlichman a series of earnest, wonky questions that were impatiently waved away. "You want to know what this was really all about?" Ehrlichman replied, with the bluntness of a man who after public disgrace and a stretch in prison had little left to protect. "The Nixon campaign in 1968, and the Nixon White House after that, had two enemies: the antiwar left and black people. You understand what I'm saying? We knew we couldn't make it illegal to be either against the war or blacks, but by getting the public to associate the hippies with marijuana and blacks with heroin, and then criminalizing both heavily, we could disrupt those communities. We could arrest their leaders, raid their homes, break up their meetings, and vilify them night after night on the evening news. Did we know we were lying about the drugs? Of course we did."

In 1973, the harshest drug laws in the nation had been passed under New York Governor Nelson Rockefeller, authorizing mandatory minimum jail sentences making it impossible for judges to be lenient in appropriate cases. Under Ronald Reagan's presidency the numbers behind bars for nonviolent drug law offenses continued to climb, increasing from 50,000 in 1980 to over 400,000 by 1997. In the late 1980s, a political hysteria about drugs led to the passage of draconian penalties that rapidly increased the prison population. In such an environment bail reform was a dead letter.

That there was no active community-based constituency supporting reform certainly was important. Some legal changes, say gay marriage, were energized by committed activists who coordinated efforts even if they didn't always agree on tactics. When gay marriage cases were framed by lawyers, litigants were chosen who looked stable and respectable. This is not an easily come by option in the bail reform world. When LDF brought the Gonzalez case in the 1960s, it was not part of litigation campaign but a lonely lawsuit,

reflecting that it was more an exercise in constitutionalism than a source of large-scale community activism. I
was keenly aware of this limitation built into the case but,
blinded by the hope that the Warren Court's reformist zeal
would carry the day, argued we should proceed anyway.
Gonzalez soon disappeared from the radar; it evoked no
demonstrations of outrage.

Bail reformers have a well-considered set of arguments
but often little support outside of the academy and from
Vera, ACLU, and LDF-type organizations. In contrast, when
arguing to establish and preserve the right to bear arms, the
National Rifle Association boasts a large bankroll, a committed membership, and ballot box suasion. While such
factors were all in play and operated in a society thought to
be overly punitive, the most important reason for the demise
of bail reform was the difficulty of finding an acceptable
practical solution to the conundrum of detention or release.
There are accused who are overwhelmingly likely to show
up in court. Holding them in detention because they are
too poor not only is bad policy but also requires the expen-
diture of scarce resources. Just as certainly there are others
who can find enough money to purchase a bail bond; their
release on such terms only serves to enrich insurance companies. Then there is the group of accused who are charged
with more serious offenses. Regardless of whether they are
detained to protect the community or for likelihood of
flight, public arousal will quickly follow news of a revolving

door—that shortly after arrest for a serious felony an individual would merely walk free out of the courtroom.

Even a committed reformer is likely to feel tremors of uncertainty if someone charged with a serious crime returns to their neighborhood soon after being apprehended. In short, there are accused who are viewed either sympathetically or indifferently as well as those who understandably provoke the fear of further criminal activity. Thus, the selection process is politically risky for the bail setter. Judges and prosecutors who go along with broadened release policies are vulnerable to variations of the Willie Horton syndrome should a crime be committed by a person whose release was agreed to. No wonder they find detention an attractive option. Resistance to immediate release, moreover, cannot be understood without taking account of the relationship of incarceration to plea bargaining. While bail is usually described as pretrial release, it is more accurately preplea release; it operates as an incentive to plead guilty. Days in jail are lost forever. People who plead get out of jail faster than those who cannot make bail and claim they aren't guilty.

When concrete practical barriers exist to resolution of a complex social problem, one where fear of crime is as important as the actual rate of crime, one is reminded that the presumption of innocence is a legal exhortation, not an empirical fact. What the public sees in a case that has been reported in the media is more often than not someone who may stimulate fear and who may very well be guilty. This reality clashes with the more benign narrative of a different set of accused described by Judge Wald. As a result, serious and significant changes have eluded fearful officials.

Nevertheless, after decades of escalating incarceration and attendant costs, concern over the failures and costs of criminal justice system have surfaced in efforts to mitigate mass incarceration, solitary confinement, and mandatory minimum sentencing. A grassroots movement has led to the creation of charitable bail funds in aid of certain accused in several communities. Disillusionment with the drug wars and prodding from a Democratic Administration also has led to the release of offenders designated nonviolent. These developments have contributed to moves to moderate the money bail system. In 2011 Attorney General Eric Holder allied the Obama Administration with Robert Kennedy's efforts in the 1960s. Holder was blunt, "Across the country, nearly two thirds of all inmates who crowd our county jails—at an annual cost of roughly nine billion taxpayer dollars—are defendants awaiting trial. . . . Almost all of these individuals could be released and supervised in their communities." The following year, a report by the Justice Policy Institute concluded that "money bail is a failed policy that does not protect public safety, discriminates against those without financial means, and causes huge costs to taxpayers and those who are unnecessarily jailed while awaiting their day in court." Then in 2015 the DOJ filed papers in a court case of a Georgia man who was jailed for six nights on a misdemeanor charge of being a pedestrian under the influence because he could not afford $160 bail. The Department basically adopted the reasoning of the long-forgotten Gonzalez argument: "Incarcerating individuals solely because of their inability to pay for their release, whether through the payment of fines, fees, or a cash bond, violates the Equal Protection Clause of the Fourteenth Amendment."

Rising detention rates and stressed budgets have recently brought these issues wider attention—New Jersey and several other states have largely abandoned the money bail system—but "their basic contours haven't changed for decades." The glacial rate of change led Professor Samuel R. Wiseman—writing in the *Yale Law Journal*—to propose a right to be monitored, arguing that "In a world in which scientists can monitor and recapture wolves, snakes and even manatees," electronic monitoring can ensure presence at trial and significantly reduce jail populations.

Indeed, as the 2016 election turned the country to the right, technology may be the only hope for resolving the tension between costly overdetention and fears of releasing the accused. In his essay Wiseman lays out potentially available methods of electronic monitoring that could "sharply reduce" the need for detention of the nondangerous, by using GPS satellite tracking technology or voice recognition to locate those who would otherwise be jailed.

With such proposals in the offing, the bonding industry has mobilized to lobby against any change that undermines its business. Despite studies indicating that 18–25% of defendants released on surety bonds fail to appear at least once, commercial interests can be expected to exercise significant political clout. Wiseman sees little hope that state legislatures will act "for the benefit of the poor and unpopular against the will of the commercial bail industry" but pins his hopes on the courts finding that detention of supposed flight risks will be successfully challenged as "excessive" when "less expensive, less burdensome and judicially administrable" alternatives are available that reduce flight risk. The main obstacle he identifies to widespread adoption of the monitoring right he proposes is concern for privacy but at least in the case of those who would otherwise be detained release with monitoring can hardly be compared in intrusiveness to jailhouse surveillance.

In 2015, New York State's Chief Judge Jonathan Lippmann proposed a pilot program that would significantly limit the use of money bail by a package of changes that included allowing judges to use electronic supervision through bracelets linked to smartphones as an alternative to cash bail. At first, it may seem ironic that after years of debate, pilot projects, official recommendations for change, legislative debates, a few test cases, fearmongering, and many thousands of contested bail decisions, true reform may be made possible only by a technological fix but such a turn of events fits the electronic, automated world that has intruded even in the relatively primitive universe of the criminal justice system. Banks of computers, video feeds, and a monitoring staff may raise many touchy policy questions but their allure is obvious. Not the least of attractions is technology's capacity to convince society that it has found a practical solution that avoids resolving intractable moral dilemmas.

Tales of Reform—Success

Hubert Eaton was trim and intense. A champion tennis player who won tournaments sponsored by the American Tennis Association at a time when the American *Lawn* Tennis Association was for whites only, he moved with the grace of an athlete well into middle age. As a young man he left the South to study at the University of Michigan Medical School, and then returned to North Carolina, to practice medicine in the port city of Wilmington, until his death in 1991. Working with his friend and tennis buddy, Dr. Robert Johnson of Lynchburg, Virginia, Eaton and his wife took in Althea Gibson, then a troubled Harlem teenager, and nurtured both the education and the athleticism of the first black woman to win the Wimbledon tournament. In Johnson's garish basement den, while we prepared for a court challenge, the two doctors poured glasses of Wild Turkey and took deserved credit for also mentoring tennis great Arthur Ashe.

Dr. Eaton brought his competitiveness from tennis courts to the law courts. Despite initial rejections, he facilitated the ultimate integration of Wilmington's public schools, library, and municipal golf course. He ran for local public offices, knowing he would lose, to stimulate voter registration in the black community and to remind those in power he wasn't going away. In 1958, Jack Greenberg represented him and two African American colleagues in an unsuccessful attempt to reverse the refusal of Wilmington's James Walker Hospital to grant them staff admitting privileges. The case turned on whether the government's involvement in the hospital was sufficient to bring the federal Constitution's antidiscrimination provisions into play. James Walker's nineteenth-century will provided that his executors give the building over to the City to be used as a hospital for the sick and afflicted but while Wilmington had appropriated funds for the Hospital, it turned the facility over to a non-profit, independent board as early as 1901.

Eaton and his colleagues did not contend, as the Court of Appeals in Richmond put it "that the exclusion of qualified physicians solely because of their race from an institution devoted to the care of the sick is indefensible . . . but rather that the hospital was still closely intertwined with government." The court finally ruled that the connections were too tenuous to permit it to regulate the policies of a private board of managers.

In 1961, however, the law looked different. The US Supreme Court ruled that a black man had been wrongly denied service at a Wilmington, Delaware, coffee shop located in a government-owned parking garage. The coffee shop "constituted a physically and financially integral and, indeed, indispensable part of the State's . . . plan to operate its project as a self-sustaining unit." The Parking Authority had "made itself a party to the refusal of service." constituting a violation of the Equal Protection Clause.

The following year I would be the responsible attorney on two cases dealing with hospitals that excluded or segregated blacks. One was to consider bringing another suit on behalf of Dr. Eaton against the Walker Hospital claiming that the Delaware case had changed the rules. The other was a much broader attack on segregation in Southern medical facilities. It would challenge one of the few federal statutes that explicitly sanctioned "separate but equal" facilities, the Hill–Burton Act of 1946 which had appropriated millions of dollars for construction and renovation of the nation's hospitals. I still felt I was just learning the rudiments of my craft but when Greenberg told me these were my cases I decided to drown fears of failure by devouring everything I could about the field.

A ruling that federal regulations and money were enough to bring the Constitution into play would challenge the entrenched practices of hundreds of Southern medical facilities that excluded African Americans from the most modern and sophisticated medical treatment in their communities, likely a contributing factor to starkly different mortality outcomes for whites and blacks. Lister Hill, cosponsor of the law, a senator from Alabama, had written into the statute a proviso that resulted in legalizing exclusion of Negro doctors and patients in over 90% of Southern medical facilities.

Until mid-twentieth century when black doctors affiliated with the National Medical Society and LDF lawyers began to call attention to a system where the best hospitals and most highly trained physicians were reserved for whites, the health discrimination story got little attention. Direct action campaigns tended to skip medical facilities, though there were exceptions like my client school teacher Gloria Rackley who challenged emergency room segregation at an Orangeburg, South Carolina, hospital and was fired in retaliation for her activism. Earlier in 1963, three black nurses at Dixie Hospital in Hampton, Virginia, decided to have lunch in the hospital's spacious white-only cafeteria. The room, which looked out on Chesapeake Bay, was built with federal money. Black employees had to take their food to an empty classroom. The women were fired; it took three years before I was able to get a federal court order granting them back pay and reinstatement.

A 1959 survey concluded that 83% of Northern medical facilities took patients regardless of race compared to 6% of Southern Hospitals. Stories of exclusion after being denied treatment despite critical need for care—the most famous, though incorrect factually, involved the deaths of Blues singer Bessie Smith and pioneer blood researcher Charles Drew, father of my LDF colleague Sylvia Drew—were commonly passed between members of the Southern Negro community. The persistence of these beliefs was powerful evidence of a general anxiety of what might happen to any black needing medical attention.

The situation was similar for doctors and dentists who sought to admit their patients to hospital without turning them over to white doctors who were total strangers to the patient. Indeed, at the time the doctors in charge of American hospitals, especially those that were nonprofit, tax exempt, and managed by private boards of directors, would commonly deny admitting privileges to those whose religion, ethnicity, medical specialty, or even personality they found wanting. Resistance to change was as intense in the medical world as elsewhere. The North Carolina and Georgia dental societies, for example, had been designated by their states as the entities that selected state boards charged with regulating the profession. Both societies were all white as were the state regulators they selected and both also claimed they were totally private. LDF successfully sued them, forcing their integration.

The Hill–Burton case was decided first and it was a stunner. A dentist named George Simkins was the Greensboro, North Carolina, version of Hubert Eaton. He started his efforts by organizing a "drive in" gathering of a group of Negro golfers who suddenly arrived to tee off at the white-only municipal course. They were promptly arrested. A similar move led to the closing of the City swimming pool rather than open it to blacks.

Greensboro had three hospitals; Wesley Long was all white; Moses Cone, known as the "Jewish Hospital," would admit a black patient if it had space and the condition in question could not be treated elsewhere; Richardson was the Negro Hospital, the place where black doctors and dentists had admitting privileges. It was overcrowded and short on the treatment options available at the white hospitals. One day a Simkins patient suffering from a serious jaw condition could not receive needed treatment at Richardson and was denied admission to Cone. The dentist was outraged; he called Jack Greenberg, insisting something had to be done. He promised to gather a group of doctors, dentists, and patients for a lawsuit if one could be brought. Greenberg's response was to order me to North Carolina to meet Simkins and take a look at the three hospitals.

A strategy quickly emerged. First, doctors and dentists filed applications drafted with the help of Durham lawyer Conrad Pearson for staff privileges at Long and Cone hospitals, which were, of course, denied. One of the seven physicians was a prominent surgeon, Alvin Blount, who had served in an army MASH unit in the Korean War. Two patients were included who sought treatment where they could get "the most complete medical equipment and the best facilities available in the Greensboro area" and be treated by their personal physicians. They were rejected. As with Hubert Eaton's case, the key was establishing that hospitals receiving federal money were shaped by government policies. While the United States had appropriated $1,269,950 to the Cone Hospital (15% of two construction projects) and $1,948,800 to the Long Hospital (50% of three projects), it was necessary to demonstrate more than a payment of funds. Study of the approved construction proposals revealed how the development plans of the hospital closely fit Hill–Burton requirements for creation of a statewide system of hospitals by inducing the states "to undertake the supervision of the construction and maintenance of adequate hospital facilities."

Because the Simkins case involved a constitutional challenge to a federal statute, the Department of Justice was presented with an opportunity to enter the case. Usually the government will defend a federal law that has been attacked but in the United States, Robert Kennedy's DOJ—shifting to stronger support of the civil rights movement—told the court the "separate but equal" language of the Hill–Burton Act was no longer valid. The hospitals must stop discriminating. On joining the program North Carolina, in effect, assumed as a state function the obligation of planning for adequate hospital care. It didn't matter that the hospitals chosen would otherwise be nominally private if their actual operations were closely intertwined with government. Through January 31, 1963, a total of 350 Hill–Burton projects had been approved by North Carolina, involving 10,210 inpatient beds and 106 health units. The total cost of the projects was over $180 million, 40% of which was federal money. In short, as the Court of Appeals would put it: "Participation in the Hill–Burton program subjects hospitals to an elaborate and intricate pattern of governmental regulations."

The Greensboro hospitals tried to use the first Eaton case to defend themselves but Chief Judge Simon Sobeloff would have none of it. He concluded, "The previous decision didn't consider . . . that the 'private' hospital is fulfilling the function of the state." Later the same court would decide that new evidence of government involvement would also force the Walker facility in Wilmington to abide by the Fourteenth Amendment even though it had never taken Hill–Burton money. Following this decision, the court took an even more dramatic step toward ending hospital discrimination by ruling a Newport News, Virginia, hospital had wrongly barred two black doctors who had specialized training on the basis of their race. This was the first decision that had delved into the qualifications of the doctors—here supported by expert testimony based on thorough investigation of credentials from two nationally prominent physicians—surgeon Samuel Standard and pediatrician Allan Macy Butler—to find them fully qualified for staff membership. Both doctors refused payment for the time they had spent on the case when I offered it to them, a phenomenon that happened often in the 1960s when LDF sought the expert advice of academics and professionals.

Segregation and discrimination by Southern medical facilities was now dead legally but, much like the response to public school desegregation, Jim Crow practices remained the same.

It would, in fact, take a massive effort to overcome resistance and bring about lasting change—requiring the passage by Congress of two major pieces of legislation followed by the willingness of a previous complacent federal bureaucracy to change its ways, replacing apathy with vigorous enforcement of the new laws. Closely modeled on the Judge Soboloff's opinion in the Simkins case, Title VI was added to the Civil Rights Act of 1964 prohibiting discrimination on the part of recipients of federal funds. Responsibility for enforcement was given to the Office of Civil Rights (OCR) at the Department then called Health, Education, and Welfare (HEW). While the responsibilities of OCR were suddenly enlarged, the staff remained at a number that made serious enforcement impossible. At first, all OCR could do was to assume compliance by accepting the nondiscrimination assurances contained in forms that were returned by the hospitals.

At LDF, we soon realized that the hospitals had simply adopted the strategy of most Southern school boards: take the position that you aren't discriminating, relying on the claim that no one has come forward insisting on different treatment. Then sit on your hands and wait. Perhaps you won't be sued, and if you are successfully sued, well then you can tell the local white community the evil government in Washington made you integrate. When it became clear that this was the common response of those running white hospitals, we mobilized LDF's network of Southern lawyers, asking each of them if the hospitals in their communities had fully integrated. So little progress was reported that we soon netted 300 complaints that when filed first elicited anger from our potential allies at OCR. They responded that they only had a small staff with little capacity to do field investigations. They were overwhelmed.

OCR was also stymied by a second consideration. The only sanction that was available under Title VI for a stubbornly noncompliant hospital was a shut off of federal funds. The bureaucrats knew that were they to invoke such a remedy in any but the most egregious case, members of Congress, some of whom could scuttle the Department budget, would go ballistic. Cutting off funds for medical treatment would appear so serious that it was not an effective threat. We continued to bring as much pressure as we could on OCR but the challenge was real and seemed intractable. It was theoretically possible to sue individual hospitals but hauling into court every discriminating medical facility was impractical. But then something unexpected happened. A process of change began from a push for action not from a line employee but from a consultant who had come to the Department with a strong recommendation from Robert Kennedy. Her name was Sherry Arnstein and she had a fancy title—special assistant to the assistant secretary of the Department of HEW—but in reality she was a gadfly who because she looked like RFK's emissary and wasn't part of the career bureaucracy could propose an aggressive strategy to desegregate the nation's hospitals.

Arnstein's successful intervention was aided by a new law that went into effect in July 1966—Medicare required hospitals to be approved for treating patients without regard to race before they could gather in federal dollars. Goaded by Arnstein from within HEW and LDF and the National Medical Association president John Holliman from the outside, John Gardner who became HEW Secretary in 1965 now had the weapons he needed to enforce Title VI. He arranged the transfer of 1,000 civil servants and the hiring of additional temporary employees to inspect and monitor compliance. As a study by David Barton Smith concludes, "No hospital would be cleared if there were any distinctions by race . . . [soon] 97% of the acute hospital beds in the United States were compliant with Title VI and the Medicare program." One result of the change was especially gratifying—racial differences in infant mortality and life expectancy narrowed in the twenty years after implementation. Smith concluded, "The Medicare program, at least in how it was implemented, was the gift of the civil rights movement." In short, none of this would have been possible without the courage and determination of doctors like Simkins and his colleagues who were willing to speak out and put themselves on the line publicly to advance the initial litigation.

In academia there has always been a dispute over how social progress comes about, sometimes focusing on the utility or disutility of litigation as opposed to other methods like legislation or intensive media campaigns. As these two tales of reform, bail reform and hospital integration, illustrate such generalizations tell only a small part of the story. The bail case was a lawsuit without a constituency to back it up and amplify its message. There was no social movement pressing the courts, only a limited if successful regional reform movement, an uncertain contribution from a federal legislative enactment, and an unappealing class of putative beneficiaries. Hospital patients and their doctors were a very different group of potential beneficiaries. The Medicare–Medicaid programs and Civil Rights Act were huge national commitments. Desegregating the hospitals was characterized by persistent lobbying from organized players. Prompt success was possible because most of the institutions in question valued receiving the pot of money promised by Medicare admission more than resisting integration. Once a critical mass opted for compliance, the holdouts were under huge competitive pressure to join in.

Only a nuanced approach to case studies like bail reform and hospital integration can serve to evaluate credibly the role of litigation in effecting social change. An example of how not to conduct such an inquiry is Gerard Rosenberg's 1991 book *The Hollow Hope*, which argued that litigating school segregation accomplished little and, more generally, that lawsuits don't usually produce liberal reform. I've critiqued Rosenberg's thesis at length elsewhere[1]: my position

---

1. *The Making of a Civil Rights Lawyer*, pp. 170–91 (2006).

is that while *Brown v. Board of Education* itself never produced widespread public school integration, it brought about enormous changes in status, law, and consciousness that were radically different than existed before—the character of American life changed because of the decision. Litigation, of course, is but one tactic among many. In some situations it is necessary because the rights or policies involved have not been recognized by a political majority; in others the value of litigation depends on how it is positioned amidst a flow of other tactical moves, most especially engagement with key community stakeholders; in still others it fails to be of much consequence. There are, in fact, many examples that suggest how variable and situational approaches to social change must be. Gay marriage was a concept reviled, prohibited by state law in a majority of US jurisdictions, and sought by a maligned group, yet public opinion and ultimately court decisions accepted it. The 1970s claims of discrimination against welfare recipients on the other hand were turned away by the courts despite an arguably solid grounding in precedent, plaintiffs living below the poverty line, and numerous backers in the nonprofit community. But they ultimately involved a politically unpalatable reallocation of income and a lack of effective sympathy for those on welfare.

The successful use of the antidiscrimination principles set out in Title VI of the 1964 Act to end segregation in medical facilities has not often been repeated. In 2001, the

Supreme Court ended the opportunity of private citizens to enforce Title VI, restricting suits to those who can prove intentional discrimination and rejecting disparate impact proof. Otherwise, enforcement is up to government agencies that are not always able or willing to act with vigor. When, for example, poor and minority communities are faced with discriminatory location of potentially polluting facilities, hazardous waste and other toxic landfills, only a few employees at the Environment Protection Agency are tasked with potential enforcement of Title VI principles; even before the Agency's powers were drastically limited by the Trump Administration it has been characterized by an investigatory report as lacking the "skills and expertise necessary" to do the job.

The powers and practices of our courts have here also been dramatically narrowed, limiting the place for law reform and impact litigation to advance any change agenda laid out by progressives. Even when access to the courts is assured, however, success of these efforts is likely to be incremental, uneven, and contingent on the strength of attendant social movements. Twenty-first-century problems like dumping environmental hazards on minority communities do not feature the animus that characterized much of the 1960s civil rights movement. They are generally of systemic origin, meaning that individualized intentionality requirements are obstacles to the mobilization of forces necessary to press for real reform. Of course, so are budgetary restraints and bureaucratic intransigence both of which hark back to political decisions that are visible to interested constituencies but rarely to the general public. With a country deeply divided over the impact of racism, it may take still another civil rights movement to expose the multiple ways in which the deprived are left to stay that way.

The Difference between Rights and Remedies

As the Hill–Burton litigation demonstrated even winning big in court doesn't always translate into success on the ground. To make civil rights laws and court decisions practically effective often takes years of enforcement and compliance work. Sometimes the obstacles are insurmountable. I learned this lesson early on when a victory I savored was snatched away at the last moment.

On May 20, 1964, on behalf of my clients—James Farmer, the leader of the Congress of Racial Equality (CORE) and other civil rights activists—I sent a telegram to Robert Moses in his role as president of the 1964 New York World's Fair. I requested permission for CORE, which had come to prominence by initiating the 1961 Freedom Rides, and the NAACP to conduct peaceful picketing in public areas of the Fair near the Florida and Louisiana pavilions as well as permission "for a reasonable number of persons to distribute handbills relative to racial discrimination." Lawyers send messages like this to likely adversaries to show courts that before a suit is brought they have previously sought what they claim they are rightfully due. I did not expect a reply from Mr. Moses and I was not disappointed.

Under a threatened massive auto "stall in" on the highways approaching the Flushing Meadows-Corona Park site in the borough of Queens, the Fair had opened four weeks earlier. Despite a bow to higher cultural tastes owing to the presence of Michelangelo's Pieta surprisingly lent by the Vatican and paintings by El Greco, Goya, Velazquez, and Picasso, the Fair was dominated by corporate marketing of a technologically rich, prosperous future. Spreading out from its signature Unisphere—a 140 foot high, 700,000 pound steel globe, one of the few Fair structures that still exist—American business and its belief in human progress was on display. There was a Pool of Industry, a Hall of Science, and a Carousel of Progress. Ford used the Fair to introduce one of its most popular cars, the Mustang; the RCA Company showed the public color television; in "Futurama II," General Motors created a fantasy world where the moon was colonized, and traffic-free highways swiftly sped commerce and commuters to blemish-free urban centers. Seated in rolling chairs, Fair goers were told by GM that they would be able to vacation under the sea in the "Hotel Atlantis" or travel in comfort on roads through previously untamed jungles that had been cleared by giant automated machines. Nations would cooperate through the "common language of science" to reap the rewards of mining the world's natural resources. Seawater would be converted to drinking water "fresh as rain."

Almost as popular as Futurama, Walt Disney created a looming, mechanical Abraham Lincoln for the Illinois pavilion. Robotic Abe spouted sanitized bromides about liberty but failed to mention slavery. It was estimated that fifty million visited the Fair before it closed in 1965 but by footing the bill for infrastructure and highways the city and state lost money anyway. According to the *New York Times*, the Fair was a "financial failure," losing seventeen million the first year alone.

Today many know how Robert Moses, working from a collection of state- and city-appointed official positions, transformed the New York metropolitan area with major highways, housing projects, bridges, playgrounds, beaches, and parks. The story of the autocratic methods he used was told unforgettably in Robert Caro's *The Power Broker*. Moses bullied his way through opposition, completing major construction projects, displacing mostly low-income residents, easily acquiring public funding, and demonstrating intractable hostility to interference from community groups until late in the 1960s when key politicians grew tired of him and he was defeated by a grassroots movement spearheaded by reformer-journalist-self-taught urbanist Jane Jacobs.

Moses' talents and dispositions were all on display in the creation of the Fair. But three weeks before the April opening, with hundreds of thousands of visitors expected, the Brooklyn and Bronx chapters of CORE embraced an idea raised the year before by journalist Louis Lomax— protest the indifference of the city and state establishment to ghetto housing and poor-quality schools, as well as the failure of the Fair to hire decent numbers of minorities, by staging a giant "stall in" on the roads leading to the site. "While millions of dollars are being spent on the World's Fair, thousands of black and Puerto Rican people are suffering." Hundreds of cars would simply stop on the highways and access roads, crowded under normal conditions, causing a massive traffic jam. As a CORE handbill put it, Moses was running a "Symbol of American Hypocrisy."

According to Joseph Tirella's history of the Fair— *Tomorrow-Land*—"The backlash began immediately. The first to react was James Farmer, Core's national chairman, who felt his leadership was under attack. He called the notion promoted by the local branches a 'harebrained idea.'" Opposition from Farmer and NAACP executive director Roy Wilkins, who also became my client, would be followed by a chorus of public officials—the mayor (Robert F. Wagner), the chief of police (Michael J. Murphy), the governor (Nelson Rockefeller)—and the media at large. President Lyndon Johnson due to speak at the opening ceremony worried the disturbance would empower the enemies of integration; Martin Luther King Jr. thought the proposed blockage was poor tactics but did not go public with his opposition. Threats to impound cars and rescind driver's licenses abounded. In the end the "stall in" never happened but the threat was effective, cutting expected opening-day attendance by two-thirds. Protesters shouted "Jim Crow Must Go" at the President and assembled dignitaries; 299 were arrested but by day 2 the Fair would be in normal mode, handling throngs of visitors well into the next year.

National CORE had vigorously opposed the plan to block traffic because Farmer saw little gain in angering commuters and Fairgoers but he and his staff felt something had to be done to keep the public aware of the indifference of Fair sponsors to the plight of minorities. Also of great importance to him was fighting the attacks from youthful black power adherents, plainly influenced by the nationalism of Malcolm X, claiming that while he was committed to integration he was insufficiently active in challenging the establishment on issues that counted.

Farmer devised two tactics to keep the heat on the Fair and bolster his position. The first was the opening-day protest demonstration. The second led him to ask our help at LDF. Jack Greenberg was skeptical that the case would accomplish much but his philosophy of leadership involved giving discretion to staff members who were highly motivated and willing to do the scut work that is commonly involved in even the most majestic of lawsuits. To say I was in favor of suing Robert Moses, who I thought was the defiler of New York City neighborhoods, was an understatement. I relished the opportunity. Even more so because a suave, experienced New York attorney, Howard Squadron, had been brought in to help by CORE'S general counsel, Carl Rachlin.

We quickly filed a civil rights suit in federal court seeking an order requiring the Fair to permit CORE and NAACP members to "disseminate handbills in a peaceful and orderly manner" and engage in peaceful picketing. After alleging that the Fair was a public body that couldn't have existed without governmental involvement and support, we urged the court to protect potential demonstrators' First Amendment rights to speech and assembly. A small army of expensively suited lawyers representing Moses and the Fair Corporation filed into the Foley Square federal courthouse to disagree. They claimed that the Fair was a private entity not subject to the Constitution and, second, that picketing and leafleting would be dangerous and disruptive of the Fair's activities.

I was elated when by chance the judge assigned to the case was Harold "Ace" Tyler who, though a Manhattan business lawyer, had served as the attorney in charge of the civil rights division of the Department of Justice during the Eisenhower Administration. It was 1964 and there were few federal trial judges with a civil rights background so we felt we were very lucky. Despite being a Republican, he had even been nominated for the judgeship by President Kennedy. Tyler was quick to find that Moses' nongovernmental activity argument fell apart of its own weight. New York City had leased the grounds to the Fair, spending twenty-four million on construction of the Fairgrounds. Moses had promised to pay the City all its "net revenues," foolishly estimated at the time at fifty million. Investments had also come from the State of New York and the federal government, both of which declared the Fair Corporation a tax-exempt educational corporation. Even the security detail hired by the Fair from the Pinkerton Company was given a governmental role: its members were by New York State statute treated as "peace officers under the law." Citing the case I had handled against the hospitals in Greensboro that had received federal construction money, Tyler found that the Fair Corporation was so infused with public involvement that it was like government itself—subject to the constitutional restrictions abridging free expression.

But when it came to the substance of the dispute, Tyler gave each side half a loaf. As to picketing he ruled that crowd density at the Fair would be "not inconsiderable" with several hundred thousand daily visitors expected plus 30,000 workers on site. He thought picketing was not a pure First Amendment right and could be abridged at the Fair due to the crowds, the number of restricted areas and spaces, the "coercive" aspect of picketing, as well as "the convenience and enjoyment of visitors who pay admission." Our half of the loaf permitted distribution of handbills, "normally given a higher position in the hierarchy of constitutionally protected activities than has the right to picket." As long as CORE and the NAACP did so "quietly and peacefully," they could disseminate informational literature and handbills.

As a final comment Judge Tyler told the Fair its total ban on expressive activities was vague and arbitrary and should be redrafted but he gave little guidance over what should replace it, concluding with language that told the Fair that despite having to change a flawed regulation it still did not have to "to permit all kinds of demonstrations."

Of course, I was disappointed about the picketing, though I had to recognize that given the law at that time the Judge was on firm ground in treating picketing differently than handing out leaflets. Still the picketing issue for me was whether it could be managed on the huge Fair site in an orderly and nonthreatening manner, not its abstract nature. Judge Tyler could have drafted an order protecting the right to picket by stressing that it was conditional, permitting it only under strictly regulated conditions. But at least we had a right to distribute leaflets and handbills. A victory that might allow James Farmer to show he had gotten a foothold in the Fair to reach visitors with a civil rights message for the duration as well as potentially helping him deal with the local affiliates that had promoted the "stall in."

Or would it? When it came to putting the terms of the court order on paper, the Judge wouldn't sign off to protect the right to leaflet unless CORE and the NAACP posted a security bond to indemnify the Fair should the leaflet distribution cause it property damage. Civil rights organizations, shoestring operations at the best of times, were in 1964 financially stressed having had to come up with huge amounts of bail money to keep antisegregation protesters out of Southern jails. They could not meet the cost of a hefty premium for what in reality would be a somewhat unusual insurance policy, especially when it was justifiably feared that the Fair with 1,000 police on hand could ascribe abuses to even peaceful protesters.

The World's Fair, in contrast, had been bankrolled by government and large corporations to the tune of millions. What imagined damage distributing handbills or leaflets the Judge thought might be caused was never specified. The bond requirement was certainly authorized by law—when a judge issues a preliminary injunction as would have been the case—but what function it would play in a situation like this other than to burden the important constitutional rights that had just been acknowledged was hard to fathom. Sadly, both civil rights organizations decided they could not afford the bond; as a result, Judge Tyler never signed an order enforcing the free speech rights he had found the Fair denied. In the end the case of *Farmer v. Moses* stood as both a reminder of the risks of depending on litigation to vindicate rights *in fact* and the capacity of the law to hide from ordinary citizens the truism that rights were only as meaningful as their practical realization—the remedies and monetary resources that went with them.

My Hour with Lenny

In their effort to deny admission to an African American, the all-white University of Mississippi claimed that James Meredith was a "troublemaker." On appeal in 1962 from the University's rejection of his application, Judge John Minor Wisdom brushed aside the argument, commenting that "Meredith's record shows just about the type of Negro who might be expected to try to crack the racial barrier at the University of Mississippi: a man with a mission and with a nervous stomach."

Sometimes it just takes a "troublemaker" to upend the struts that keep the status quo in place. One such was Lenny Bruce whose challenge to obscenity laws did him no good but fatally exposed the prosecution of public performers to ridicule.

"Law books, legal documents from his earlier trials, drug paraphernalia and spools of unwound and twisted audio tape were heaped up and strewn about, virtually filling every square inch of space." So *The Trials of Lenny Bruce*, the authoritative version of the doomed comedian's legal life and death by Ronald K. L. Collins and David M. Skover, describes what one of his lawyers, Martin Garbus, saw when he visited his client's room at Greenwich Village's Marlton Hotel. Several months later, I found the scene little changed except for the presence of a comely blonde who primly held a steno book and number two pencil at the ready to record my words of wisdom. In the hour I spent with Bruce she said not a word.

What had brought me to a narrow room in this down-on-its-luck hotel on a Manhattan street known more as a tourist entry point to the Village than for a good night's sleep was a phone call from Albert Goldman, a Columbia professor and Bruce's confidant, friend, and eventual biographer.

"Lenny has been convicted of an obscene performance, as you probably know, for his act at the Café Au Go Go," Goldman explained.

"He is up for sentencing but he has dismissed his lawyers and wants to represent himself. He needs someone to coach him. I want to make sure that he doesn't hurt himself. You've been recommended."

"Wasn't he represented by Ephraim London and his assistant Marty Garbus?" I asked. "London is the most highly regarded anti-obscenity lawyer in the country and Garbus is young but hot."

"Lenny can't communicate with London. Their relationship is poisonous. Anyway Lenny wants to do his act for the judges before they sentence him and London won't have it."

"Do his act. What does that mean?"

"Look, he is going to be sentenced because of what he said while performing at the Club. He thinks he can show the judges that there is nothing prurient about his performance. All the judges know is what came from notes taken by some cops and a hard to hear tape recording."

"Well, I like Lenny. My wife and I saw his act at Fillmore East on Second Avenue. He was hilarious. What I liked most was the way he would say things people wouldn't easily acknowledge doing or thinking."

"Yeah, that's Lenny. What did he say?"

"He walked out on the stage half an hour late, complained about suffering from pleurisy. He looked awful—though it was hard to see him clearly through the weed smoke. Then apropos of nothing, he said, 'You know every guy in this place has a secret.' Then a big theatrical pause. 'He has pissed in a sink, and never admitted it.' The place broke up. I mean it was really packed; the crowd was totally with him."

"Well, he now needs friendly advice."

"I can't represent him. There's no race issue so he isn't a Legal Defense Fund case but even if there was one I have a full docket. I have a group of capital cases. We're in the middle of trying to end segregation in Southern hospitals. We're trying to influence the language used in the Civil Rights Act. I could go on."

"No, no, you don't have to represent him. That's not necessary. Just prep him; talk him for an hour; take him through what a sentencing hearing is like. Be an informal advisor. I'll arrange it. He's at the Marlton on Eighth Street. He'll be happy to see you. How about it?"

"I don't know."

"Look, he has run out of options. All these big lawyer names buzzing around, but he's broke. Just talk to him."

I was about to tell Goldman again I'd think about it but I realized that was just game playing. I knew what I wanted to do. "Ok, Ok," I said, "set it up." The lure of the celebrity, and stepping in even for a moment where the big name in the field had failed, was more than I could resist. It helped that I was protected from further involvement because it would not be possible to take him on as a client while I was working at LDF.

A few days later I took the subway as I had so many times as a teen to Sheridan Square, crossed Sixth Avenue, and easily found the Marlton. It was early so I walked down to number 17 Eighth Street to what was then for New Yorkers like me the City's most important bookstore. In the obituary of its owner Eli Wilentz who died in 1995, *The Times* would correctly call the Eighth Street Bookstore "a literary nerve center of Greenwich Village." I had often lost myself in its three floors getting a breather from walking around the Village after leaving my morning session at Stuyvesant. From a collection heavily represented by affordable paperbacks, I took the first steps toward a lifetime of reading

English and French fiction, little of which had been mentioned in my high school English classes. The obit writer
captured the larger spirit of the place when he wrote:

". . . the person riffling through a book in the next aisle
could be W. H. Auden, E. E. Cummings, Marianne Moore,
Kenneth Patchen, Delmore Schwartz, Michael Harrington,
Jack Kerouac, or perhaps Allen Ginsberg, Gregory Corso
or Leroi Jones."

I never encountered any of these literary worthies at the
store but I did try to chat up numerous browsing young
women. They were almost all older and recognized I was
not at their level; still they were usually polite. I was disappointed that all they did was recommend some really good
reads.

The Lenny Bruce who opened the hotel room door was not
the assertive, unrelenting hipster of his public reputation.
His hair needed a comb, his clothes were disheveled, he
had a beaten-down look but he was extremely courteous—
though he had trouble looking me in the eye—and very
soft-spoken. He told me right off he had a clear idea of how he
wanted to proceed at sentencing—apparently he felt he had
to explain his planned approach to me precisely and carefully. First he cut to the chase by sweeping away Ephraim
London and their relationship in a few words: "I just can't
get through to him what I want. He is only interested in the
appellate courts. I can't wait for that."

Bruce then made the mistake, common to all autodidacts
confronting the lingo, jargon, and folkways of professional

talk: he translated literally. Pulling law books from the flotsam mostly covering a sagging single bed, his blonde amanuensis silently standing by, he started reading out statutory language touching on rights guaranteed by the Constitution, forms of redress, privileges of citizenship.

His voice rose as he got to why court decisions were on his side: "They say there has to be proof of obscenity, which means prurient, which means gives you a hard-on. And that's not the way I go!"

Sensing he had more to say, I held back on the traditional lawyer talk I had planned, though I nodded and smiled as he spoke as often as I dared. He turned to the day of sentencing. "They say my act is this or that. I have to show them what I do. They have the bogus notes of a cop or two and a terrible tape. Once they see the act they'll know they have to let me go."

Thinking of the images that crowded Bruce's act—Jackie Kennedy "hauling ass" when JFK was assassinated, Eleanor Roosevelt's and a display of "tits." Saint Paul giving up "fucking." Tonto and sodomy or was it fellatio? The "pissing in the sink" riff. I finally asked full of innocence: "Why would London oppose you doing your act?"

"He is only interested in the appeals. I'm bleeding money; dying to work."

Then Lenny went back to first principles, though there was a bit of the supplicant here: "If only they heard it and saw it they'd know I was something they didn't like but that I wasn't obscene."

At this point, I intervened to justify my purpose in being present. "I'm not here," I began, "to tell you not to do what you plan to do. I have basically three points. The first is to be as polite and respectful of the setting as you can. Judge Murtagh is a stickler for decorum. He loathes you already so don't give him any more ammunition."

"Secondly, ignore the prosecutor, Richard Kuh. Yes, he is after your blood. Yes, he is trying to make a career out of prosecuting you. There's nothing you can say about him at this point that helps you."

"Finally," and here I felt like a doctor telling a patient the disease is terminal, "Nothing you are likely to do at sentencing will help you. They have probably made their minds up before. So do your thing if you want. Consider it therapy or education for the unwashed but don't fool yourself into thinking you are going to win anything in that courtroom."

Bruce responded to this central casting lawyer speech not at all. I had the distinct feeling that despite what Al Goldman had said, Lenny had heard all the prep talk and caveats he needed before. All he said was: "I'm going to sue in federal courts to stop this."

"Well give it a try," I replied, looking around the room for my coat, "but don't expect anything from that either. The feds don't like intervening in state criminal cases. But you know that, right?"

My question hung in the air as we shook hands, as the blonde smiled goodbye. "Look," I said as a parting shot, "I

can't represent you; the court will probably appoint someone to advise you at the hearing itself, but I'll be there for
support."

A few weeks later I found the courtroom at 100 Centre
Street, the depressing Manhattan criminal court building I'd visited too often. Familiarity with its rooms and
hallways—where Bruce had famously joked, "In the halls
of justice, the only justice is in the halls"—never eased the
pain. It was crowded with lost lives, peeling paint, black
and brown faces, and suppressed anger.

Lenny disregarded everything I had suggested, as I guess
I knew he would. His act was laced with what would offend.
Murtagh took most of it in silently, giving a good imitation
of a slab of granite. Judge Creel, the liberal who had dis-
sented from the guilty verdict, spent a good deal of time
studying the contours of the wood grain on the bench
behind which he sat. It was Justice Phipps, the swing vote,
who caught my attention. Of the three, only he seemed to
enjoy Lenny's humor, though he showed it subtly with a
twinkle in the eye and slightly raised cheeks. Of course, I
realized, so much of Lenny Bruce's slashing talk was that
of an outsider, a view of mainstream society that evoked its
piety, bigotry, and hypocrisy. Of course, a black man would
right away be more likely to connect with Lenny.

Then it was Richard Kuh's turn. He went right after him:
Bruce had shown no remorse; has tried to continue doing his
obscene act even after he had been charged. He should be
imprisoned and the owners of the Café Au Go Go should

be fined the maximum allowed. (Years later, I learned that Gerald Harris, a young prosecutor in the DA office, had been assigned the case first but begged off because he found Lenny's act "hilarious.")

This was too much for Bruce. He jumped up: "I am a Jew before this Court. I would like to set the record straight that the Jew is not remorseful. . . . I come before the Court not for mercy but for justice."

He was sentenced to four months in the workhouse but never served a day. On August 3, 1966, he was found in his San Francisco bathroom, as Collins and Skover described the scene—"head tilted to his left side, eyes closed. Naked but for the blue denim trousers gathered at his ankles. Dead of an overdose. A hypodermic needle spiked into his right arm, a blue bathroom sash loosely tied below his right elbow. A syringe, burned bottle cap, and other narcotics paraphernalia scattered about." As is the law most everywhere, his death meant that because the obscenity conviction was still on appeal, it was vacated. It would not be entered on any criminal rap sheet he carried into the hereafter.

The Eighth Street Bookstore is now a shoe shop. The renovated Marlton charges big bucks for its rooms. Most of the students in the course I teach on the First Amendment have never heard of Lenny Bruce. But a half-century later obscenity law is radically different. After years of judicial confusion and turmoil over the definition of obscenity it now largely leads only to prosecutions of those charged with child pornography. Even in rural or evangelical dominated areas, much less New York City, Bruce would never be charged much less convicted. After rap, hip hop, public consumption of porn, Larry Flynt and *Hustler* magazine, prosecution losses in appellate courts, the staggering costs of contested prosecutions and shifts in public attitudes, as well as the enormous presence of pornographic images on the Internet, law enforcement now usually intervenes only where children are involved or personal privacy is invaded and not always then.

To the generation that listened to him, enjoyed his act, and watched the way he was harassed, Bruce broke the mold. He could make you wince but also remind you that there was a First Amendment and that it needed a transfusion.

Serendipity

In 1967, after being promoted along with my colleague Leroy Clark to the post of First Assistant Counsel at LDF, I began to lobby Muhammad Ali's personal lawyer, Chauncey Eskridge, a member of the informal network of civil rights lawyers across the country we worked with, to let me try and get back Ali's New York State boxing license—taken away because of his unwillingness to accept induction in the armed forces during the Vietnam War. Ali was later convicted of a federal crime and sentenced to five years in prison but his criminal case was on appeal.

Every chance I get I remind Chauncey that we should do something. Ali has been shunned largely because he has revealed that he is a follower of the Nation of Islam and its leader Elijah Mohammad. I press Chauncey on the obvious—that New York State Athletic Commission denied the champ an opportunity to defend himself before his license to box was rescinded. I'm not sure why but defending Ali is something of a crusade with me. Behind his café au lait–colored, speckled mask of a face Chauncey is often difficult to read but his message this time is clear.

"No, not yet." He says it, and not much more, again and again. So much so that I think I better stop asking.

In refusing induction, Ali famously stated that he has "got nothing against no Viet Cong," a line that was falsely circulated as him saying "no Viet Cong ever called me nigger." Across the nation, he has been condemned and shunned. The governor of Illinois calls Ali "disgusting" and the governor of Maine says that he "should be held in utter contempt by every patriotic American." The New York Athletic Commission pulled his license to box and vacates his heavyweight championship on the ground that he is charged with a crime; other states fall in line immediately. Soon he can't box anywhere.

While a succession of lawyers, including my colleague Jonathan Shapiro at LDF, take his draft conviction to higher courts, Ali earns what he can as a speaker on the college circuit, acts in a ridiculous short-lived Broadway show, and publishes a ghosted biography but despite increasing financial troubles Chauncey still insists the time isn't ripe. He volunteers that he is waiting for a change in public opinion. Another shrewd lesson in a legal life of such lessons that law is not made mechanically as the public often thinks. And Chauncey is right. It isn't until Vietnam War fatigue becomes general, until it's clear President Johnson will not run for reelection that Chauncey at last gives me the green light. But he still has his doubts of our chances and he is right about this too: the law doesn't usually protect felons from the collateral consequences of their conviction. "I'm going to get him a fight in Atlanta if I can," he insists, "but you do the law thing."

Having fought to get this case, I must now "do the law thing" by finding a winning legal basis to support Ali's claim that he is entitled to box—at least until and if he is incarcerated. There is an insight here that shows itself through clouds of self-protection. I am only sometimes suited to my profession. A better legal approach would start out with a survey of the available arguments and then move on to an evaluation of their likelihood of success. I came to Ali because his treatment strained my sense of fairness but as even a first year law student would tell me the odds were that only the right legal doctrine, not a sense of injustice, could get him back in the ring.

As a convicted felon, a dodger of the draft (like me, only he did it publicly), winning the return of his license is no easy task: the law in this area has not been made by sympathetic litigants. Mostly those who have challenged barriers to subsequent employment have failed to vindicate their claims. There are procedural arguments available going to the crude way the chair of the Athletic Commission, a hack politician who got his job by threatening Governor Nelson Rockefeller that he would otherwise force a Republican officeholder into a primary battle, handled pulling of the license without holding a hearing but winning on this ground won't get us very far—the stacked Commission will just hold a pro forma hearing and reach the same result, putting us back to square one.

The real reason Ali was refused permission to box, I think, is because he is a bigger-than-life, provocative, assertive black man perceived as having a grudge against white society expressed by his ever-working, unfiltered, mouth, and his affiliation with the Nation of Islam. Most Americans think the black Muslims are a hate group, a threatening and violent religious sect. But proving that Ali is a victim because of his race or his racial allegiances in a form that merits legal redress is tricky. In court, what everybody knows to be the case gets you just so far. Admissible evidence is necessary. The proof available here is gossamer.

But I am rescued miraculously by childhood memories showing me the path. I remember sitting next to my father in front of our stand-alone Philco radio, a model in what looks like a wooden case that must be three or four feet high. We are listening to the regular Friday night broadcast of boxing from Madison Square Garden. Ira, who often had a bet down on one of the fighters, would be in his teacher mode. I have to understand about gambling, he said, so later in life not be taken for a sucker. What I learned from him, from the sports pages he followed, from his gambling habits, which sometimes brought Christmas gifts from his bookmaker into our modest household, was that the fight game was full of shady characters, violent men outside the ring as well as inside, and all manner of fraud, corner cutting, and high jinks. Great New York sports writers like Jimmy Cannon and Milton Gross reinforced Ira's pedagogy: they were always telling readers of their *New York Post* columns about the presence of criminal types in the fight game.

These boxers all were licensed, I think, so why not Muhammad Ali?

At this time I have a younger colleague whose job situation is tight; she has only temporary work at the Legal Defense Fund. Ann is the toughest woman I know as well as one of the most attractive. Among her talents is that she gets people of all backgrounds and classes to listen to her. Most lawyers know how to think; she knows how to think *and* talk. In her free time she plays the bass; her husky voice, like her instrument, commands attention, cuts through the cacophony. When she wants something badly, I secretly think she sounds like a cop. And she usually gets what she wants. She is looking for a better job so I give her the assignment: find the felons who have boxing licenses from the state. She soon reports that we need a court order to gain access to the Athletic Commission's files. The State resists so it takes almost a year before we get the permission we need. When Ann finally gets to examine the files, she finds numbers that shock us both—some 244 licensed fighters have criminal records, often very serious ones, that haven't led New York State to interfere with their boxing careers. We return to federal court with our evidence and are ultimately assigned Judge Walter Mansfield, an ex-marine, in fact a war hero, who surprisingly rules that the state has acted so arbitrarily that it violated the federal Constitution.

Ali gets his boxing license back and begins his epic battles with Joe Frazier to regain and then hold his champion's crown. The criminal case against him soon collapses for technical legal reasons that actually have little to do with his supposed crime and which are as serendipitous as my recollection of Ira's lessons about the fight game. It turns out that after the Supreme Court takes a preliminary vote against Ali, a law clerk gets ahold of African American scholar C. Eric Lincoln's *Black Muslims in America*, the leading book about the group. After learning more about the Nation of Islam, he persuades his boss, Justice John Marshall Harlan, that Ali has a decent defense of the sort put up by my colleague Jonathan and that he is entitled to a ministerial exemption from the draft. Chief Justice Warren Burger is outraged at Harlan's change of mind but another Justice, Potter Stewart, suggests a way to set aside the conviction without forcing the Court to delve into racial politics. Improbably, Ali is now a free man as well as free to fight.

Soon he is on the road to redemption. Never has the hero to coward to hero route been covered so fast and so successfully. Of course, very little happens for one reason. Ali needed lots of luck and a lot of lawyering but I don't believe his principled stand against the war would have yielded a happy future for him if the war itself hadn't turned sour, a lethal set of bad decisions that more and more Americans came to regret. Yes, yes, the Justice Holmes' endlessly quoted line has it just right: "The Life of the law has not been logic, it has been experience." Ali is saved, I believe, by the nation's experience of the Vietnam War. Ann and my arguments are justification, not motivation.

Chauncey Eskridge was clearly correct to resist moving fast by following the urgings of my youthful enthusiasm. But from the Ali case victory, I get my fifteen minutes of fame. My name appears in a few columns on the Sports pages, childishly giving me more satisfaction than if I found it in a law review; I hear from junior high classmates; more students than I expect sign up for my classes at Columbia Law School. It's true that I receive no proposals of marriage but then also absent is the hate mail featuring death threats and ropes tied in nooses that occasionally arrived at LDF after I returned from litigation trips across the South.

Later Jack Greenberg complains that despite his millions, his subsequent triumphs, the champ never makes a substantial financial contribution to LDF's work. The lawsuits themselves fade from view, until 2017 when journalist Leigh Montville publishes a book he calls *Sting Like a Bee*. Of the millions of words written about Muhammad Ali, his grace in the ring, the interviews, and the documentary films, relatively little has been said to explain that without them his fabled career would have been short lived.

In 1994, the Center for Sport and Society at my university conferred on Ali its Sportsman of the Year award. I get to introduce him at the ceremony and in accepting the award Ali says a few words in thanks but they are barely audible. Suffering from what is called a parkinsonism syndrome, he is nothing like the dashing, challenging figure of his youth but even humbled as he is a dignity has emerged. The crowd stands and wildly applauds, as thereafter will many crowds in many places. He is a figure to respect. When he dies at seventy-four in June 2016, he is mourned everywhere, by politicians of all stripes, celebrities, common people. His final Wikipedia entry is over 20,000 words. Tributes come from across the globe. His journey from when I represented him to the modern pantheon is so remarkable that it restores a sense of hope about the capacity of humans and their audiences to change and grow. Invisible to most, the law played a role in this.

Though Mohammad's conviction was eventually quashed and his license restored, his case brought to my attention the destructive way our law treats persons finishing a criminal sentence, a path that I think hurts society as much as the individual. Teaching at Columbia gave me both the time and the incentive to learn more about the difficulties encountered by ex-offenders, usually released without any guidance or financial support, in getting the jobs that are likely to keep them out of jail again. Ali had gotten his right to fight back because the Athletic Commission acted arbitrarily; ordinary Americans were, I thought, treated unfairly when they were denied employment or state licenses because they had a criminal record even when the work opportunity they sought had nothing to do with whatever had got them in trouble with the law. Two of my brightest students looked into the available research and concluded that employer fear of doing something risky as well as punitive urges often kept ex-offenders from employment that was known to be the best hedge against recidivism. With their help, I drafted a model law restricting both public and private employers in New York State from denying opportunities unless the type of crime had a direct relationship to the work that was sought.

We decided to publish an article setting out the new law that we proposed and the thinking behind it in an upstate New York law review. Our hope was that it might then reach legislators who would be less likely to dismiss it as merely the work of Manhattan elitists. Still we know our model law was likely a hard sell. No state had enacted anything like it; nor do most state legislators pour over law reviews. Nevertheless, we were pleased when the editor of the *Syracuse Law Review* immediately accepted the article for publication.

Months later, after I distributed reprints to a few friends and colleagues and otherwise moved on to other issues, I received a phone call in my Columbia office from a man who said his name is John Donne. After a weird moment where my thoughts flashed on the famous English poet, I realized I was talking to the most powerful state legislator who dealt with criminal law matters. He came to the point quickly: "I read your law and I'm going to get it enacted."

And so he did. Article 23-A of the New York Correction Law hasn't always been treated well by the courts but the

amended statutory version of our model law for the rehabilitation of offenders that was signed by the governor in
1976 is to this day the broadest protection ex-offenders have
against irrational discrimination in any state. As I write, its
formulation is being promoted for adoption by activists
urging a number of states to act in ways that permanently
reduce the prison population.

Of all Muhammad's many achievements this may by the
one fewest know about. It's a law he gave us because without the experience of confronting his mistreatment, it never
would have seen the light of day. I give Ira an assist too.

Babs

My mother-in-law Babette requested that I speak to the inmates in a class she was teaching at a high-security prison in Walpole, Massachusetts. From the get-go, Babs, as friends called her, and I have had a troubled relationship. Early on it was uncertain exactly what upset her but that she worried about her first son-in-law was all too clear from dour facial expressions, snippy asides, petty criticisms— "You didn't say 'Good Morning.'" Later on doubts about me merged with disapproval about how her first grand-child was being raised: We were too attentive to Jessie's needs for her likes; our home was excessively child centered such that, as she told Heli, "She had to intervene. It was like having to grab a child off the tracks to save her from an on rushing trolley."

In an autobiography written in the 1930s when she was a student at Swarthmore College, Babs complained bitterly about an upbringing that too stridently emphasized being the best at everything, one that left her doubting her-self. Still the standards she complained about had been internalized. They had become her own. She was never shy of letting people know they had not met her expectations and she had a lot of them, especially about me. Years later Babs was described, in a tribute to her husband published after his death, as a "woman of decided opinions." True enough, behind those opinions were a set of rules when it came to language, table manners, colleges for her four children, and a long list of other items.

At first, I thought she was just reacting to never having heard of me before learning that I was going to marry her daughter. That seemed reasonable enough given that we'd decided to marry so shortly after having met but little changed when I became a more familiar figure. I concluded from the way she intruded into our marriage with subtle and not so subtle digs about everything from word choices to furniture choices that this product of a tight-knit German-Jewish Chicago community felt her first-born daughter, said to be a look-alike, had been stolen from her by some uncouth character from Manhattan. It didn't help that the brief courtship had taken place far from her sight in foreign countries and that the subject of mother–daughter pillow talk from Heli's earliest year was "The kind of wedding you will have," including even the fabric of the dresses.

For the first five or six years of our marriage, there was little improvement. We remained civil but kept a football field's length of emotional distance, avoiding any overt confrontation. Both of us mellowed when she was diagnosed with what were thought to be breast cancer cells in her lymphatic system. She also came to respect my work more after I had argued a few cases before the Supreme Court and some of her friends gave testimonials to my character, including my former teacher, Harvard Law professor and Supreme Judicial Court of Massachusetts judge Ben Kaplan and his wife the poet Felicia Lamport. But even as illness softened her attitude, she found a way to remain a critic, though a much more constructive one: shortly after her death a copy of my first book was found on her bedside table; she had read a third of it, tattooing the margins with apt editorial queries about syntax and grammar.

Despite the adversarial tenor of our relationship, I thought her intelligent and creative; even when her opinions about everything from racial politics to food choices were to my mind totally wrong, they usually made you think. As a young woman she had walked away from a dream job with a Broadway producer when her recently widowed mother insisted she was needed at home. Later Babs published romantic fiction in mass circulation magazines like the *Saturday Evening Post* and *Woman's Day* only to cut short her writing career to raise her children when her husband was serving as a flight surgeon in North Africa during World War II. After moving to Cambridge from Chicago in 1953, she was a feature at neighborhood play readings and living room musicals often populated by big-name professors. Some she cowrote with songwriter-satirist and math professor Tom Lehrer. She was beloved by a large circle of accomplished female friends, many of whom she kept in contact with by regular letters and cards.

As I came to learn firsthand about the many failings of the criminal justice system, I was particularly impressed by her work on prison education. One of the first graduates of a then new Harvard masters in teaching graduate program, she was told that a correspondence course she had assembled on American history had been taken by large numbers of prisoners. She became interested in how giving prisoners educational opportunities could ease their lot, perhaps reducing recidivism; soon after finishing the Harvard program she won a grant from the federal government's Law Enforcement Assistance Program. After adding her own financial contribution, she arranged to place a group of Harvard graduate students in the state prison at Walpole with the goal of training life-term- and other long-term-sentenced inmates to teach other prisoners how to read and write.

The inmate trainees met with their Harvard tutors regularly but there was also a weekly class for the prisoner group where Babs tried to encourage discussion of contemporary policy issues, often by inviting as her guests big names in the Harvard–Cambridge intellectual axis to talk about their specialties. It was for such a class that she asked me to speak about criminal law reform. I was glad to do it both because I had been working on several tough criminal cases and, more importantly, because I saw the invitation to visit as a way of her showing me an olive branch. I wanted peace, not competition.

On the drive to the prison, after she astonished me by pointing out the pond-side plot at the Mount Auburn Cemetery where she wanted to be buried, we talked only about family topics, mostly the doings of my six-year-old daughter Jessie. After getting searched and clearing security, we found the room she had been assigned full of chattering inmates. I had barely entered when a short, sharp-eyed prisoner came toward me with hand outstretched. He was wearing a gray prison work uniform and a huge smile.

"Michael Meltsner," he exclaimed. *"Biggers v. Tennessee!"*

The man's name was William "Lefty" Gilday, a convicted bank robber. He was referring to a case about eye witness identification I had lost in the Supreme Court because the Court was spilt four–four on our argument that sixteen-year-old Archie Nathaniel Biggers had been subject to suggestive identification procedures that led to his rape conviction. Counting votes before the Supreme Court argument, it looked like I had the case won five to four until Avon Williams Jr., the local counsel and first African American senator to serve in the Tennessee legislature since Reconstruction, told me that Thurgood Marshall would recuse himself because he and Avon were cousins. The eight-member Court went on to split evenly, thus affirming without any resolution of the constitutional issues the decision of the Supreme Court of Tennessee that my teenage client's conviction for rape should be upheld. At the time I visited Walpole, Avon and I were trying to get the federal courts to reexamine the case. (Eventually, the Supreme Court looked at it again and found that Biggers' identification "show up"—he'd been viewed by the complainant alone in a room full of police—was not unduly suggestive.)

No sentimentalist about her charges, Babs leaned over and whispered, "Beware of the charm offensive."

Either this guy, I thought, is an accomplished jailhouse lawyer or he is one slippery con artist.

Turned out he was both.

The program Babs had created in 1968 was called the Student–Tutor Evaluation Project or STEP; it was the first higher education program in the Massachusetts prison system. She persuaded both Northeastern and Brandeis Universities to certify its courses for academic credit and very soon started collecting encomiums from reformers across the country. The aim of STEP was to boost the education of men serving short prison terms in the hopes they would continue to study once they were released or paroled. The unique feature that attracted funding and accolades was the use of the academic tutors to convert the long termers into teachers. It was thought—as Ray Jones, an inmate analyst, wrote in 1992—that the Massachusetts prison authorities were reluctant to allow STEP to go forward but allowed the "program into the prison because she had political influence . . . but it demonstrated its discomfort from the outset by restricting participation to fifteen carefully selected prisoners per session."

That Babs had important friends in the professions and the Brattle Street area of Cambridge was incontrovertibly true but STEP also filled a real need for rehabilitation-related services. She had little connection, however, with Massachusetts' rowdy political world. A relentless advocate for STEP, she did know how to get mileage from her image as an effective do-gooder, especially as she was also willing to shell out her own money to increase the program's budget. In the rest of her life, she was outspoken, even intrusive, when she grabbed onto an issue or a critique but a different, more tactful Babs emerged where STEP were concerned. She certainly may have pulled strings but she never mentioned the particulars so I don't know if STEP was allowed in because of political pull or just the perception that it met a need by the usually resistant of novelty Massachusetts Correction Department. But I'd learned one thing about Babs very early: when she was engaged in a crusade, she came across as one determined and powerhouse of a woman.

As it turned out, her innovations were a remarkable success until they were thwarted by shocking events of the sort no one could have predicted.

In the months after my visit, Gilday and another STEP student, Stanley Bond, were paroled. Bond was young, heavyset but still good-looking and a war veteran. He was also a sociopath. He'd been convicted after a massive lone wolf crime spree, sent to prison for holding up dozens of Western Union offices; as subsequent events would confirm, he had no regrets for his crimes. He had the knack of persuading people he was much more interested in them than he actually was and because he was convinced of his charm, better educated than many of his fellows and a master manipulator, he saw excelling in the STEP program as his route out of prison.

Once released, he was quickly able to enroll in Brandeis University where Heli's father John Spiegel, previously teaching social psychiatry at Harvard, had been serving as the first director of the Lemberg Center for the Study of Violence. The Center was a research facility set up in 1966 to probe the causes of urban violence. John was well known in the academic world for being the coauthor of *Men Under Stress*, a path-breaking study of the mental and emotional breakdown of servicemen during World War II. The Lemberg Center job converted him from a highly respected but largely unknown outside of academia professor to a national figure, a widely quoted and interviewed commentator on the riots of the late 1960s. In a major investigation funded by government, leading foundations, and the philanthropy of a New York businessman, the Center sent field investigators into six cities to develop an early warning system that might detect impending civil disturbances and racial violence. Four of the six—Cleveland, Dayton, San Francisco, and later Boston—would end up experiencing significant racial conflict.

Babs was not naïve about some of the Walpole men she was trying to help but it's clear that much like Gilday, Bond was an accomplished con man. Soon after his arrival on the Brandeis campus he joined a group of students who were trying to mount a campus strike to protest the Vietnam War. One would later tell the press that not knowing what to make of the ex-inmate and veteran students assumed he was an undercover cop. But Stanley Bond played the student radical game well, often using his experience in the world of war and prison to gain influence over young people whom he criticized as parlor revolutionaries. In fact, he was more interested in bedding as many women as he could than in the student protest movement or purely academic pursuits.

Gilday and Robert Valeri, another paroled STEP student, were more concerned with getting back to robbing than an education but they made a bow to their parole cover story by gaining admission to Northeastern University, though apparently they never attended a class. Despite his criminal record, Gilday who was proud of his jailhouse lawyering even tried unsuccessfully to persuade the dean of the law school—a job I would hold almost a decade later—to let him study for the bar.

After Ohio National Guard troops killed four students at Kent State University who were peacefully protesting against the war, Bond joined with two Brandeis student activists, Kathy Power, who was a principal in a student strike movement, and her roommate Susan Saxe, a magna cum laude English and American Studies major soon to graduate, along with his Walpole buddies, Gilday and Valeri, in one of those fantastic jumbles of crime, violence, and veneer of political protest that was a late 1960s and early 1970s specialty. The pack armed themselves, robbed a Newburyport Massachusetts National Guard armory for ammunition, and then went after several banks with the aim they claimed of financing antiwar activities. As the five were robbing a branch of the State Street Bank in the Brighton neighborhood of Boston, Gilday shot a police officer responding to an alarm, killing him.

The group of five, previously unknown to the police, were now the subject of an intense national search. Gilday was arrested first at the Massachusetts–New Hampshire border after several home invasions, hostage taking, and the theft of three cars. Hundreds of officers, said to be the largest manhunt in New England history, finally cornered him in a heavily wooded area. Later he would thank a Worcester newspaper photographer for saving his life, believing that if the newsman hadn't been there taking pictures, the police would have shot him dead. He never, however, thanked me—not that I care a whit—but ironically after receiving one of the last death sentences handed down by a Massachusetts jury, Gilday became a lifer, a beneficiary along the other 600 plus other men on American's death rows of

LDF's 1972 victory declaring the death penalty unconstitutional in the Supreme Court case of *Furman v. Georgia.*

Valeri was quickly picked up where he was living in the
town of Somerville. He freely told the police everything he
knew, including tips that the women had a planned escape
route and that Bond was heading West. Packing a 9mm
pistol and $10,000 in cash, as well as other weapons in his
luggage, Bond was soon seized from a plane about to take
off from the Grand Junction, Colorado, airport. He had
been fingered by a passenger who had seen media coverage
of the robbery. In statements to the press from jail, Bond
voiced a narrative that would soon become familiar to
Americans featuring claims that his revolutionary organization, the Revolutionary Action (RFA) group—there was
no proof it existed—was preparing a revolution against the
establishment. He was, he claimed in a largely incoherent
manifesto, not a criminal but a political prisoner.

In 1973, a small group, probably no more than eight,
called the Symbionese Liberation Army (SLA), would
become national news when it murdered Oakland California school superintendent Marcus Foster (and seriously
wounded his assistant, my Oberlin College classmate Bob
Blackburn). Later, the SLA captured the front pages again
when it kidnapped heiress Patty Hearst who then partici-
pated in a series of California robberies claiming she had
been converted to its antiracist, anticapitalist, and feminist
struggle. Ultimately convicted of bank robbery, her sentence was commuted by President Carter; she was later

pardoned by Bill Clinton. There was no known link between the SLA's rebellion and rhetoric to the actions of the five in Massachusetts. The SLA had been conceived in California prisons and while certainly the revolutionary justification for murder and robbery was similar to Bond's RFA palaver, the two cohorts were unconnected responses to the same social disarray, one in the liberal East and the other in the liberal West.

Bond was returned to Massachusetts; sentenced to a long term at Walpole but would die when a bomb he was secretly making as part of an escape plan went off accidentally and killed him. Susan Saxe and Kathy Powers, both placed on the FBI's Most Wanted list, adopted new names, went underground, and successfully escaped discovery. They soon split up and the trajectory of their lives diverged. Saxe avoided arrest for almost five years, until the police claimed she was seen walking with her lover on a Philadelphia street by an alert officer; a women's group supporting her asserted she had in fact been found due to illegal wiretaps or surveillance. Brought back to face charges she eventually pled guilty, telling the judge defiantly that she was doing so to end being "harassed, hounded and vilified" by the government: "I do not recognize the right of the state to a single day of my life, but I do recognize its power to take that and more. I will never abandon my political commitments in exchange for favors from the system." Represented by one of the best young lawyers in the Commonwealth, Nancy Gertner—eventually a federal judge—she was sentenced to ten to twelve years but was released after seven years in prison.

Power's story took a very different turn. She created a new identity and changed her way of life, having a son, later marrying, working as a cook and restaurateur, living a quiet, community-based life in an Oregon college town for twenty-three years. But troubled by her responsibility for the death of the officer and missing her extended Catholic family she sought the help of a psychotherapist. As a result of their conversations, Power decided to turn herself in and take full responsibility for her actions. Pleading guilty in 1993 to robbery, she was sentenced to eight to twelve years and ordered not to profit from her crimes, a condition of dubious validity under the prevailing First Amendment rules. But her story would be fictionalized by others in several novels and a television series. After she was paroled in 1999, she wrote a memoir about her life on the run, went back to school, and worked on the AIDS crisis for a nonprofit. Power's story of conscience was so powerful that her lawyer Rikki Klieman, later also a television personality married to New York Police Commissioner Bill Bratton, would also write a book about the return of the fugitive. In 2012 Power attended her 40th Brandeis reunion where she was generally welcomed; at the time she published an essay in a University publication called "My Surrender and Return" where the contrast with Susan Saxe, who apparently never apologized for the crime spree, was evident:

"I offered my body for imprisonment to begin to pay for my years of living as an outlaw. I offered my suffering to balance in some small way the suffering of . . . [the police officer's] family and community over his death. And, when the first offering was not seen as enough, I offered more by withdrawing my request for parole and spending an additional year and a half in prison."

After the bank robbery and shooting, Brandeis and Northeastern wanted out of the STEP program. Babs ultimately moved it to the University of Massachusetts but her health was declining and the parolee's crime spree had diminished STEP's potential reach. Through gifts from the family in her memory and a selfless administrator at the University of Massachusetts Boston, STEP kept going on a shoestring budget for another decade until it fell victim to a wave of 1980s restrictions imposed on any rehabilitation efforts in the state's prisons. With the perspective of hindsight, programs like STEP look like the last gasp of efforts to provide restorative services to those convicted of crimes before the era of mass incarceration, mandatory minimum requirements, life without parole sentences, and draconian sentencing guidelines kicked in—developments which are only now over forty years later being actively opposed by those calling for reform.

The liberal agenda represented by Bab's modest effort to induce Massachusetts correctional officials to support greater educational resources for the incarcerated was very much of the times but like President Johnson's ambitious

War on Poverty such efforts demonstrated the drastic limits of laws and programs when confronted by general fears
of crime and desires among many Americans for isolation
from the poor and minorities, distance from government
regulation, and freedom from taxation. Just the way true
revolutions are usually made by the disappointed middle
class rather than the totally disfranchised, a society that
promises reform, and then supports only slender, half-
hearted efforts, both raises expectations and then is likely to
bitterly disappoint them.

As I worked my way through hundreds of reform-minded
lawsuits and years of active civil rights lawyering I decided
that it would take more than winning these cases to confront the radical impulse that found a place in the post–
civil rights era. Even when the cases resulted in eloquent
opinions and celebrated triumphs, subsequent events often
demonstrated how difficult it was to translate court orders
into changed lives.

The Clinic

My first year of law school was tense. I feared most not being able to understand the cases. Many dealt with commercial relationships of which I was ignorant; they used a language totally foreign to me, talking of "proximate cause," "consideration," "promissory estoppel," "unjust enrichment," and "offer and acceptance."

My immediate reaction was to question the choice to enroll. After all, I thought, what does this have to do with political freedom and antidiscrimination, the issues that I care about? It would be a while before I understood the importance to my concerns of how private parties deal with each other and how the law oversees these arrangements. Years later when I spent every day working on civil rights and civil liberties legal questions, I learned how foolishly narrow minded it was to believe that progress with rights and liberties can be divorced from the way the private sector is organized and behaves. Reformers who are blind to the workings of the economy don't get very far in this society.

If I initially found it difficult to come to terms with the commercial context of so many of my courses, I felt almost as uncomfortable with many of my classmates. They were bright and usually friendly, though like most all Yale Law students of the day they had to cope with unruly competitive feelings of their own and their peers. These feelings created an environment where grades and class rank could color the way students treated each other, though there was also a strong sense that the urge had to be fought off—we ought to be a band of brothers—there were only seven women in my class—especially as most assuredly it was gospel that everyone with a Yale Law degree would do well. I tried to keep my distance from these dynamics but it was almost impossible because first year grades determined law journal membership; an editorship meant you were on track for coveted judicial clerkships or job offers from the best firms.

I was struck by the confident appearance of so many of my classmates. From the vantage of my own insecurity, it was as if they had all taken a course in how to win the law school game before they actually came on the field. They dressed for success: while not all wearing jackets and ties to class, they dressed neatly, looking put together well with pressed slacks and dress shirts. A far cry from the frayed wardrobe and disheveled look that passed for the Oberlin College dress code I followed. My survival in this alien environment had to do with supportive roommates and two extraordinary teachers—Alexander Bickel and Benjamin Kaplan. After watching them in class and learning about their careers, I decided that if they valued the law so could I.

Amazingly, after the first year ended I began to feel things would change. A friendly third year student had told me early on that everything would look different and it did. My grades were high enough to put to rest worries about basic competence and I saw that classmates had been struggling with fears and doubts similar to mine; not were all superbrainy as in my insecurity I had made them. Most of all I felt a growing sense of professional identity, a potential working role from the cacophony of signals that come my way from the institution, the faculty, classmates, and a legal world around us that was struggling with the very issues of fairness and liberty that concerned me.

Ironically, feeling more comfortable about being a law student in the second and third years my attention shifted away from school. Once the basic analytic methods had been understood, in most of my classes I felt a strong sense of needless repetition; of going through the motions with decided cases that may have no relevance to the work I wanted to end up doing. I was much more interested in books and articles spelling out the policy implications of the cases than the judicial opinions themselves. Even with the good teachers, and there were many, I compared class discussions invidiously—zeroing in so often on the particulars of how a judge decided whether A or B had the better argument—with the open-ended though often overly abstract Oberlin classroom. I also began to realize in a rudimentary way that the law was a living thing, much more than even learned judgments from appellate judges who were often remote from the gritty reality of the disputes they decided. It hit me that most law was actually made by lawyers in their offices. I was probably too young to appreciate the irresponsibility that comes from not testing abstractions in the concrete of actual cases but as my attention wandered I was lucky to have picked up enough in the subjects that I cared about and the procedures governing litigation so as not to feel like a fool when I began to practice.

There were, however, two important exceptions to a feeling I was just serving time until the remaining two years were up. One was an experience that seemed a failure but that later proved crucial when after leaving LDF I confronted the job of creating a legal clinic at Columbia Law School where under supervision students would themselves practice law. The New Haven public defender was a single practitioner tasked with representing most of those charged with crime in the City too poor to afford a lawyer. I can still see him, a slight man, shirt untucked, tie slightly askew, eyes not looking at me but perhaps focused on the particulars of some new case on his overcrowded docket. Given the number of criminal cases in the City, it was an absurd arrangement. To do his job, he needed a team of assistant lawyers but none had been budgeted. Help from Yale students was necessary for him to barely survive. By joining a student-run legal aid organization—no course credit was then available for this work—my roommates and I became part-time assistants, getting our first taste of actual legal practice. We did field investigations, wrote research memos, and ran errands like filing papers with the courts. We hoped to work closely enough with the defender to learn the details of his strategic and tactical thinking but he was so over-whelmed that he had little time to do more than point us to work he wanted done.

For my first assignment I wrote a memo arguing that certain evidence unlawfully seized by the police should be suppressed. He converted the memo into a formal motion, filing it with the court, but when I asked him if my draft was any good he was evasive. At first, I worried that I'd missed something important that he was just too polite to call out but it soon became obvious that he gave my research only a few seconds' attention, decided it was good enough to use, and then moved on to the next of his endless list of cases. One thing stood out: practical experience is extremely valuable but only if the mentor-supervisor sets the bar high enough. Otherwise what is learned from experience is just how to get by. The lack of oversight from the public defender was disappointing but aside from a first brush with the criminal law, I had learned something about what to avoid that would stand me well when I became a teacher myself.

The second experience came from a seminar taught by the most eccentric member of the faculty, Fred Rodell, where eight of us had to write a short essay every week about a legal topic that would be intelligible to a layman. The seminar met in the fabled Yale confines of Mory's Temple Bar, where only men were welcome. Such was the sensitivity toward gender equality at the time that when a female student elected to take the course, the professor persuaded her to withdraw. Every week we'd sit around drinking beer and critiquing each other's pieces with Rodell, who had probably chosen the venue because he had trouble going long without a drink. He hated conventional legal scholarship and believed judges make up the rules as they went along to get the results they wanted but his serious work was well behind him. His more recent writings were scorned by his colleagues but he was still a devastating critic and a cunning journalist; he opened the door for me to see how important it was to defang the mystique of the law so that a larger public would be able to appreciate what was going on and, perhaps, mobilize to do something about it.

Soon professional journalist Anthony Lewis of *The Times* would show the way to do this to a larger public. He has been followed by a long list of able commentators who today accurately explain legal developments to a wide audience. Sometimes I imagine my students rely more on Lyle Denniston, Nina Totenberg, Jeffrey Toobin, Dahlia Lithwick, Emily Bazelon, and a host of others than on the judicial opinions they comment on.

Despite the distance I kept from full involvement in the life of law school while at Yale, most of my teachers made a huge impact on the way I saw the world. Even when they didn't have overwhelming pedagogical skills, they were full of ideas and demanding questions. Outside of class men like Tom Emerson, Boris Bittker, Bickel, Joe, and Abe Goldstein played a variety of impactful public roles—litigating, consulting, testifying before Congress, and germinating new policy ideas—while they shuttled between Washington jobs, New York firms, and New Haven teaching. When I entered the academic world at Columbia, I asked myself if I could possibly play such roles when I'd been such an indifferent law student. I had already taught an advanced criminal law seminar at NYU Law School but I thought of that as a special assignment with a small group of highly motivated third year students. I was probably a suitable teacher only because of my unusual caseload at LDF that gave me experience in a species of law reform cases that few others had. But returning to law school to teach, to live the life of a full-time faculty member, was a very different matter. I feared it might be too formal an environment for me; it was not something I had ever imagined for myself. Perhaps that's why I almost rejected the Columbia offer before teaching my first class when Dean William Warren, a tax law expert who'd been dean for eighteen years, informed me he'd gone along with the faculty vote to set up a clinic but wasn't particularly comfortable with the idea. If that wasn't disconcerting enough, then he told me:

"For budgetary reasons I'm cutting your salary by several thousand dollars."

That left me with a first year paycheck even smaller than
it had been at LDF. Our family could survive without the
money but I worried that Warren's attitude reflected faculty
ambivalence about the new program. And I was right.

During my first six months on the job I treaded water.
After all, when I was a law student, I'd never taken a clinical
course. So far as I knew, neither Yale nor any other school
offered them. Trying to figure out how to begin to create
one, I dodged the larger implications of student practice by
continuing to handle most of my LDF cases with a cohort
of assistants. I simply met my clients in the company of my
students, who helped write motions and briefs; then we
went off to the courts from a Morningside Heights instead
mid-Manhattan office. The logistics were particularly challenging; I didn't have a knowledgeable support staff as I did
at LDF where the secretaries were a source of both spiritual
and practical wisdom.

I was often stretched thin making sure each of my eighteen students had a decent assignment. As a practitioner, I
had to worry only about myself. Now I had to keep everyone busy. At times, I felt like The Sorcerer's Apprentice,
coming up quickly with tasks for the students as soon as
they finished their previous assignment, even when I could
get the project done myself more easily. In the first months
I made little progress putting together the kind of materi-
als about the practice of law I wanted students to read. In
truth I was beginning to feel beleaguered but suddenly this

all changed when at my suggestion the law school hired Philip Schrag to join me as a second clinician.

Philip was a phenomenon. After working at the Legal Defense Fund for a few years he'd been named the New York City Consumer Advocate, an ombudsman-type post he pretty much created himself. I'd been at LDF for nine and a half years, tried and argued all sorts of civil rights cases before the federal courts. Philip's tenure had been much shorter but he'd mounted inventive challenges to the way businesses treated low-income consumers, an area rarely touched by progressive lawyers. He had also written about the law while practicing, a factor that made him particularly attractive to more traditional faculty at the Law School.

It quickly turned out that Philip was perfectly suited to the challenge of setting up a clinic. He was full of energy, arriving every morning at Morningside Heights with a proposed agenda scrawled on a 3×5 card. While his primary allegiance was placing students in real lawyering situations, in short order he became one of the more prominent thinkers in the emerging field of preparing students to represent actual clients. Articles we wrote together about ongoing struggles to figure out new ways to teach the Columbia clinic met a need for the growing presence of such courses across the country. To my surprise, our work was devoured by newly hired clinicians, not that they always followed our lead, because the new field suffered from a lack of guidance. We were cited with our names as if we represented a special path to approach student practice. In the early days of this movement the new teachers were consumed with start-up challenges: few were yet chronicling, as we were, what we were doing. That will change.

A particular challenge that consumed us was the search for the best way to manage the tension between client care and student learning. A key issue emerged: How much responsibility should we give a student for decision making about a client's case? It's a dilemma encountered in all professional training programs and particularly difficult to resolve because obviously the novice can compromise the needs or interests of the client. In medicine, of course, life or bodily integrity may be at stake but there is no other way to learn surgery, for example, than finding a way to accept the risks for the newcomer to actually do it. In law, the skill of the practitioner can mean avoidance of jail or loss of housing or employment. It's plainly necessary for students to take responsibility for the cases they handle but it's also predictable that they will make mistakes.

It's not an easy call to know at what point it would be malpractice to let a student continue on a course of action we aren't sure is the right one. After all, the students may be closer to the case than we are so to an extent we have to rely on their judgment but they are also inexperienced and untested. We hope to resolve the dilemma by staying as close as we can to the cases, telling student lawyers we are a resource freely available for feedback and advice. We insist they check in regularly. To be sure, the students are motivated to succeed, fully aware that they have the well-being of clients in their hands, but the ultimate responsibility for their performance will be on our shoulders.

Shortly after his arrival at Columbia, Philip dropped a bombshell. He would take six students to serve the local community up close by working at a law office run by the New York Legal Aid Society in central Harlem for an almost full semester of academic credit. Today it's hard to imagine how unusual a step this was in the early 1970s. Faculties then were anxious about clinics, fearing students wouldn't learn how the best practitioners did things. Here Philip was taking them away from the school and into a neighborhood where few white professors had ever lingered.

I heard more about these worries than Philip because I remained at our 116th Street offices, litigating complicated cases with the help of my student interns. I still had a full docket including many of my LDF race cases. I was representing Muhammad Ali in his quest to return to the boxing ring, defendants in criminal cases, and Chinese restaurateurs struggling against dragnet raids from immigration agents. I took my students to Albany and Washington to watch me argue before the New York Court of Appeals and the US Supreme Court. Soon a surprising case demonstrated how far from pure classroom learning clinical work can be. At his sentencing, I represented a black seaman convicted of an assault on the high seas. During his hearing at the Foley Square federal courthouse he became agitated and appeared to have a heart seizure. As the judge was about to send him to prison, he made a strange gurgling sound. I turned to look at him and he suddenly rose from his chair, gasped, and then fell to the floor of the courtroom.

The bailiff rushed to his phone to call for emergency assistance but immediately the elderly sentencing judge stood up from behind the bench and began to wave his arms madly—his fluttering black robe made him look like a bat in motion—and started shouting like a crazy man:

"He's malingering, malingering."

I was stunned and began to speak when I saw my student assistant run to the client.

It turns out she was a former hospital nurse. Before an ambulance arrived, she leapt into action and quickly administered apparent lifesaving CPR. As the client was carried out of the courtroom on a stretcher to a local hospital, the judge continued his rant, leaving me still speechless.

I'd been before a few judges who behaved strangely but never one as out of control as this. Fortunately, the client reached the hospital and was successfully treated, though he was then transferred to federal prison.

I was sure that my student would never forget the way she acted in the face of uncertainty, stress, and challenge. At Yale I had brilliant teachers and peers who I knew one day would have distinguished careers but nothing that was actually a stress test of sorts could have happened in a curriculum dominated by the idea that learning has to take place in classrooms. Litigation is full of pressures, often unpredictable in shape, but it doesn't take a client's seizure to understand that (like the old joke about getting to Carnegie Hall) it takes practice, practice, practice to manage the tension. The earlier you start, the better.

But I have some difficult moments when I tell the story of the sentencing hearing to my faculty colleagues. Several are unimpressed. "But is there valuable learning here?" one asked. "Couldn't these experiences," says another, "wait until after graduation?" And one professor was caustic: "Well, she certainly now knows where the courthouse is." At this point, I decided there was something deeply threatening to traditional academics in learning by doing.

Philip and I soon decided the traditional curriculum implicitly conveyed that lawyers work as individuals; our experience, however, was that good lawyers knew how to be collaborative. In what may be the most unpredictable turn in our work lives, we committed to model an effective team approach by concentrating on our own working relationship. Though I was a therapy veteran, our interest was not primarily psychological but on how to interact, make decisions, and present them to students. We knew that we often approached problems differently. Philip easily saw the complications that lurked in every task. My tendency was to simplify. He can be devastating in a cerebral analysis of a legal problem while I am often trying to escape the letter of the law to locate the equities. He knows numbers; though I will pick up much about statistics from him, I start from point zero. He is supreme at civil litigation but has never, as I have, handled complex criminal cases.

As we linked our courses, we learned to talk through most decisions, including personal dimensions and potential conflicts. Previously, we would have made individual decisions—we are both decisive, self-directed individuals—and never looked back. Now we identify every choice point we can. We agree often but if we disagree then we negotiate. If we hit a stumbling block, we negotiate some more. If we still can't work it out—and this is important—we ask a third party for advice. As we sort this out, it helps that we have fun; we get through the tough places by finding humor and irony in the legal world around us.

Out of this work we hope comes a message of effective collaboration and unitary leadership. With our linked courses, we organize competitive exercises between the two classes. Coincidentally, Philip, and his wife and two sons, move to an apartment in the same Westside Manhattan building where my wife and I live with our daughters, Jessie and Molly. We are two floors away. In the rear of my apartment is a rarely opened door that leads to a dingy and dimly lit back stairway meant to provide egress in case of fire. Some evenings Philip and I meet on these stairs, plan our next-day classes, and share the day's gossip. We feel like conspirators.

Increasingly, we have a lot to say about how lawyers should learn their trade. We feel we can be as conceptual about lawyering as our colleagues are about legal rules, standards, and doctrines but because the clients we serve are mostly poor or otherwise disadvantaged we also have a social mission that cannot be avoided. I get the feeling some of my faculty colleagues are jealous because we have lured so many good students to the clinic but I also notice a shift toward greater acceptance of what we are doing, often showing up in small civilities and courtesies. Though most of the time it's just below the surface, Philip and I are engaged in a serious ideological battle with conventional modes of legal education. We believe, against the dialectical evisceration of appeals court opinions that traditionally makes up law classes, students also need to work with actual players in legal world, or crafted simulated versions thereof. We want them to bang up against the hard surface of practical difficulty, cultural traditions, and bureaucratic constraints, not just the intellectual focus on judicial reasoning. We couldn't imagine doctors dealing with tough cases and critical life decisions without training in practice; why should it be any different with lawyers?

Early on, we realize that while the vast majority of legal conflicts are concluded by a negotiation between the parties, unlike today, virtually no American law school offers a bargaining course. As a result we introduce negotiation exercises into our classes; students are divided into pairs, given the same problem like in a bridge tournament, and then evaluated on how they come out. We hope they learn something about how to negotiate from this approach because it is obvious that bargaining skill will become important at some point in most legal careers. We write a model negotiating problem called the Bins case based on a minority student's wrongful arrest in a criminal case that ends up being adopted by teachers in other schools. Without our permission, one creates a video version of the case. We confront a question of principle: should we assert our rights under the copyright laws and license our work for a fee *or* allow free use of our work to help in the development of a new field? We decide anyone can use what we produce, though when we publish a set of readings for clinical students our publisher insists the book has to be protected in the usual way.

We find that when an arrogant and confident student negotiates against a student we feel is more intelligent, brashness and belief in your own powers seems associated with success. In these early years of the women's movement, men of perhaps lessor intellectual ability end up achieving better settlements than women who appear less willing to display the power they have inherent in the facts of the problem, a finding that shifts the way I go about training negotiators. When one of my favorite students, a woman of undoubted ability and rare personal strength, is trounced by an arrogant male who bullies her, it dawns on me that success depends as much on the way power is displayed as on the power one has.

Our most telling experience, one that leads to disconcerting consequences for me, comes when we publish an article in a newsletter called *The Clearinghouse Review* that is read by many lawyers who represent clients without funds. The article is titled *"Negotiating Tactics for Legal Services Lawyers"*; it argues that poverty lawyers spend an enormous amount of time working out settlements but have actually received little guidance in developing best practices. The article goes on to list approaches that should be known to lawyers representing the poor. We make extremely clear that we do "not endorse the propriety" of every one of the tactics but note that they might be used against legal services lawyer so they have to be identified and understood. One of the ploys, for example, is "Appear irrational when it seems helpful"; another is "Raise some of your demands as the negotiations progress." These ethically questionable techniques were commonplace in the lower courts; often used against lawyers trying to protect clients from losing apartments, bargaining over the length of misdemeanor sentences, or aiming to quash unconscionable commercial contracts entered into by low-income consumers. These were years of great expansion in the availability of legal services to the poor. As recent graduates took up these new positions they demanded training in how to represent poor people's interests. *"Negotiating Tactics for Legal Services Lawyers"* gathered a large audience. The editors at the Clearinghouse told us it was the most sought-after reprint of any article they had published. A few years later we were asked to permit republication.

But soon the article stirred controversy from an unexpected quarter. A Louisiana federal judge—ignoring that we were informing lawyers of certain tactics that might be used against them—attacked us in a law review for recommending unethical behavior. To some who never bothered to read our original article, this no doubt tarnished our reputation. It was rumored that the dean of the Stanford Law School vetoed a proposal that I be appointed to the faculty because I coauthored the article. I found this preposterous especially as I had never applied for a job at Stanford. I certainly would have enjoyed the honor of being asked but leaving the East wouldn't have happened. I loved visiting California but as my wife joked when someone asked her if we would ever move there, "Its too far from the coast."

When I inquired of someone who knew the facts, I was told the story was true. And over thirty years later, I was astonished to read an article in one of the nation's leading academic journals asserting that Philip and I had recommended questionable tactics for legal services lawyers. When I protested, pointing to the clear language in the article that the author had ignored, an apology was forthcoming, and the language was withdrawn and even scrubbed from the online legal research platforms of Westlaw and Lexis.

Our next controversy arrived when we created a simulated case that my class litigated against Philip's. We videotaped interactions between the students. They had to take depositions in role, file and argue motions before faculty judges, and attempt to negotiate a settlement. The simulation was a controlled environment, allowing us to challenge them (but in a safe space) with problems they would confront in practice and give them extensive feedback on their performance. "What's going on here?" we asked when periodically stopping the tape to review what the students had done. "What do you see?" At first, the class was passive. This student generation had grown up watching television, not visibly interacting with what was going on in front of them. But we learned to wait them out; even a little silence pressed them to fill the space. Eventually the observations poured out. Soon we could hardly keep up with the visual critiques and buried clues the students exhumed.

Simulation is a form of educational gaming—"serious games" is what one writer labels them—that we conclude can offer an efficient way of training lawyers how to do their work. But our peers in the clinical community aren't so sure. Some clinical teachers think simulating litigation is abandoning the mission to serve the underserved. A former Ford Foundation executive named William Pincus is the key man here. A true visionary, he founded the Council on Legal Education for Professional Responsibility (CLEPR), the chief funding source for new clinics. Without his leadership, it's doubtful most of the new programs would exist. Pincus values providing legal services to the underrepresented more than anything. He believes the way to do this is to start students with real clients and real cases early on. We agree that student practice is essential but argue that simulation is a practical and powerful mode of preparation for actual lawyering tasks. While he still thinks we'd be better off opening a legal services office—something that we plan to do as soon as we can command the necessary resources—Pincus gives us a qualified blessing to try it out.

At the annual conference of the American Association of Law Schools in San Francisco, I present our approach to a crowded meeting room, playing representative videos for the assembled cadre of teachers. Pincus is in the audience, sitting next to Bill Greenhalgh, a Georgetown Law School professor who is a fierce opponent. He thinks educational games will divert students from actual practice. I sneak looks at them while I lecture. Pincus is frowning but Greenhalgh looks like he is ready to explode. Still a few months later Pincus decides to subsidize a book we planned to write for those who want to explore simulations.

We dedicate the book to Gary Bellow, a Harvard professor who is a leading light in our field. Bellow has told me that he thinks the best way to approach teaching would-be advocates is to look at how stage actors prepare. He suggests I give actor training a try myself. Eventually, I take him up on it, traveling down to Greenwich Village one night a week to join an acting class taught by Carol Rosenfeld at the HB Studio, Uta Hagen and Herbert Bergdorf's famous school for aspiring stage actors. By subjecting myself to the discipline of actor preparation, I try to find out if Bellow is right about the potential of performance training methods developed first in Russia by Konstantin Stanislavski and his disciples.

Carol is a great teacher. She has the knack of looking at the outer shell of a performance and reading what is going on inside the mind of the performer. At first, I was skeptical that she could really divine so much from the exterior but the would-be actors in the class assure me she has a gift I previously associated with talented psychotherapists. But in their case the insight was usually based on familiarity; hours of sitting with a patient. Carol, however, does her work after observing for just minutes. When my first turn comes, I am quickly converted. The task is to display total concentration while doing a common task. I bring an old brass pitcher covered with a rusty brown patina, go to the front of the room, and set to rubbing it shiny with a rag soaked in chemical cleanser. The class turns silent. The minutes pass. I rub away. At first, I focus intently on the action of the rag on the metal but then my mind wanders. I drift to remembering how I took my young daughter, Molly, to school that morning. She was silent on the bus. What, I wondered, was on her mind.

How long is this going on? Shouldn't Carol have stopped me? It feels way overdue. But in fact it has taken less than three minutes before she calls a halt. "Michael, you are thinking too much," she tells me. After some detailed comments, she bores in, "Let the action speak."

She sized me up perfectly and did it in the same way I like to work—in few words. The trick, I now decide, is to help advocates find a way to use their own experience to bring the emotional reality of their beleaguered clients' plight to the attention of legislators, judges, prosecutors, and bureaucrats who often inhabit a different social world and aren't always aware that middle class assumptions don't necessarily work for the poor. Carol's approach has lodged inside me and makes me a better teacher.

When Philip and I have learned what we could from simulating litigation, our Columbia Dean, Michael Sovern, agrees to fund our dream—a working law office for students to represent clients in the community. We interviewed every student who applied to the clinic making clear that while we will be there for them they were going to be primarily responsible for their clients' interests. The students nod in agreement but we know some will later feel they've been thrown too early into the swimming pool. We hired a managing attorney, a talented young lawyer named Holly Hartstone. She has less experience than we have but blends easily into our collaborative teaching style. Most striking, she had no hesitation telling us when she thinks we are going in the wrong direction. When I want to jump in to rescue a student from what may be a mistake, she cautions me to wait a bit to see if she can find a solution on her own. In warning me not to hover, Holly reminded me of the approach of my parents for whom helicopter parenting was a no-no. Philip and I had come full circle, starting with a hierarchical notion of our students as assistants observing us model lawyering to a place where we emphasize student

responsibility while we observe their work for later discussion. Though we were always ready to help, we forcibly
intervened only in an extreme situation.

When we decided to give students primary responsibility even at an early stage of their careers, we thought we'd
discovered a form of educational gold. We asked ourselves
regularly whether we were graduating better advocates;
lawyers who would be more sensitive to client needs. Would
the lessons from the clinic carry over to the years ahead?
Research into the professional development of lawyers
made it clear that practicing attorneys highly valued their
education for its emphasis on analytics but many also felt
important skills like drafting, negotiation, fact gathering,
counseling, and dealing with communication and human
relations were insufficiently covered. We tried to address
these lacks but in truth framed the educational mix presented to students with motives that were not purely
pedagogical.

In a decade of intense interest in social change, we hoped
our students would work against inequality, insecurity, and
segregation. We had, perhaps, a naïve faith that the kind of
lawyering modeled in the clinic would ultimately suggest a
satisfactory way of defining a professional life but we were
far from sure. In writing about our work we lamented that
"When we ceased being litigators, we may have lost much
of the power of example and may have been left trying to
make up what we say for what we no longer do." We wanted

our students to emerge as champions for the disadvantaged and while many did we, of course, had no control over the development of their careers. For us this created a dilemma that we described thusly:

". . . we get better and better at teaching lawyers to serve their clients effectively, but to what social end? For all our pride in our improvement as teachers, we remain saddled with the guilt that, to the small extent we influence our students, we are helping to produce a greater concentration of wealth and power in a nation that needs less."

The response was quick. One of the teachers who brought clinics to Columbia was an eminent academic named Walter Gellhorn. A man with a stern countenance and ramrod posture, his name may not mean much to many today but he was in his time a highly influential figure. Walter never wavered in his support of our work but that didn't mean he relaxed his opposition to what we were doing if it clashed with what he thought right and proper. When he read the language quoted above, he fired off a damming critique:

"I was not very sympathetic with your emotional dissatisfaction. . . . I don't think that you, as instructors, are either obligated or in a sense, empowered to utilize your pedagogical power to reshape society or students' choices. . . . You say you feel 'guilt' because you teach students effectively without teaching them also to serve . . . clients whose interests seem to you most worthy of good lawyers' concern. That seems to me mistaken zeal. If we were training other kinds of professionals—pediatricians, let us say—we would be concerned with equipping them to be effective deliverers of professional service; we might hope that they would deliver them to where we discerned the greatest need but I doubt that we would feel guilt if a topnotch graduate chose to practice on Park avenue instead of in East Harlem."

Of course, such guilt is exactly what I *would* feel but I still had great admiration for Walter Gellhorn. Early in his career he had given expert testimony in support of ending segregation in Southern law schools; later he started a program to train civil rights lawyers long before it was fashionable, one of whose graduates was my LDF boss Jack Greenberg. He had also advanced the career of Julius Chambers, who became a star lawyer decades later succeeding Greenberg as Director at LDF, when he arranged a graduate fellowship for him at Columbia. So I went to see him immediately to make clear any idea we were in the business of choosing paths for students other than what they wanted for themselves was a red herring. Our problem, I emphasized, was deeper. The dilemma we alluded to had nothing to do with undermining student autonomy. Rather it was a question of how we felt about our own role. Philip and I were merely recognizing that while we respected what we were doing as educators, we also cared about the social consequences of what we passed on.

As the years Philip and I worked together waned, New York City seemed to be unraveling. During the mid-1970s it had to be rescued from bankruptcy. The 1977 City-wide blackout caused by the failure of Consolidated Edison to respond effectively to lightning strikes at upstate power stations led to widespread looting, hundreds of fires, and thousands of arrests. The hostility of the rest of the country was confirmed when President Carter refused an emergency assistance designation because the disaster wasn't "natural." The common fear of violence was ratcheted up to hysteric proportions by the siege of David Berkowitz, the Son of Sam or .44 Caliber Killer, who stealthily murdered six, injured seven, and brought widespread panic to the populace.

As the decade closed we both felt it was time for a change. Clinics barely present in 1970 were setting up shop everywhere. Philip decided to go to work for the United States Arms Control Agency, dealing with nuclear proliferation issues he'd first confronted in college working on the Massachusetts senatorial campaign of university professor Stuart Hughes. I was offered the deanship of the most practice-oriented law school in America, but because it was in Boston I hesitated. My wife was for it; my eldest daughter hated the idea but finally it was up to me—could I leave Manhattan? Heli quipped, "You act like you'll need a passport."

Philip would help negotiate a nuclear proliferation agreement with the Soviets before joining the faculty of the Georgetown Law School. I like to think the bargaining skills he put to good use were honed by the "serious" games we played with our students. Among a long list of his subsequent accomplishments was creation of a pioneering clinic where students represented refugees seeking asylum before government hearing officers. In the years that followed our departure, Columbia added a raft of clinics giving students the opportunity to work on criminal cases, domestic violence, and economic development.

It was not alone. All American law schools, and many across the world, now offer students opportunities to practice where, until the creative philanthropy of William Pincus, there had been none. So many have been established that clinical work has earned its own academic jargon—now it is called "experiential education," a phrase that aims to enhance the dignity conferred by involvement with clients and courts before a student has passed the bar. Thomas F. Geraghty of Northwestern put the present understanding plainly: "Students learn best when exposed to interactive teaching methodologies that enable them to learn skills and when those skills are used to produce concrete results on behalf of individual clients and/or in support of improvements in our system of justice."

Even state schools under budgetary pressure have increased their commitment to clinical work. The University of California Law School at Irvine bragged that it had eight different "Core" clinics and that students are required to take a course with one of them. They ranged from "international justice" to "intellectual property" to representing veterans. At Yale, where I'd had my frustrating first experience with practice in the public defender's office, the

faculty for years resisted awarding credit for student practice. Today, however, the dean can write to alumni that, "A
modern law school must train its students to turn their
intellectual pursuits to practical account." The Law School
now has more than three dozen live-client clinics. Students
have helped prevent deportation of hundreds of refugees;
its Supreme Court Clinic has been involved in seventy
cases before the High Court. Recently an army of clinic
students helped stop the first Trump administration travel
ban in its tracks.

In short, clinical legal education ultimately triumphed.
Law firms and government employers could invest only so
much in training; they came to find clinic experience an
add-on to a job applicant's value. When Philip and I started,
only a couple dozen other teachers were doing what we
were. Their future employment status was uncertain, their
pay lower than colleagues, and many were often denied
access to collegial faculty decision making. But clinicians
have now arrived; the last time I looked at 200 or so law
schools there were over 1,400 teachers who do most of
their work supervising and training future advocates and
negotiators.

A main reservation about this rosy picture is that my
ultimate goal of a clinical law school has yet to be fully realized. From the beginning I believed that if the learning
through practice method was successful, it ought to be used
generally in almost all classes, not sequestered in subject

matter–specific electives. It's true that now interactive exercises, role plays, simulation, field investigations, mock trials, and video and audio playback resources can be found at all levels of a law school education where before they were nonexistent. Teachers are much looser and more active learning centered; the autocratic Professor Charles Kingsfield of the popular movie of the 1970s, *The Paper Chase*, is no longer to be found in many classrooms but I'm not sure this would have happened if more women and minorities hadn't found their way into the profession. What's missing, however, is still missing, the piece of my dream that has "experiential learning" on an equal plane with conceptual and doctrinal approaches. Both are necessary, along with more than the usual thin veneer of ethical imperatives to serve the poor, the disabled, and the unpopular.

Violence and the Word

I loved my work at Columbia but it was painful to no longer share the camaraderie of working at LDF. The frustration only increased as the courts slowed and then stopped the momentum for equal treatment of the poor that had bubbled up in the 1960s. In 1970, the Supreme Court ruled that it would not interfere with legislative choices in allocating welfare funds by setting aside maximum grant caps to families regardless of the obvious impact on families with many children. The following year the Court approved warrantless home visits, which if resisted by welfare recipients resulted in a loss of benefits; in surely one of the more bizarre Court decisions of the era, in 1973 a majority of Justices decided that an indigent had to pay a court fee before seeking bankruptcy protection. The same year the Justices issued what might be considered the deathblow to efforts to constitutionally protect against class discrimination when it approved a discriminatory Texas property tax–based public school financing system. Domination in the years ahead by Republican presidents resulted in a right-leaning judiciary, increased income inequality, "law and order" politics, and a dramatic reliance on incarceration to solve social problems.

An exception to these developments was a series of LDF employment discrimination victories. In a case against the Duke Power Company a unanimous Court adopted what became known as the "disparate impact" doctrine so that the law proscribed "not only overt discrimination but practices that are fair in form"—like the tests that Duke had used to deny jobs—"but discriminatory in operation." In short, if minority employment suffered from use of a particular practice, the practice had to be shown truly necessary to successful job performance. As important, the Justices indicated that the burden was on the employer not the employee to show that a discriminatory practice was a "business necessity."

The decision led to victories in scores of suits, some against major corporations like United States Steel, Lorillard, and Kaiser Aluminum. Jack Greenberg hired lawyers who could digitize the employment and promotion records of corporations with the result that the overwhelming proof of discrimination assembled led to favorable settlements for black workers and counsel fees to LDF, payments that were turned into resources for the next case waiting on what looked like a long line. But all too soon an increasingly conservative and business-oriented Supreme Court blocked progress under antidiscrimination employment laws; as a result, Congress had to pass the 1991 Civil Rights Act to overrule many of these decisions.

But the news about LDF's campaign against capital punishment was hardly encouraging. Despite the 1972 victory in *Furman v. Georgia* eliminating the death penalty because of the way it operated in practice, state after state adopted new sentencing schemes to bring it back. California voters overruled a state Supreme Court decision that determined capital punishment was unconstitutionally "cruel *or* unusual" by amending the state constitution. The new laws reached the Supreme Court of the United States in 1976 and capital punishment was restored.

As if he knew how much I missed being absent from the battlefield, especially while the fate of *Furman* hung in the balance. Tony Amsterdam sent me a note that's intended to make me feel better: It said, "Look at page 378 in volume 58 of the Minnesota Law Review." Today I would turn to my computer and with a few clicks find the source but in the 1970s I took a well-worn path between my office and the Law School library stacks. The volume wasn't to be found on the shelves but a friendly librarian fished it out from a pile of newly arrived publications that had yet to be cataloged. Standing at his desk I read:

". . . but as Michael Meltsner—my soul brother and collaborator in many litigations against police abuse—has recently written: 'no one feels so irrelevant as a lawyer in a shoot out.'"

My first reaction was to bask in the warmth of "soul brother." For an only child, one who imagined what it would be like to have an older sibling, acquiring a "soul brother" like Tony (he has a year on me) who I greatly admired shook me to the core. But after a while I regained my Manhattan-bred balance between irony and emotion, noting how he characteristically conferred excessive praise on those he works with.

Having forgotten, I actually questioned whether I did, indeed, write the words he quoted. But then I remembered precisely where they'd come from. When I reread the full quote, it occurred to me that here again on my part was the avoidance of conflict by choosing a lessor, and the cynic in me says less personally threatening, form of conflict. Lawyers are the true undertakers of violence. To choose such a profession is to vacate the brain space where the immediate response is physical and move to a place that, while at times may seem equally aggressive, even cruel, is dominated by words, not deeds. Yet how thick are the walls of this façade if beneath the surface, there is a force barely contained struggling to get out? Perhaps lawyering as many of us do it is simply violence that just lurks behind nice words.

Certainly this is true of the legal process as a whole, and the role of judges within it. Though Alexander Hamilton famously observed in the *Federalist Papers* (No. 78) that judges possessed only judgment, not the "sword or the purse," behind every decree is the power of the state, no matter that deploying that power is usually unnecessary. Indeed, the orders of a court whether they mention the iron fist in the velvet glove or not cannot be understood as anything but commands for obedience that implicitly suppress dissent.

It is true, of course, that insisting "This is the way things will be because I say so" (speaking as the law) is often a way of employing a threat of violence to defeat greater use of it. Examples of this kind of force of law are not hard to find in the criminal law; they are often raised and praised when terrorism is at issue. When, however, in 1957 President Eisenhower sent in the 101st Airborne Division to ensure the integration of Little Rock Central High School, Little Rock, Arkansas, he was acting to enforce a federal court injunction prohibiting state officials from interfering with the decision of the courts, one obtained by the joint efforts of the Department of Justice and LDF. One of the most memorable days of my time at Yale was when after the President acted, Alexander Bickel, in our constitutional law class, departed from the day's assignment to scrupulously analyze the laws authorizing and the documents implementing the dispatch of troops to ensure the court order was honored. The following year in ultimately affirming the supremacy of federal law, the Supreme Court made clear that "No state legislator or executive or judicial officer can war against the Constitution without violating his undertaking to support it." In Arkansas, Governor Faubus and state legislators were also making claims under law, both

local law and their view of the federal Constitution as subject to a state veto or "interposition."

The winner in this clash is ultimately the institution with
the most power, a matter where race is involved that ultimately goes back to who won the Civil War. Depending on
whose ox is gored, the implementation of law can be understood as either a screen for violence or the best use of government authority to promote public safety, order, and
equity. But regardless of which side you are on, once the
shooting begins and the bodies are being carried to the
morgue, the lawyer has failed.

Tony's *Perspectives on the Fourth Amendment* was three
lectures sponsored by what is called the Oliver Wendell
Holmes Devise. The Justice left funds in his will to which
Congress later added to document and disseminate the
history of the Supreme Court. While the Fourth Amendment with its fluid interpretive gloss on when search and
seizure is authorized (they cannot be "unreasonable")
remains something of a constitutional problem child even
today, no analysis of its preferred interpretation has been
more influential. He urged police departments to set their
own standards and rules governing searches and seizures
because by owning them they would more likely see that
they were followed. Rather than continuing to decide a flock
of poorly related and understood random individual cases
under the Amendment, the judicial role would become
reviewing the content and application of police regulations.
The Supreme Court has never gone this far but present

statutory law confers on the Department of Justice the opportunity through negotiation and, if that fails, litigation to exercise the sort of oversight role Amsterdam suggested when a police department has engaged in a pattern and practice of violating constitutional rights. Before the Trump administration took over, the DOJ increasingly used these powers, often in inflammatory racial controversies like that which followed the police shooting of Michael Brown in Ferguson, Missouri, to require local departments to adopt policies more guaranteeing of Fourth Amendment values of privacy and security. But nothing illustrates the vortex of contending forces attending the societal mix of violence and law than the history of the police practice known as stop and frisk.

"I am married to Raymond Fullwood, a Negro. Because I am a Caucasian, in the five years of our marriage, we have been stopped no less than twenty times by Los Angeles police officers. . . . I am certain the reason they chose to stop us is because we are a mixed couple. Mrs. Marilyn Fullwood."

So began LDF's brief in the 1968 Supreme Court cases that empowered police officers to detain individuals on the street without the usual probable cause to believe a crime had been or was about to be committed, if the officer had only a reasonable suspicion that the person may be engaged in criminal activity. The Court was asked to rule for the first time in American history to permit police to restrain and search when they did not have sufficient evidence to hold the person to answer criminal charges.

LDF's brief was a passionate attack of both the constitutionality and the practice of stop and frisk. It argued that
police are trained to be suspicious and to rely on intuition.
As a result, approving stop and frisk is a "broad all purpose
rubber stamp for validating police intrusions." The stops, we
contended, were actually as intrusive as arrests; excepting
the trip to the stationhouse, the loss of personal liberty was
much the same. Likewise, frisks turned out to be much like
searches. Initially described as a quick pat down for officer
safety, the frisk we predicted correctly would soon morph
into a means for an officer to search for a weapon or drugs.

Approving stop and frisk meant that the fruits of the
frisk would now be admissible in evidence if a judge found
the officer's suspicion was reasonable. Of course, the judge
would not have an opportunity to review the legality of the
stop and frisk if no charges resulted from the police conduct. Because this was the outcome of the vast majority of
stops, unless an individual initiated a complicated, costly,
and often futile lawsuit to challenge police practices, the
character and frequency of illegal stops would be invisible
to the public and the courts. Our brief warned that relying on a vague suspicion test conferred such broad discretion on police to detain citizens that it violated the Fourth
Amendment's protection against unreasonable invasions
of privacy.

But like so much of the way the criminal law plays
out, stop and frisk was really all about race—approval of
this essentially subjective power to police would lead to an

escalation of dangerous conflicts with members of minority communities. If the police and the ghetto dweller view each other with fear, suspicion, and often hatred, any enforced stop is a potential source of conflict. But when the stop is based on the inarticulate, unregulated judgment of the cop on the beat, the potential is magnified. To avoid the intense danger of igniting destructive community conflict, LDF argued that authority for stop and frisk should be rejected.

In a statement that we reprinted in the brief my father-in-law, John Spiegel, wrote that research into the origins of the riots of the 1960s suggested police and blacks often regarded each other in a way that was particularly dangerous—they viewed the other as "animal-like, brutal and sadistic." These attitudes resulted in a vicious circle of behavior that John concluded only "serves to confirm the image which the Negro males and police officers hold of each other." Cops viewed blacks as inherently violent; black men believed that the way they were seen so frightened the police that they overacted with excessive use of weapons and physical force, behavior that led to contempt of the police on the part of the men. These attitudes stimulated and intensified the whole cycle of fear and excess again. In such a situation, the brief concluded, to legitimize detention and search on suspicion—without probable cause—"is to give free reign to police intervention in the most dangerous way."

The Supreme Court rejected these arguments, significantly focusing on the specific facts of the Terry case and holding that the officer's actions were reasonable, thus comporting with the Fourth Amendment, when:

". . . two men hover about a street corner for an extended period of time, at the end of which it becomes apparent that they are not waiting for anyone or anything; where these men pace alternately along an identical route, pausing to stare in the same store window roughly 24 times; where each completion of this route is followed immediately by a conference between the two men on the corner; where they are joined in one of these conferences by a third man who leaves swiftly, and where the two men finally follow the third and rejoin him a couple of blocks away."

The Court's opinion avoided the thrust of LDF's systemic argument—urging wholesale street detentions would cause hostility and disruption—by responding that "The wholesale harassment by certain elements of the police, of which minority groups, particularly Negroes, frequently complain, will not be stopped by the exclusion of any evidence from any criminal trial."

The only dissenter from this view, Justice Abe Fortas, pointed out that the Fourth Amendment ban on unreasonable searches and seizures was drafted by the Framers to prohibit allowing the police to arrest and search on suspicion. Fortas, however, also failed to deal with the consequences of stop and frisk on relations between the races. No one can say with certainty whether a different decision by the Supreme Court in 1968 would have made for a different reality on the streets of America's cities but it is clear that LDF accurately predicted what eventually occurred and tried to prevent it. The chickens came home to roost in major cities like Philadelphia and Chicago but New York City became the prime case after it initiated a policy of aggressive policing in minority neighborhoods, often for truly minor offenses. Under the City's program, hundreds of thousands of people were stopped every year, creating enormous tension between the police and minority communities. Police soon justified their stops on the basis of claims like "furtive movements," or "area has high incidence of crime" or presence of a "suspicious bulge/object." It's not difficult to see the way stop and frisk played out as a giant step toward the massive move toward imprisonment and related forms of social control that has meant the United States has the highest incarceration rate in the world.

Crime statistics are consistently twisted to support whatever argument the user is making but the data that emerged from studies of the City's use of stop and frisk were hardly a testament to the effectiveness of a tactic that had dramatic social costs. In 2012, for example, the year before the trial in the case that successfully challenged the New York practices, only 5% of the stops recorded on police contact forms resulted in a summons, 6% in an arrest, and a minuscule 0.15% in the confiscation of guns.

But did stop and frisk affect crime rates? The *New York Daily News*, once a supporter of the practice, admitted that it was wrong to believe it stopped crime—the justification for the decreased standard of proof. "We are delighted to say that we were wrong." When the NYPD began scaling back its stops, the number reported fell 97% from a high of 685,700 in 2011 to 22,900 in 2015. Not only did crime fail to rise, but also New York hit record lows. Whether wrongly or rightly, however, the constitutional question—substituting the lower "suspicion" standard for probable cause—had been settled. In individual cases the application of the lessor standard can, of course, be challenged on the facts, though no one should believe that this is easily done; however, the systemic question—discriminatory use by a police department—remains. The decision in the challenge case was based on finding that the police had profiled and targeted black and Hispanic young men in particular areas of the City. They suffered a potential arrest record, a frightening invasion of privacy and humiliation along with consequences passed on to their children, families, and neighbors. In 2013, to remedy the widespread constitutional violations Judge Shira Scheindlin ordered a court-appointed monitor to oversee a series of reforms to NYPD policing practices. After the Court of Appeals for the Second Circuit stayed this remedy a new City Administration decided to accept the lower court's decision and drop an appeal.

Judge Scheindlin refused to consider as a defense evidence of the effectiveness of stop and frisk as a crime-reducing mechanism. But the question remains how the social costs of the practice, illegitimate as it was found to be, related to potential gains in law enforcement. Does crime reduction outweigh the hostility and pain it generates? Can we strike a balance in this case between the competing interests of a government with the responsibility to maintain safe streets and the rights of Americans to be in public without fear of police interference? It was widely reported that stop and frisk gained traction in the City as a way of reducing gun violence. If that's the case, did it work? In answering, it's not enough to point out that the detentions failed to produce significant numbers of arrests; rather the more difficult inquiry is whether the fear of stop and frisk reduced the presence and use of firearms. The argument that it did is not insubstantial, as put by one scholarly professor Jeffrey Belin: "The facts suggest, at least tentatively, that mass stop-and-frisk, along with related aggressive policing strategies, while inflicting harmful privacy intrusions on a large swath of innocent citizens, may decrease violent crime and incarceration by deterring" carrying and use of weapons.

Here's the conundrum. Prevention and deterrence of carrying weapons in public is an obvious value yet as the New York experience shows it depends on violating the Constitution by harming vast numbers of minority men. Even though only a tiny fraction of those stopped and frisked will have anything to do with weapons, the message to weapon holders is that the risks of carrying are significantly increased. But as Professor Belin concluded, "while isolated 'stop and frisks' will always be available to individual police officers as a crime-fighting tactic, crime-deterring strategies based on massive applications of stops and frisks cannot lawfully be sustained at least absent dramatic shifts in longstanding constitutional doctrine." New York was not alone in grappling with the fallout from stop and frisk. In 2014, the Chicago Police Department (CPD) conducted more than a quarter of a million stops of civilians that did not lead to an arrest. Chicagoans were stopped more than four times as often as people in New York. While street detentions are just one of the police department problems facing relations between the CPD and minority communities, the numbers are deeply troubling.

Can a court-appointed monitor working with a police department under court supervision—the kind of action suggested by Tony's Holmes Lecture approach—produce policies that reduce gun violence *and* racially targeted enforcement? The monitor appointed by the judge to check on compliance and develop better guides for NYPD action was as good a choice as can be imagined for such a demanding task. Judge Scheindlin chose attorney Peter Zimroth, an eminent lawyer with an extraordinary set of relevant experiences. A partner in a major law firm, he had been the much praised corporation counsel of the City—its chief legal officer. Earlier in his career he served as an assistant US attorney, the chief assistant district attorney in Manhattan, and a law clerk to liberal jurists, US Supreme Court Justice Abe Fortas, and Chief Judge David Bazelon of the District of Columbia Court of Appeals. He even had a stint as a summer intern at the Legal Defense Fund.

Zimroth soon set up a process that would train, monitor, supervise, and discipline officers adequately to prevent
a widespread pattern of racial profiling, arbitrary, and race-
based stops. His agenda included:

- helping the Department develop a body camera
  program;
- requiring police to collect data on all stops and make
  the data public to be analyzed and assessed;
- requiring regular training for officers on legal requirements for stop and frisks;
- requiring police officers to issue a receipt for every
  pedestrian stop, with the officer's name, the time of the
  encounter, the place of the encounter, and the reason
  for the encounter—making it possible to facilitate a
  civilian complaint regarding the encounter; and
- issuing regular progress and compliance reports to the
  supervising judge.

Enforcement of these and forthcoming new rules is, however, a work in progress. Until recently, New York cops still
used stop and frisk over fifty times a day. Focus groups for
officers suggest a poor understanding of obligations under
legitimate stop and frisk procedures. But a 2017 report from
Zimroth showed overall progress while indicating a lot
more was necessary. Street stops had decreased, which ironically raised fears by activists of underreporting, but the
racial disparity in stops had narrowed. Hispanics remained
more likely to be searched and arrested but blacks were less

likely than whites to be found carrying guns, the report concluded.

Can what is basically a rule of law approach advance two legitimate but seemingly conflicting goals? According to Professor Belin, "a program of aggressive policing designed to deter unlawful gun carrying like that employed in New York City can be either effective or constitutional, but not both."

The Supreme Court ignored LDF's rejection of stop and frisk but offered a few words to mitigate the damage its new standard might cause by insisting that police are not entitled to seize and search every person of whom they make inquiries: "Before he places a hand on the person of a citizen in search of anything, he must have constitutionally adequate, reasonable grounds for doing so. In the case of the self-protective search for weapons, he must be able to point to particular facts from which he reasonably inferred that the individual was armed and dangerous." As a text this sounds clear and convincing. Yet the reality of stop and frisk on the streets and highways of America is replete with instances in which the Court has been totally disregarded.

A few examples from a pool of thousands make the point:

1. A college police officer responded to a call to investigate a man pushing a woman in a public area on a college's campus. He found a student who had been hanging out with and kissing his girlfriend.

Invoking stop and frisk, the officer demanded he submit to a search for a weapon believing that officers are free to conduct a frisk whenever they are investigating a potential "domestic violence" incident, regardless of the specific circumstances of the call or the facts encountered. When the student refused the search, the officer tasered him. A court later found the officer employed excessive force but excused him from any liability because the use of force did not violate clearly established law.

2. Former Arizona's Maricopa County Sheriff Joe Arpaio has been convicted of contempt of court because of "stop and frisk" practices that indisputably profiled Hispanics. The Sheriff, who declared a law enforcement war against suspected illegal immigrants, stated in an interview that an individual's manner of dress alone is sufficient reasonable suspicion to stop and frisk. Arpaio was, of course, pardoned by President Trump.

3. Here is what the National Rifle Association says about Stop and Frisk:

> The basic effect of the [stop and frisk] decision is that police can stop and frisk you for weapons and drugs for pretty much any reason whatsoever and never will they either face a . . . lawsuit or have evidence get thrown out of court.

4. A man was riding his bike down the Gulf Coast Highway in Escambia County, Florida, when a police car pulled up behind him. As the officer later explained, he had no reason to suspect that the man was doing anything illegal but he hadn't seen the man before and wanted to make his acquaintance. As they talked, the man started fidgeting—he had a pocketknife on his person, he explained. The officer conducted a search, and found crack cocaine. In Florida, cocaine possession is a third-degree felony; the sixty-four-year-old African American was sentenced to the maximum five years in prison. An appeals court affirmed the conviction, denying that the cocaine was seized in an illegal stop and frisk because the officer "never ordered him to stop, but merely engaged in a conversation with him." Fidgeting was enough suspicion to initiate a search.

5. Pennsylvania state legislator Jewell Williams had just picked up his dry cleaning and was driving home through North Philadelphia when he noticed officers had stopped a car with two elderly black men inside. The officers frisked the driver, and when a cop set his cash down on the trunk of the car, the loose paper bills fluttered away in the wind and were scooped up by patrons from a nearby bar. "So I got out of the car, and I was yelling to the people, 'Yo, leave that man's money

alone!'" says Williams, who is black. The cops got angry. They swore at and handcuffed the driver and passenger, a city employee and a retired tailor, and put them both in a patrol car. Williams, standing next to his vehicle with legislative tags, pulled out his state representative ID and even pointed to his home, which was on the other side of an overgrown lot. "Get back in your fucking car before I give you a bunch of tickets," one cop told him. Williams said he was then handcuffed and pushed into a police vehicle. The lawsuit he filed forced Philadelphia to change how it stops and searches its residents. But a subsequent report written by the lawyers representing Williams found that police were not obeying the terms of the settlement.

6. Just moments before she passed a black man walking on the shoulder of a street, seemingly to avoid construction along the sidewalk, a woman noticed an unmarked police car. The vehicle pulled in front of the pedestrian and cut him off; a plainclothes officer emerged and accused the man of walking in the middle of the road. The allegation shocked her, the woman later said, and as she witnessed the officer take the man by the back of his jacket. She told the officer, "You were the one who incited this." But the man was placed in handcuffs.

The gap between African Americans and police is apparently as enormous now as it was when John Spiegel lamented it in 1968 but in a speech to police chiefs, FBI Director James Comey took a different view. He thought video images of police shootings had given the public an inaccurate impression that there was an epidemic of police violence against black people. Comey told a gathering of police chiefs that despite a wave of protests prompted by fatal police shootings of black men and boys, "Americans actually have no idea" about how often police use lethal force because nobody has collected enough data. His views, however, contrasted with those of one of the nation's most respected criminologists who concluded approximately 1,000 Americans were killed each year at the hands of the police. According to Franklin Zimring of the University of California many of the deaths were unnecessary, caused by foolish rules governing lethal force and failures of police leadership.

The conflict between the police and minority communities existed for decades before it was forcefully labeled as a danger to the public peace by national commission reports in the 1960s but it endures, sharply intensified by the use of stop and frisk and the failure of efforts to deter excessive use of lethal force. Sadly, aggressive policing is just part of an increasing use of the criminal law—through mandatory minimum sentencing, excessive incarceration even of low-level offenders, denial of safety net protections, and prison rehabilitation programs—to exercise control over the consequences of social dislocation, alienation, poverty, and mental illness. Ironically, anxiety over violence diverts attention and resources from efforts to curb it by increasing economic opportunity and improving education.

We live with the consequences.

Charleston and Beyond

What I remember most about Charleston in 1963: the August heat that no courtroom fan could defeat and the performance of my LDF colleague Connie Motley, a woman I once described as "solid as an oak tree . . . who suffered little nonsense" from segregationists. LDF lawyers might get away with calling her "Connie" but to the world she was Constance Baker Motley, Mrs. Motley, Borough President Motley, State Senator Motley, Judge, and finally Chief Judge Motley. The daughter of a Yale university chef, her career was meteoric. Hired by Thurgood Marshall after graduation, she once commented about entering law school that at Columbia "men were being drafted, and suddenly women who had done well in college were considered acceptable candidates for the vacant seats."

By 1962, she was second in command in the office hierarchy and had compiled a formidable record bringing cases that integrated all-white universities in the deep South. Charleston was the first time I would get to work closely with her and I wasn't disappointed. Years later when she was a judge in New York (the first black female to be appointed to the federal bench), she occasionally appointed me to represent prisoners asking that their convictions be overturned for constitutional violations. I always tried to put my best efforts into these cases; there was something about the gravity of Mrs. Motley's demeanor that made you aspire to the highest standards of the profession.

The Supreme Court had declared school segregation unconstitutional in 1954—one of the cases came from South Carolina—but nine years later when we journeyed to Charleston no black child had stepped foot in a previously white school. One reason was the gloss put on *Brown v. Board of Education* by a North Carolina federal appeals judge—John J. Parker—who had been denied Supreme Court Senate confirmation in 1930 because of his antilabor and racial views. In considering how courts should handle school segregation cases after Brown, Parker took the narrow view that "Fourteenth Amendment rights are only individual rights; that therefore Negro school children individually must exhaust their administrative remedies and will not be allowed to bring class action suits to desegregate a school system." Because the Supreme Court had followed Brown a year later with a decision that integration should proceed at "deliberate speed," school boards across the South were allowed for over a decade to seize on Parker's words as justification for doing nothing to dismantle segregated schooling.

Enraged by his state's resistance, J. Arthur Brown, the South Carolina NAACP president, finally organized a small group seeking to end segregation by suing the Charleston school board. The case dragged on and was finally named for his daughter, Millicent; when it was called for trial, Mrs. Motley and I were sent by LDF to represent the children and their parents.

At first, there was nothing different about the case than dozens of others we'd brought across the South. There could be no factual dispute about the school district policy of segregation. The real question was how much desegregation Kennedy appointee Robert Martin would order and how long a delay he would countenance. But then there was a shocking development. White parents retained a Washington lawyer, George Leonard, to intervene in the case. Funded by covert right wing sources, with the judge's permission he proposed to present factual "proof" that the Supreme Court's 1954 decision was wrong: it need not be followed, Leonard submitted, because the decision assumed blacks and whites were created equal but blacks were in fact inferior beings.

Human rights lawyers take as a given that for every court victory, the opposition, especially if they have power and money, will take steps to circumvent the result. Leonard's dog and pony show—he aimed it at a number of Southern school systems—was just a more blatant version of the type.

He brought with him to Charleston well-paid but on-the-fringe academics who testified that Negro test scores and brain weights—they were more like dolphins!—were consistently lower than those of whites and that black and white children were so different in intellectual capacity and behavior that they should not go to school together. On the radio I had debated the death penalty with one of the witnesses, Ernest van den Haag, who taught at Fordham and NYU. He opined that blacks and whites should never live in the same community (it turned out he lived in Manhattan, in Greenwich Village) and that school integration would produce high crime rates, social disruption, and poor health.

There was no jury in a case like this; Judge Martin could have barred the testimony but he let Leonard have his day in court so that he couldn't complain later he wasn't heard. Because the testimony was both junk science and legally irrelevant, we declined to cross-examine Leonard's witnesses. But it was difficult to sit silently listening to what was really hate speech, especially as the jury box was filled—this being the first serious effort to get the state to actually integrate its schools—with a clutch of reporters avidly scribbling in their notebooks. A usually impassive Mrs. Motley did her share of squirming, as did I, as we listened to the parade of pejorative testimony masquerading as science.

After the "experts" testified, the school board lawyers took over from Leonard and called to the stand local superintendent of schools, Thomas Carrere. After his direct examination concluded, Mrs. Motley suddenly decided to question him. I expected she might ask about the logistics of converting a dual system to a unitary nonracial one but to my surprise she was interested in only one issue: "You've heard the testimony," she said irritably. "Do you agree that the Negro children you were hired to educate are so different than whites that they can't learn together?"

Panic spread instantly across Mr. Carrere's face. He had the look of a man torn between his calling and his need for a job. In answer to her question, he mumbled something about how he had to believe what he'd just heard from the witnesses. She expressed astonishment, asked a few more questions, and dismissed him, but when he left the witness stand he passed between this tall, striking-looking black woman and the jury box. Not looking at Carrere, she fixed a hard stare at the assembled journalists; speaking in a voice they could plainly hear she laid the man down: "You should be ashamed of yourself."

At her words, the superintendent physically cringed and fled the courtroom. If the judge heard what she had said, he gave no indication of it. After the trial, he basically ignored the white superiority "science" but he also left the biracial school system untouched. Following Judge Parker's lead, he ordered only the eleven black students involved in the lawsuit to enter the white schools the following month.

Millicent Brown was one of them. Now a history professor at a local college, she and another black girl soon began to attend the white Rivers High School but while she made one close white friend as with many integration pioneers Brown found the experience painful and isolating. Like many Americans, Charlestonians often believe they've put their racism behind them but in truth the City has much to overcome. Between 1783 and 1808 when importation of slaves was banned, 100,000 Africans were delivered from the harbor to its thriving slave markets. Many were dispersed across the South but according to the *New York Times*, South Carolina's slave population grew over the years to 400,000. The state's agriculture production and building trades were dependent on them.

A tourist mecca today, Charleston has been led a by a relatively progressive mayor since the 1970s; locals heralded creation of a new International African American Museum due to open in 2019. But race relations in Charleston are as muddled as in other places in the country, exacerbated by economic inequality between the races. In 1980, the Charleston peninsula, the most attractive part of the City, was two-thirds black, but by 2010, the area became two-thirds white. The Charleston *Post and Courier* attributed this dramatic shift to black flight. "The city's black residents have fled to nearby suburbs, most likely as a reaction to gentrification, which often brings inflated rents and an overall higher cost of living to urban neighborhoods."

In April 2015, a white police officer shot and killed a fifty-year-old black man after a traffic stop for a broken brake light. A few months later, the infamous Charleston church shooting took place at the historic Emanuel African Methodist Episcopal Church in downtown Charleston. During a prayer service, nine black worshippers were gunned down

by twenty-one-year-old Dylann Roof who confessed that
he committed the shooting in hopes of igniting a race war.
Charleston may be a different place today than it was in
1963 but, while I hope so, the evidence is decidedly mixed.

Despite recent events like the Charleston shootings,
which are hardly restricted to a city in South Carolina, one
of the more unsettling notions in today's America is the
belief that white people still shouldn't be labeled as "racist"
even when they consistently support policies that single out
racial minorities for harmful treatment. Take the view of
one prominent linguist, John McWhorter, that the way we
use the word "racism" has become imprecise and so abusive that we should retire it. He argues that while "people
of color still labor under the fact that their color makes
them likely to be raised by people with less money, less
access to solid schooling and health care, and less likely to
obtain or keep a solid job," use of the term "societal racism"
to describe these conditions blocks us from dealing with
these conditions effectively because "it is thought more interesting to teach whites to acknowledge their 'privilege' than
[for example] to espouse reading programs . . . proven effective in teaching (black) kids to read." "Racism," he argues,
has been turned into "subjectification," changing from an
"objective" to a "personal" reference. In other words, it now
describes not a belief in the inferiority of a race but something a minority person *feels* when a "societal discrepancy"
is tagged "racism." He would replace societal racism with
"racial inequality" because it somehow avoids "scolding white

people." After all claims of implicit bias can lead to a "witch hunt."

McWhorter's essay, published in *The Boston Globe*, days after the election of Donald Trump whose selection he deplored, should be taken seriously because it stands as one of the more elegant and carefully reasoned justifications for continuation of the "racial inequality" he earnestly wishes to reverse. To be clear, most, though certainly not all, of the actions that maintain inequality come from white people. But the results of these actions are impossible to dismantle unless we take seriously that context matters. Our problem is hardly confined to those who sneer or engage in hate speech. In a democracy what large numbers of people feel when confronted with instance after instance of what the legal scholar Lawrence M. Friedman calls efforts to create a "hierarchy of dominance by the majority-white citizens at the expense of non-white citizens, [is] an effort that infects multiple aspects of public life."

It takes a certain kind of blindness, even when self-interest is *not* factored in, to downplay the racial imperatives that lurk behind key public events in American history, a history that persists despite the transformative changes in millions of lives that emanated from the Civil Rights Movement. In short, humiliation is not some transient sentiment. It is both a feeling that affects behavior and a consequence of messages sent by hundreds of years of actions by lawmakers, law enforcers, as well as private citizens. What some like to label as the country's "original sin" can be seen in our cherished Constitution that sought to ensure slaves never became a decisive factor in electoral politics by defining them as counting as three-fifths of a person in determining political representation in the House of Representatives and the compromise over slave status that brought us the antidemocratic Electoral College. These foundational compromises reflect an ambivalence about race that has never left us—the South wanted slaves counted the same as their masters; delegates from Northern non–slave states wanted only free inhabitants to be counted for seats in the House.

The Framers "split" the difference. The infamous Dred Scott decision of 1857 defining African slaves as chattels ("An item of Personal Property that is movable; it may be animate or inanimate") had to be reversed by the Civil War at the cost of hundreds of thousands of lives. But reconstruction efforts to integrate the freed slaves into full citizenship were canceled by the Hayes–Tilden electoral compromise of 1876, awarding the White House on the understanding that the new president would remove federal troops from the South. The Supreme Court in *Plessy v. Ferguson* enshrined segregation in the Constitution for fifty-eight years but it did so under the mask of "separate but equal," a proviso which was still another way that allowed those in power—read white men—to claim they were not really racists. Then *Brown v. Board of Education* began the process of toppling the formal structure of segregation and discrimination but tellingly it did so without indicting the history of white supremacy beliefs that traveled in the same compartment as slavery, segregation, and discrimination. In the words of Harvard professor Randall Kennedy:

[Chief Justice] "Warren insisted upon writing an opinion that was non-accusatory, he omitted a central aspect of the segregation story: the reason why segregationists separated students racially pursuant to the coercive force of governmental power. Perhaps Warren's choice was prudent. Maybe euphemism was part of the price for a unanimous repudiation of the separate but equal doctrine. Maybe unanimity was essential. But whatever the merits of the judicial strategy, Brown is notably lacking in clarity and candor. Missing from the most honored race relations decision in American constitutional history is a straightforward reckoning with deplorable racism."

This was the attitude that expressed itself also in the regular denial of the racism, or as Professor McWhorter would call it "racial inequality," involved in efforts to eliminate economic, educational, and criminal justice disparities. Take the way the Supreme Court dealt with capital punishment. In 1963, Justice Arthur Goldberg courageously opened the discussion by urging the Justices to consider declaring the death penalty for rape unconstitutional. His opinion listed both moral and penology arguments but in order not to offend white America the opinion was sheared of its most profound constitutional objection, that death for rape had been crafted almost a century earlier and applied thereafter to look like it applied to all offenders but was in fact almost always a penalty reserved for black men convicted of raping white women. Ignoring this history was a bow to continued power of the mythic belief in uncontrolled black sexuality. It's no accident that the death penalty was oft-supported in the South by self-identified "moderates," men who thought it would lead to less lynching.

When the Supreme Court decided *Brown v. Board of Education* in 1954, it confronted constitutional provisions meant to ensure, as the Justices put it as early as 1872, "the freedom of the slave race." Yet in 2007 a plurality of the Court turned the Amendment on its head in an important case from Seattle, Washington, by holding that a white student could not be denied a choice of school under a voluntarily adopted school assignment plan that sought to reduce segregation and increase diversity by employing racial criteria. In his opinion Chief Justice Roberts brushed aside evidence that a racially diverse environment is highly beneficial for minority learners, basically equating the community interest in fostering integration with the desire of a single white student to attend a particular school. To do otherwise, he concluded, would be unconstitutional racial balancing and famously "The way to stop discrimination on the basis of race is to stop discriminating on the basis of race."

One dissenter, Justice John Paul Stevens, replied, "There is a cruel irony in the Chief Justice's reliance on our decision in Brown. . . . Before Brown, schoolchildren were told where they could and could not go to school based on the color of their skin." Roberts "fails to note that it was only black schoolchildren who were so ordered; indeed, the history books do not tell stories of white children struggling to attend black schools. In this and other ways, the Chief Justice rewrites the history of one of this Court's most important decisions."

Roberts answered that according to Stevens, the Court "equate[s] remedial preferences with invidious discrimination," and ignores the difference between "an engine of oppression" and an effort "to foster equality in society," or, more colorfully, "between a 'No Trespassing' sign and a welcome mat," but it "does nothing of the kind . . . it simply means that whenever the government treats any person unequally because of his or her race, that person has suffered an injury that falls squarely within the language and spirit of the Constitution's guarantee of equal protection." In a retort to another dissenter, Roberts wrote that Justice Breyer speaks of bringing "the races" together—as the justification for excluding individuals on the basis of their race—but "Absent searching judicial inquiry into the justification for such race based measures, there is simply no way of determining what classifications are benign' or 'remedial' and what classifications are in fact motivated by illegitimate notions of racial inferiority or simple racial politics."

In short, the Court has said that all racial classifications imposed by government "must be analyzed," which on the surface seems to make sense when dealing with the volatile issues of race and public policy. But as scholar John Hart Ely pointed out the usual reason for strictly examining the grant by a white-dominated process to advantage minorities and disadvantage whites lacks the suspicion that invidious discrimination against the minority has taken place. The Chief Justice joined the historical parade of those upholding fair on its face, though not so fair at all in practice approaches that have consistently characterized efforts to cope with the legacy of our slave and Jim Crow past. The context and contrast of exclusion as between blacks and whites are totally different. Of course, other minorities have suffered from discrimination but their persecution, harsh as it might have been, simply doesn't compare with the length, depth, and persistence of racist acts and beliefs targeting black Americans. If, however, a similar case can be made for another minority, be it ethnic or economic, well then the best remedy is to treat that group also with training, skills, and meaningful allocation of resources.

The "strict scrutiny" test Roberts relied on to reject affirmative efforts to redress the legacy of deprivation and inequality is narrow and rigid. In one of the few exceptions approved—the policy of the University of Michigan Law School to ensure a diverse student body—the Court felt it necessary to express the expectation "that 25 years from now, the use of racial preferences will no longer be necessary to further the interest approved today." That hope might be an encouraging aspiration if it came as part of a national consensus to deal with the present remnants of past policies and attitudes. The time limit, however, only makes sense, as Andrew Vallis put it, if "what is envisioned is a (transitional) period during which race-conscious policies are necessary to overcome the legacies of the past." As of the post-2016 election period there is absolutely no sign of a sustained effort in that direction. Ironically, it may be that the elimination of formal legal support of segregation allowed many Americans to decide racism was a thing of the past.

The wishful thinking that we can simply by the passage of time without taking rigorous and persistent action inhabit a color-blind society is hardly new. Only eighteen years after the adoption of the constitutional amendment that ended slavery, the Supreme Court declared:

> When a man has emerged from slavery, and by the aid of beneficent legislation has shaken off the inseparable concomitants of that state, there must be some stage in the progress of his elevation when he takes the rank of a mere citizen and ceases to be the special favorite of the laws, and when his rights as a citizen, or a man, are to be protected in the ordinary modes by which other men's rights are protected.

The "beneficent legislation" in question was most probably the Act that created the Freedmen's Bureau, an early affirmative action effort to ease the transition of the former slaves (as well as poor whites) to the new era. The Bureau distributed food to the poor and set up hundreds of schools but it was opposed by leading Southerners and lacking sustained support from Congress it died along with the rest of Reconstruction. There you have it in a nutshell. Forced enslavement from across the world, families ripped apart, deprived of education and the liberty conferred on others, legally treated as chattels, then held in peonage, and landless. Well, we've given you a few years of federal welfare and eighteen years of equality under the law so now pull up those bootstraps! Sadly, this way of thinking is still with us.

The primary question for me never has been to succor the victims. Anyone with a sense of history knows that human beings are capable of humanitarian assistance but, valuable as it may be, such steps are time limited, and never enough. No, the question is what kind of a country you get if you don't make "special favorites" of those you have made "special victims." Do we want a country where, for example, more than half of African American men in their thirties have served time in prison (the case, e.g., in Wisconsin), a status that effectively blocks most of them (and perhaps their families) from becoming middle class? A country where the wealth of white households is thirteen times the median wealth of black households and ten times the wealth of Hispanic households? Still pursuing a route away from caste system policies will never be successful if the approach taken ignores that no group has a monopoly on losing out. Ninety percent of those born in 1940 will earn more than their parents; only 50% born in 1980 will do so. Inequality ultimately affects the entire spectrum of Americans.

Because for many years ending capital punishment was at the top of my personal agenda, the most egregious recent example of rejecting proof of racial bias when it marks a system rather than a proved intentional act against an individual was the decision in 1987, in which the Court ruled in the case of *McCleskey v. Kemp* that even solid statistical evidence gathered by stellar researchers of racial disparities in the administration of the death penalty did not offend the Constitution. A majority of the Justices chose to require proof of direct intent to discriminate that is impossible to find—no longer do officials or jurors admit or publicize and even brag of their bias against blacks as they did a century ago. The evidence ultimately rejected was a study of 2,484 murder cases in Georgia put together by criminologist David Baldus. His team looked into hundreds of factors that might influence sentencing decisions; they found one dominated—killers of white people were four times more likely on average to be sentenced to death when the victim was white. David Bruck, a veteran capital case lawyer, wrote that, "The correlation that the Baldus study shows between race and death sentencing in Georgia is two-and-a-half times greater than the proven correlation between cigarette smoking and heart disease." He added: "If this case involved race discrimination in the way Georgia hires prison guards or assigns first graders to public schools . . .

Georgia would almost certainly lose. Ordinary civil rights lawsuits rarely involve evidence of race discrimination as detailed and as powerful."

The Supreme Court assumed the findings of the Baldus study were valid but nevertheless held that there was no violation of the Constitution. Proof of massive sentencing disparities based on race wasn't enough; Justice Powell, the opinion writer, feared such disparities could be found throughout the justice system. In dissent, Justice William Brennan called Powell out for being fearful of "too much Justice." A frustrated Tony Amsterdam compared the decision to the infamous 1857 decision that black slaves were property and not citizens. He called it the Dred Scott decision of our time. If you credit the story, after he retired his biographer Professor John Jeffries Jr. asked Justice Powell whether, given the chance, he would change his vote in any case.

"Yes," Justice Powell said. "McCleskey v. Kemp."

The Justice's apparent remorse is not widely shared. Bold efforts to eliminate racial disparities continue to face legal as well as political obstacles even though their elimination was emphasized as early as the first Civil Rights Act in 1866. In one telling instance, the Court restated its position on the validity of efforts to devise compensatory relief from discrimination in a 1989 case involving the Richmond, Virginia, City Council's plan to increase the share of municipal contracts for minority-owned construction businesses. In a City with a black population of about 50%, only 0.67%

of the contracts had gone to minority-owned business. Justice O'Connor writing for the Court rejected the plan, because it would open the door to competing claims for "remedial relief" for every disadvantaged group. Once again the wish for color blindness triumphed over the reality of racial disparity: "The dream of a Nation of equal citizens in a society where race is irrelevant to personal opportunity and achievement would be lost in a mosaic of shifting preferences based on inherently unmeasurable claims of past wrongs."

Among the many criticisms of the decision one law professor, Patricia Williams, was particularly outraged at O'Connor's explanations: "What strikes me most about this holding are the rhetorical devices the court employs to justify its outcome:. . . It sets up a 'slippery slope' at the bottom of which lie hordes-in-waiting of warring barbarians: an 'open door' through which would flood the 'competing claims' of 'every disadvantaged group.' It problematizes by conjuring mythic dangers;. . . It describes situations for which there are clear, hard statistical data as 'inherently unmeasureable.'"

In 2013, a slim majority gutted another form of remediation—the portion of the 1965 Voting Rights Act that required preclearance of electoral system changes by the Justice Department when states or political subdivisions had maintained tests or devices as prerequisites to voting, and had low voter registration or turnout in the 1960s and early 1970s. The Court said things were different now, ignoring evidence that many of the changes had led to a wide range of efforts to disfranchise or render irrelevant the votes of African Americans. Of particular interest was the fury of Justice Antonin Scalia who complained that a key provision of the Act was a "perpetuation of racial entitlement."

These rulings of the Justices hardly exhaust the avenues for reform and redress of the racial divide in this country but they do limit the possibilities open to legislators, agency players, and the executive branch should political realities dictate they wish to act. With this shaping but not determinative role in mind, the actions of the Supreme Court set out three restrictive principles: (1) In the vast majority of cases racial discrimination must be established only in individualized settings rather than as a result of proof derived from the impact of systemic factors. (2) National patterns of discrimination in an industry or profession such as historic patterns of disfavoring minorities are a form of societal discrimination that will not justify preferential efforts to remedy the legacies of the past. (3) To advance a goal of ultimate color blindness, decision makers can ignore the extent to which the present has been effected by a history of wide-ranging governmental and private actions that had racial impact.

The damaged lives ignored by using these principles can be glimpsed by a look at the background of the riots that erupted in August, 2014 in Ferguson, Missouri. National attention focused on the details of still another fatal encounter between a black youth and a white officer. The DOJ investigated the killing and the practices of the Ferguson police, ultimately forcing a restructuring of the local department. Frustrated by a failure to get at the root causes of the turmoil, the Economic Policy Institute (EPI), a nonpartisan think tank created to include the needs of low-and middle-income workers in economic policy discussions, published a report by Richard Rothstein entitled *The Making of Ferguson: Public Policies at the Root of Its Troubles*.[1] Rothstein's conclusions make tough reading. The history he documents makes clear the way laws and practices influence economic relations as well as personal opportunity long after they may have been reversed. According to the report, governmental actions that ended in the late twentieth century continue to determine today's racial segregation patterns:

> No doubt, private prejudice and suburbanites' desire for homogenous affluent environments contributed to segregation in St. Louis and other metropolitan areas. But these explanations are too partial, and too conveniently excuse public policy from responsibility. A more powerful cause of metropolitan segregation in St. Louis and nationwide has been the explicit intents of

---

1. In his 2017 book, *The Color of Law*, Rothstein expanded the story of local, state, and federal government support of segregation.

federal, state, and local governments to create racially segregated metropolises.

In the case of St. Louis, these included:

- Segregated public housing projects that separated blacks and whites who had previously lived in more integrated urban areas;
- Restrictive covenants, excluding African Americans from white areas, that began as private agreements but then were adopted as explicit public policy;
- Government subsidies for white suburban developments that excluded blacks, depriving African Americans of the 20th century home-equity driven wealth gains reaped by whites;
- Denial of adequate municipal services in ghettos, leading to slum conditions in black neighborhoods that reinforced whites' conviction that "blacks" and "slums" were synonymous;
- Boundary, annexation, spot zoning, and municipal incorporation policies designed to remove African Americans from residence near neighborhoods, or to prevent them from establishing
- Urban renewal and redevelopment programs to shift ghetto locations, in the guise of cleaning up those slums;
- Government regulators' tacit (and sometimes open) support for real estate and financial sector policies

and practices that explicitly promoted residential segregation;

- A government-sponsored dual labor market that made suburban housing less affordable for African Americans by preventing them from accumulating wealth needed to participate in homeownership.
- Racially explicit zoning decisions that designated specific ghetto boundaries within the city of St. Louis, turning black neighborhoods into slums.

For those that might deny the foregoing portrait, Rothstein recalled that as early as 1974, a three-judge federal court panel concluded that "segregated housing in the St. Louis metropolitan area was . . . in large measure the result of deliberate racial discrimination in the housing market by the real estate industry and by agencies of the federal, state, and local governments." The Department of Justice agreed this was the case but took no action in response. In 1980, another court order included an "instruction for the state, county, and city governments to devise plans to integrate schools by integrating housing. Public officials ignored this aspect of the order."

While many, though certainly not all, of these policies were ended in the past century, that they continue to exercise their influence in countless pernicious ways makes a shambles of arguments against setting things right. The most significant of these continuities for me is the political. As long as we, abetted sometimes explicitly sometimes implicitly by judges, legislators, the media, educators, and other shapers of our public culture, deny the effects into the future of the policies like those Rothstein lists, covering as they do the entire range of American life, and resist reversing their effects, the country will remain at odds with itself. Today's rules may be color-blind but yesterday's were not and we still dance to their tune.

Epilogue

In the wake of Donald Trump's 2016 election victory, the Democratic Party and its supporters fixed the blame for defeat across the electoral landscape—the misguided interventions of FBI Director James Comey, the flood of emails hacked by Russia and leaked via WikiLeaks—for ignoring the loss of dignity and good jobs by the white noncollege working class voters and their attendant resentment. Especially in Pennsylvania, Michigan, and Wisconsin, enough voters to ensure defeat turned their back on Hillary Clinton by supporting Trump despite many of them agreeing he was flawed. A counterpoint to Democratic Party self-laceration over becoming a party dominated by better off, better educated, bicoastal Americans who supported free trade and globalization and who failed to consider what was happening in the Rust Belt was the attack on liberal "fixation on diversity" and what was generally labeled "identity politics.

The charge was epitomized by widespread media attention to the identity politics issue and particularly the work

of a Columbia Professor, Mark Lilla, who claimed this fixation cost the election. Liberals had "slipped into a kind of
moral panic about race, gender and sexual identity" that
prevented them "from becoming a unifying force capable of governing." As a result they were "narcissistically
unaware of conditions outside their self-defined groups."
For this state of affairs he blamed an obsession with bathrooms for transgender students, high school history cur-
riculums, college campus diversity programs, and liberal's
belief in their "moral superiority" over Trump voters. Calling
out ethnic, racial, and gender groupings for support, he
argued, was a way to lose elections; Clinton should have been
campaigning to appeal to "Americans as Americans . . ."
speaking to "the nation as a nation of citizens who are in
this together and must help one another." Calling Clinton's
defeat a "Whitelash," was a cop-out masking a liberal conviction of "moral superiority," allowing liberals to ignore
what Trump voters said was "their overriding concerns."

Lilla's prescription for change was a high-minded but
unlikely cure: teachers who would make sure they'd produce
"committed citizens aware of their system of government
and major forces and events in our history"; an emphasis on
"democracy is not only about rights but . . . duties"; a "liberal press" that would begin educating itself about parts of
the country that have been ignored and about what matters
there, especially religion.

Thus, Lilla's diagnosis rejects the idea that Trump's victory
marks a repetition of the historic phenomenon of whites

reacting to blacks doing better. Instead, he offered still another twist in the seemingly endless American saga of diminishing the importance of racial disparity—the twist being that Trump voters don't really care about race or if they do it's only because of liberal fixation on the matter. It's hard to take this argument seriously given the racial and ethnic cast of much of Trump's rhetoric, the enthusiasm with which it was heard by his audiences, disparagement of President Obama, the appointment of right wing advisors, and the epidemic of hate speech and hate crimes that erupted as soon as he took office. It's difficult to ignore your identity when you are assaulted for it or told to go back from where you came from, even if you are at where you came from. Or if you are a black male and know the arrest and prison statistics. Michael Eric Dyson replied to such arguments by commenting that the "real unifying force in our national cultural and political life . . . is white identity masked as universal, neutral and, therefore, quintessentially American. The greatest purveyors of identity politics today, and for the bulk of the nation's history, have been white citizens." Debating identity politics as a tactic is one thing but we shouldn't delude ourselves into ignoring that for many Americans it's toxic to assert that "physical and moral violence," against minorities, as history professor Jim Haas put it, "is rooted in the endemic violence of early America and inherent in American society."

Another version of the identity politics criticism came from Senator Bernie Sanders, understandably distraught by the defeat of Clinton in a race he thought he could have won. Sanders called for a Democratic Party that would "go beyond identity politics." While it's "enormously important" to "end all forms of discrimination," "We need more African Americans" and women—"It is not good enough for someone to say, 'I'm a woman! Vote for me!'. . . What we need is a woman who has the guts to stand up to Wall Street, to the insurance companies, to the drug companies."

There are a wide range of justifiable criticisms of the Clinton campaign—she failed to defuse the email issue, took Rust Belt states for granted, made a stupid gaff calling out "deplorable" Trump supporters, focused so much on her opponent's defects she forgot concrete talk about policy, never connected with key voters over the loss of jobs through globalization—but both Lilla and Sanders caricature her approach, though the Vermont Senator played a valuable role in forcing Americans to confront their denial of the nation's class system. Sanders also had the courage, which Clinton failed to fully acknowledge, that American capitalism had developed, in the words of Nobel Laureate Joseph Stiglitz, so that the "end of making money justifies the means, which in the US subprime crisis meant exploiting the poorest and least educated among us."

Clinton, however, never claimed women should vote for her because she was a woman; pointing out the historic nature of her potential election and that she was running against a man who had displayed rampant misogyny was hardly an irrational stance. More importantly, calling attention to the identity claims of your largest supporters is what politics is and has always been about. Lilla's lame call for better civics education and focus on unity certainly sounds good but the notion that such can replace interest group politics is naïve. He ignores that the working class voters he'd love to have back in the Democratic fold constitute just another interest group with an identity that Trump successfully courted.

Imani Perry put it well. "Identity is more than a simple personal possession" but "a marker of how resources and opportunities are distributed in our society." When Senator Sanders emphasizes class interests in contrast to group affiliation, it is merely a tactic to gain support for his equality for all agenda; on the other hand, Lilla and others who disparage diversity adherents who seek policies to end societal disadvantage ultimately read more like ideological expressions than political strategies.

An outraged Lilla told National Public Radio that he had been called a white supremacist by a colleague at Columbia. That surely was unfair but it is true that he ignored the fact that identities are not only named but also claimed; living with their social meaning is not something that humans can avoid. Paradoxically, his call that more attention must be paid to "white, rural, religious" voters is simply his own version of identity politics, only this time with a group he associates more with aiming at "Americans as Americans."

There is, however, a core truth in Lilla's approach that cannot be so easily swatted away as the identity politics blame game. Mainstream Americans and the politicians they elect ignore that changing economic and social outcomes doesn't necessarily take work and dignity away from one group but rather provides the chance to create a safer and less humiliatingly hierarchical society for everyone. Second, there is no fundamental divergence between the interests of working class and poor whites and those of working class and poor minorities. Moving society away from inequality policies need not solely aim at a particular racial grouping but even when they do policies that promote "elevation" for one group that is subject to "othering" tend to do so for all.

The point was made powerfully by prominent political theorist Michael Walzer—"[P]eople without money, or without enough money; people without jobs or with jobs that barely support them; people who are frighteningly vulnerable to the smallest economic turndown, who live on the edge of destitution; people whose children are taught in overcrowded and understaffed schools . . . who are living in decaying cities or rural isolation . . . these people are not distinguished by their gender, or their nationality or their religion, not even by their race. They are so to speak naturally diverse." Walzer skips over the reality that certainly race, nationality, gender—and age—are all significantly associated with those he identifies but the general point remains: we need policies that focus on "Americans in trouble."

Most of all, widespread wishful thinking that the past was entombed, never to darken the present, is an ever present opportunity for politicians to play on the desire of those who often for personal reasons don't want to know or to believe that ending inequality isn't a zero sum game with minorities the winners but an effort to raise the quality of life for all. Millions of Americans have avoided full knowledge that their prosperity depended in part on exploiting and denigrating others. While this is hardly a phenomenon limited to these shores, recent events suggest that the exploitation has come to rest also on white working class men and their families. In the short term, they may vent their anger at minorities and immigrants but unless their needs are addressed blame will also be directed at the true manipulators of the economy and the government. For me, the most powerful words surfacing in the 2016 election were "The Establishment." My guess, and it's only that, is that our fractious, divisive identity politics can be overridden only by greater equality or real prosperity.

On the wall of my university office for many years was a photograph taken during the German occupation of France of a sign in a Parisian restaurant window that read "Restaurant JUIF . . . entrée interdite aux non juifs." Prevalent in nineteenth-century America, especially near where I work in Boston, were "NINA" ads proclaiming "Help wanted—No Irish Need Apply." I was proud that the dean of my law school, Eugene V. Rostow—no bleeding heart he— had strongly condemned the 1942 evacuation and incarceration of Japanese Americans. He said of the commanding general whose "findings" were necessary to support the

exclusion orders, "[H]is motivation was ignorant race prej-
udice, not facts to support the hypothesis that there were
greater risk of sabotage from the Japanese than among
Germans, Italians or ethnic affiliations." When my parents
took me South for the first time on a vacation at age ten, the
train stopped outside of Washington, DC, to force all the
colored passengers into racially segregated cars. I wasn't
prepared for what I saw in the forced movement of a mass of
men and women based on their skin color; I've never forgotten it. The 2016 electoral explosion of resentment
against urban constituencies was framed in terms of city
dwellers—of course, disproportionately minority—getting
the power, resources, and respect that rural voters—mostly
white—were unjustly being denied.

In short, othering takes many forms but it is everywhere:
an equal opportunity, bipartisan source of humiliation and
anger. The human brain may be organized in a fashion that
makes tribal allegiance and outsider exclusion the default
but that's no excuse for not fighting the tendency. Indeed,
all the more reason—and with passion.

I close this chapter at a time of national distress. Division seems the overriding characteristic of public life. Basic
assumptions of governmental structure and policy are
under challenge. Limits of past progress depress many.
Norms of fair treatment, courtesy, and civility are increasingly flouted. Dissent is greeted with threats of violence;
bigotry appears on the rise but is assuredly more prominently expressed. Many want to be comforted by thinking

that nothing here is new, that only an ignorant sense of history can fail to see that we have weathered the storms of Native American genocide, slavery and war, lynching and segregation, robber barons and bread lines, riots and crime waves. Patterns have influence but every era is newly minted, uniquely shaped, and formed so that no prediction is assured. For me the past is a source of ideas but more importantly a sign of work that needs to be done. One need not be a follower of George Friedrich Hegel's reactive theory of history to believe the chaos of the moment will source rapid desires to bring on a more just and accommodating future. For me, one key to that evolution is maintenance of an open and free society, one that is capable of gathering and assimilating evidence. The second crucial element is actors and activists who stay in the work. I found them in the 1960s when I emerged from my cocoon of youth. They let me be part of that work and it changed the world. I expect their like will come again and I can only hope my dear readers will join them.

Acknowledgments

Ultimately the stories we tell ourselves about who we are and where we've gone amount to best guesses. Knowledge mysteriously layers itself into character and shapes experience or the process, equally tentative, equally opaque, works in reverse. For me fortunately the relationships that have emerged are undeniable, vivid, and concrete. I couldn't have written this book much less lived much of the life it traces without the intense presence of my wife, my two daughters, Jessie and Molly, their children and spouses. As a young man, I believed in the dominance of personal autonomy but proof of its jacketed confines is confirmed by the number of those who helped, wittingly or otherwise, bring the book to rest. I mention but a few of the many. My great thanks and gratitude to Anthony Amsterdam, Roger Abrams, Matt Berger, Margaret Burnham, Brandon Garrett, Randall Kennedy, Evan Mandery, Daniel Medwed, Herb Sturz, Patricia Wald, Mark Morrill, Carol McGeehan, Victor Navasky, Dorothy Samuels, Philip Schrag, Carol Steiker, Rose Zoltek-Jick, and Margaret Woo. Library and computer–related support was exceptionally provided by Jackie LaCorte, Diane D'almeida, Alfreda Russell, and Keith Wise. Special thanks to the Editors at Twelve Tables Press and Publisher, Steve Errick.

I owe a great debt for the decades-long friendship of Stanley Fisher and the late Harry Subin. Their laughter—and example—has kept me going through many a rough patch.

About the Author

Michael Meltsner is the George J. and Kathleen Waters Matthews Distinguished University Professor of Law at Northeastern University. He was first assistant counsel to the NAACP Legal Defense Fund in the 1960s, arguing many leading civil rights cases before the federal courts. From 1970 to 1979 as a professor of law at Columbia Law School, he cofounded the school's first clinical program. He served as the Northeastern dean from 1979 until 1984. His memoir, *The Making of a Civil Rights Lawyer*, was published in 2006. Among his other writings are: *Cruel and Unusual: The Supreme Court and Capital Punishment; Public Interest Advocacy and Reflections on Clinical Legal Education* (both with Philip Schrag); and *Short Takes*, a novel. His most recent book, *Rape, Race, and Injustice*, tells the story of a group of law students sent secretly to the South during the 1960s to collect proof of sentencing discrimination. His 2011 play *In Our Name: A Play of the Torture Years* has been performed in New York and Boston. He has been a Guggenheim Fellow and has served as a consultant to the Department of Justice, the Ford Foundation, and the Legal Action Center and has lectured in Canada, Egypt, Germany, India, the Netherlands, and South Africa. In 2000, he was named a fellow of the American Academy in Berlin. From 2000 to 2005 he was a visiting professor and director of the First-Year Lawyering Program at Harvard Law School. In 2010, he received the Hugo Bedau Award for excellence in death penalty scholarship. Calling him "... the principal architect of the death penalty abolition movement in the United States," in 2012 he was awarded an honorary doctorate by John Jay College (CUNY).

Index